JOHN HAMILTON OF DONEGAL 1800-1884

This Recklessly Generous Landlord

John Hamilton, of Brownhall and St. Ernan's, Co. Donegal, 1800-1884, of whom Fr. John Doherty, PP of Donegal, wrote: 'His tenants honour him, respect him and love him for his personal kindness and friendliness towards them'.

John Hamilton of Donegal, 1800–1884

This Recklessly Generous Landlord

DERMOT JAMES

The Woodfield Press

This book was typeset in Ireland by
Gough Typesetting Services for
THE WOODFIELD PRESS
17 Jamestown Square, Inchicore, Dublin 8.

The catalogue record for this title
is available from the British Library.

ISBN 0-9528453-4-2

The author and the publisher
wish to acknowledge
the generous financial assistance
this book has received from

AIB Limited

and

DONEGAL CREAMERIES plc.

Printed in Ireland
by Genprint Limited

Contents

List of Illustrations

MAPS

FAMILY TREE

'. . . on hearing of John Hamilton's death, several thousand people had very good reason to sincerely regret the passing of this complex, but remarkably benevolent and recklessly generous landlord.'

Preface

Who was John Hamilton? Few people who know anything about Irish landlords would have to ask the same question about the Earl of Leitrim, or Sir Denis Mahon, or George Adair, whose names will probably be for ever linked with the horrors of wholesale evictions and the coffin ships. A minority of landlords strove hard, with varying degrees of success, to help their tenants and some bankrupted both themselves and their estates in the process – but can anyone now name *even one* such benevolent landlord?

This book is about such a person who, it can be persuasively argued, probably did more for his tenants – whom he frequently called his 'friends and neighbours' – than any other landlord before, during and after the Famine. Yet, outside the immediate area of his estate, the memory of him has been almost totally forgotten, and one of the few historians who seemed to have been aware of this most unusual man was the late Professor J.C. Beckett. In the space of five paragraphs in his book *The Anglo-Irish Tradition*, he succinctly summed-up the achievements of this considerate, if not unique landlord. His words are reproduced here by kind permission of Queens University, Belfast:

> A good many Irish landlords – more than is commonly recognised – did, in fact, try to improve the lot of their tenants and promote the general welfare of their neighbourhoods. But they generally found it an uphill task, in which only a determined man was likely to persevere for long. One such man was John Hamilton, of St. Ernan's, in County Donegal, one of the poorest parts of Ulster, where the population was predominately Roman Catholic and where relations between landlord and tenant were, in general, less harmonious than they were in the province as a whole.
>
> Hamilton had thus to face the same sort of social and economic difficulties as landlords in the three southern provinces; and his experience is worth examining in some detail. He had succeeded, as a minor, to a large but impoverished estate, of which he took possession on attaining his majority in 1821. He devoted the next sixty years of his life to improving the condition of his tenants. Instead of working through an agent he managed everything himself. He moved freely among the tenants,

giving advice and listening to their complaints; he visited their homes and knew the particular circumstance of every family on the estate. He built houses, drained land, constructed roads, established and maintained schools. To begin with, at least, he found the result of his efforts disappointing: Many of those for whom he had done most remained, as before, shiftless, ragged and dirty. But he refused to give up. Year after year he continued his help and his exhortations; the standard of farming and of cleanliness gradually improved; and even the local parish priest, a noted critic of landlordism in general, bore public witness to his kindness and his popularity.

Hamilton may have found it easier to win the confidence of his tenants because he held aloof from party politics, though he did issue warnings from time to time about the folly of being misled by political or agrarian agitators. But he was a strong, if not strictly orthodox, Protestant: and, while not seeking controversy, he lost no opportunity of proclaiming his religious views. Religion was, indeed, the dominant influence in his life and inspired the sense of duty that guided him in the management of his estate. His conviction that only when others came under the same influence would society be happy made him suspicious of attempts to improve the state of affairs by legislation. In an address to his tenants on Gladstone's Land Act of 1870, he warned them: 'Even if the law could make all landlords do right, it would be little use, unless it could make all *tenants* wise, prudent, industrious and good.'

Hamilton attained a considerable measure of success; but it was attained only by patient and unremitting devotion to duty, inspired and informed by strong religious conviction. And, in the end, the success was only partial. In his last address to his tenants, issued after sixty years of life among them, one can detect a note of disappointment behind the friendly style; and his statement that he now favours the winding up of the whole landlord system by a policy of land purchase reads almost like a confession of defeat.

Hamilton was certainly not typical; indeed, men of his stamp are rare in any community. But it is the very fact that he was untypical that makes his experience instructive. Here was a landlord of determined character, impelled by a strong sense of duty arising from religious conviction; in the course of a long life he won the affection of his tenants and the approval even of those who were opposed to landlordism in general; and yet, in the end, he was forced to the conclusion that there was no place for landlords in the social and economic life of Ireland. And this conclusion did not arise from any doubts about his own policy, but from a slow and reluctant acceptance of the fact that the tenants did not want any landlords at all. If Hamilton – whom even that hammer of the Irish landlords, Mr. Gladstone, felt himself obliged to praise – had to

> make this confession, it seems fair to conclude that the fate of the landlords was inescapable. Their own character and conduct may have hastened their fall, and certainly embittered the struggle that preceded it. But, once the voting power of the Roman Catholic majority had been organised in the cause of Home Rule, the landlords, who were the outstanding representatives of Protestant ascendancy and the leading supporters of the parliamentary union, could not survive indefinitely.

★ ★ ★

Like most people, I had never heard of Hamilton either, but in December 1996, less than six weeks after the publication of *The Wicklow World of Elizabeth Smith,* which I had jointly edited with Séamas Ó Maitiú, I was telephoned by a person who said that he had enjoyed reading about how Mrs. Smith and her benevolent landlord husband had treated their tenants with considerable kindness. He went on to say that he saw strong parallels between Elizabeth Smith of Blessington and John Hamilton of Donegal, because both had dealt humanely with their tenants and both had kept journals recording events as they were happening. When I admitted that I had never heard of him, my caller advised me to try to obtain a copy of a book published about Hamilton in 1894, ten years after he had died. That was the genesis of this volume.

The book in question, *Sixty Years' Experience as an Irish Landlord*, by the Rev. H.C. White, had been privately printed and proved extremely difficult to locate. When I eventually found a copy, it seemed very uneven in quality, not without errors and with a heavy emphasis on Hamilton's religious thinking – the latter causing me to wonder if this aspect of Hamilton's life had been deliberately emphasised by its reverend author. While still scouring the various libraries where much of the Hamilton papers had been deposited by past generations of the family, I discovered not only that most of John Hamilton's journals had survived on the far side of the Irish Sea but that they had recently been sent to cousins living in Dublin who required them for the Famine commemorations. This was a remarkable stroke of good luck, and with this unexpectedly easy access to the originals, I soon discovered that a great deal of very interesting detail had been omitted from White's book and this encouraged me to produce a wholly new account about this remarkable, though largely unknown landlord in a format which would appeal to present-day readers.

Another stroke of good fortune was to follow. Further journals and note books, which the Rev. White had not seen, turned up in Ireland including what may have been John Hamilton's very first journal, written when he was a seventeen year old student at Cambridge; also a small notebook in which he gave an account of a tour in the west of Ireland just as the potato famine was beginning, and several sketchbooks which showed him to be a competent amateur artist. Along with these, was a single journal kept by John's talented and very observant ten year old daughter during the family's extensive continental tour which actually provides a more descriptive account of the family's travels than the journals written by her father.

John Hamilton's writings give a good picture of the man's own character. With no formal training, he proved himself to be an innovating agriculturist and proprietor. He read and travelled widely and was something of a linguist, having taught himself Irish and German, and he appears to have had a good knowledge of French as well as both Latin and Greek. He was deeply – almost obsessively – religious, constantly questioning both himself and others, and there can be no doubt that his religious beliefs were the main driving force of his life and influenced most of his dealings with his fellow men. It was, however, his dealings with his own tenants (as well as the neighbouring poor who were not his tenants) that marked him out as an exceptional person and an unusually generous and benevolent landlord.

Having inherited a considerable fortune on his twenty-first birthday, he embarked upon an extraordinary spending spree with careless abandon so that, by the time he was fifty, not only was all the capital gone but part of the estate had been mortgaged. Hamilton had not used his money for personal pleasures – indeed, he and his family led quite Spartan lives – but he had spent on an extravagant scale to improve both his estate and conditions for his tenants, and had lost a very large sum of money as a result of borrowing heavily during the Famine years. He subsequently admitted that he could have achieved the same results with less than half the expenditure if he had been less impatient to get things done quickly. But there is no point in continuing this summary; the reader will find all these details and much more in the ensuing pages

His journals and other writings provide a good idea of what kind of complex person he was, but they do not supply the whole story. His many omissions often prove frustrating – not least the dearth of detail about what he actually did for his tenants during the Famine years, and about his life after the death of his first wife. Because his journals recorded private recollections and private thoughts, he felt no need to explain or to elaborate on his actions, and his sometimes casual mentions of people by initials can be puzzling but, where possible, these and most of the other obscure references have been clarified in the text. Wherever John Hamilton's own text is quoted, his spellings and abbreviations, his use of capital letters and some other quirks, are faithfully followed. Spellings of place-names were often rendered in several different ways at that time, but most of the variations can be easily recognised and, in this connection, while Brownhall is sometimes spelt Brown Hall, the former version has been followed with very few exceptions throughout the book. One final point concerns the value of the Pound during the middle of the last century relative to its value today: A crude but simple rule of thumb is to multiply the sum by fifty, making John Hamilton's gift of one hundred pounds to Donegal parish church equal to approximately £5,000 in today's money.

ACKNOWLEDGEMENTS

My thanks are due to, the Manuscripts Department of Trinity College Library, the National Library of Ireland, the Library of the Royal Irish Academy, the Library of the Representative Church Body, the Linenhall Library, Belfast, the Library of the University of St Andrews, and, in each case, to those staff members who were so helpful in general research. I am also grateful to Queen's University in Belfast for permission to quote from the late Professor Beckett's *The Anglo-Irish Tradition*.

I also acknowledge the valuable assistance received from many other people, including the following: John and Radine Hamilton of Brownhall, David and Joyce Hamilton of Dublin, and Judith Fearnall in Gwent – all of whom were very helpful in assisting me in matters relating to the Hamilton families including the loan of journals, family photographs and other material. For their part in the generous provision of funding of this book, I am most grateful to Michael McClean, Manager of Allied Irish Bank, Donegal, and to John Keon, Managing Director of Donegal Creameries Plc.

Also to the following in connection with illustrations: The present John Hamilton for permission to reproduce detail from a painting of his great-great grandfather on the cover, and to Bord Failte – The Irish Tourist Board for permission to reproduce detail from their photograph of the Bluestack Mountains, on the same cover; to John Donnelly, photographer, Donegal, for the photographic reproductions of three Hamilton family paintings, and to Francis Bradley, whose neat maps enhance these pages and will prove helpful to readers unfamiliar with the areas concerned.

Many other individuals assisted in various ways including: Eileen Burgess of Bridgetown, Ciaran Clarke of Ardnamona, Esme Colley and Anne Denard of Dublin, David Davin of St Ernan's, Carol and Cowan Ervine, Newport-on-Tay near St Andrews, Hazel Graham, Dublin, Helen Hartnett, Dublin, Dr. K. Moe, Dublin, Eric Montgomery, Belfast, Lettie Morrow, Laghey, Brian O'Dowd of St.Ernan's, Thomas Pakenham of Tullynally, and the Rev. David Skuce, Rector of Drumholm (Ballintra). I also acknowledge the considerable contribution made by my wife, Gladys, who is responsible for most of the typescript and who travelled with me in the footsteps of John Hamilton around Ireland and abroad. And finally, a special word of thanks is due to Terri McDonnell of the Woodfield Press who, for the second time in as many years, has taken the risk of publishing a work of mine centred on an aspect of Irish landlordism.

DERMOT JAMES

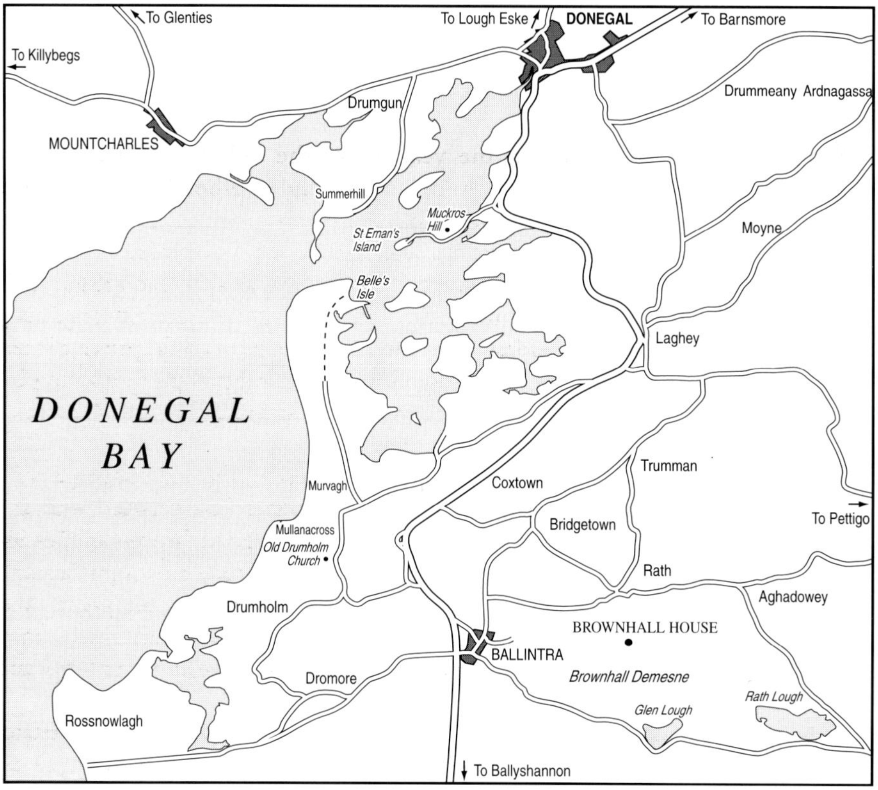

Map of the area around Donegal Bay showing the location of Brownhall Estate, St. Ernan's Isle, Belle's Isle, etc.

ONE

Introducing John Hamilton

John Hamilton was born in the year 1800, the eldest son of a wealthy County Donegal landowner. John's father and mother had died before he was eight years old so he, his brother Edward, and his sister Catherine were taken into care by guardian uncles and aunts until they came of age. After boarding at Armagh Royal School, the two boys were sent to Cambridge University where, during his second year, John discovered an extraordinary dispensation available to the eldest grandson of a peer who could prove a lineal descent from an English king. By producing a certified pedigree showing his family connection with Edward I, John was enabled to obtain his Master of Arts degree without sitting for an examination.

Even apart from the family's distant royal ancestry, the Hamiltons were a very well-connected family; and because John's father had married into the influential Pakenham family, young John had a number of famous uncles including Sir Edward, Sir Hercules and Henry Pakenham and, most significantly, Arthur Wellesley, who was later to become the Duke of Wellington. And besides his connections with a range of Ango-Irish aristocratic families, he claimed he was related to Mrs. C. S. Alexander who wrote *Once in royal David's city* and many other well-known hymns.

At the age of 21, John inherited the extensive, entailed Brownhall Estate, totalling around 20,000 acres. The main part of the estate ran inland from Donegal Bay, between Donegal town and Ballintra, almost as far as Pettigo and Lough Erne; and northwards to near Lough Eske and the Barnsmore Gap. Separated from this, about twenty miles further north, there was a further, very large tract in the Finn valley. In addition to the estate, John inherited the very considerable family fortune, its extent a matter of some debate, some sources putting it at nearly one million pounds in today's money.

John had, of course, no training whatever in managing either his property or his purse, a disadvantage shared by many landlords at that time, but in John's case he had not even had the benefit of being able to learn from watching how his father had managed the business of the estate. It was no disadvantage to him that he had seen some of the benefits of well-run estate while being brought up by the Pakenhams, even though much of this period was spent boarding at school and university. With an elitist background and so much inherited wealth, it would have been easy for John Hamilton to have become the generally accepted stereotype of an autocratic, ruthless, hard-drinking, hard-riding, evicting landlord. He had his faults but these were not among them. Indeed, from the outset he seems to have had a good idea of how he proposed to improve both his property and the lot of his tenants, regarding himself as their 'philosopher and friend'. Much of the land was mountainous and very poor, inhabited by a poverty-stricken peasantry, most of whom lived in wretched conditions. In his old age, John Hamilton recalled that when he was a young man:

> the part of my landed property which most interested me was a considerable extent of moor or, as it is called here without any regard to elevation, mountain, which was pretty well stocked with grouse. It is a district which ought not to be populous, and its soil pays ill for cultivation; but the unhappy legislation which made leases of the value of forty shillings a year give a vote for the county representative, had led my forefathers to encourage sub-division to such a degree that instead of five or six substantial tenants, I found nearly a hundred. That they were poor I need not say, but they paid their rents duly, and were a more civilised folk than, under the circumstances in a very remote corner of a very remote county, could be expected.

While still only 21 he proposed to Mary, the 17 year old sister of his college friend, Hugh Rose, and the young couple were married in her native Scotland four months later. No doubt any reservations which her parents may have harboured about permitting their daughter to marry at such a tender age were overcome by their awareness of her young suitor's wealth.

One of the first problems which John had to face when he arrived back in Brownhall with his young wife was the fact that part of the estate was held under a twenty-one year lease from Trinity College, Dublin. What John found to be especially irksome was the fact that Brownhall House was standing on leased land while there was freehold land barely a stone's throw away. He made a number of attempts to negotiate a deal with the college authorities but the harder he tried the more he convinced them that maintaining the lease was worth their while. John Hamilton did not like to lose an argument, but finding himself beaten on this point, and not wishing to be under threat of being forced out of his home at some future date, he decided to build another one in the neighbourhood. How he came to settle on St.Ernan's Island in Donegal Bay is described in subsequent pages but, fortunately for the family, his brother continued to live in the old home at Brownhall for some time and it has passed down through the family to the present day. What is now a low, two-storey wing was the original house built by John Hamilton's grandfather, another John, after moving there in 1697 from Murvagh, a short distance away, nearer to Donegal Bay. A feature of this older wing was a most unusual galleried kitchen, similar to that at Strokestown House. His son, James, completed by

1789 the three-storey cube house attached to the older house which has survived almost unchanged

John Hamilton's new house at St.Ernan's was situated a short distance from the shore at Muckros Hill and, as access by boat was inconvenient, he decided to build a linking causeway. When his tenants heard about this, such was their opinion of him even at this early stage, that they volunteered to complete it for him. Helped by local peasants who were not his tenants, they organised themselves into work parties of 50, taking it in turns to haul the rocks from Laghey quarry some miles away, and laid them across to the island, resolutely refusing Hamilton's offers to pay them for the work. This incident made a lasting impression on Hamilton who became even more determined to avoid judging his people as being ignorant, stupid and lazy, recognising instead that whatever faults they had were largely the result of past mismanagement and lack of guidance by those who should have known better.

John Hamilton's paternal grandparents, John (1735–1811), and Elizabeth, nee Stewart, (from a portrait painted by Gilbert Stuart between 1787 and 1793). (Private collection)

He treated his tenants with humanity and was 'a father to his people', encouraging them to improve their own lot, and was not only genuinely but generously interested in their welfare. Within fifteen years, after he had divided his estate into different sections, he was able to claim that in some of them 'there is not now one single pauper, though on the same spot there were a few years ago many of the population dependent upon absolute charity, or uncertain means of livelihood'. After the Famine, he was to claim that only one tenant died from starvation and not one had need to enter the local workhouse. He was repeatedly critical of those landlords who made little or no effort to help their tenants, and wrote, in 1847: 'I am not going to defend our class as free from blame – nay, I acknowledge that we have all erred more or less, and the evils and sufferings caused by neglectful or worse conduct on the part of some landlords have no excuse. . . .'

He was, by his own admission, an impatient man – a fault which was, literally, to cost him dearly – and in his anxiety to get things going quickly, he incurred unnecessary expense. At the outset, his resources must have appeared to him to be almost infinite so that he gave little thought to expenditure, but the outcome of his profligate spending was that his inheritance was almost entirely dissipated by the end of the Famine. This had resulted from his eagerness to improve the estate, but he also spent generously and somewhat unwisely to help his tenants, later admitting that he could have achieved just as much at half the cost if only he had learned to be more patient. It was hardly surprising that succeeding generations of the family found it hard to forgive him for his carelessness with the family's money and one member in particular, his grandson John Stewart Hamilton, wrote scathingly in his autobiography: 'I always think that ninety per cent of his so-called good deeds were done in the name of the Lord and to the glory of John Hamilton,' adding: 'though his family had no cause to bless his name, his tenants and the poor had much'. He also wrote that his grandfather had lived a life of 'personal and philantrophic extravagance which his descendants have never ceased to deplore'. The accusation of *personal* extravagance seems manifestly unfair given that it appears clear that he spent comparatively little on himself – indeed his whole family lived relatively frugally, and hardly socialised at all. However, while derogatory about the accuracy of others, John Stewart Hamilton's autobiography is far from free of errors of fact, whatever about errors of judgement.

When compiling this work, the aspect of his life which caused the greatest difficulty was his almost obsessive interest in religion. An attempt to give adequate coverage to John Hamilton's religious outlook would almost certainly prove utterly boring for most readers today, so this side of his character, while recognised, is not covered in great depth. For the record, the reader is here informed that by far the greater part of John's journals are taken-up with personal dissertations about religion and private prayers and, as all this indicates, he was a deeply religious person whose religion was the dominant influence in his life. To it he owed the sense of duty that directed him throughout his life and it was the guiding force in the manner in which he managed his estate. But while he held to what he regarded the essential Christian certainties, he was at the same time a questioning man who liked nothing better than to engage in conversations about various aspects of religion with learned divines and complete strangers alike. A staunch member of the Established Church, his journals indicate that for much of his life he was searching for something different but never seemed to find it. After starting a number of Bible-reading classes for adults in the area and engaging in lay preaching, he seriously considered ordination and, when discouraged in this by his Bishop, he redoubled his work with Sunday classes and opened many more of them as well as Sunday schools for children, all of which attracted attendances across the religious divide, eventually totalling well over 1,000 each week, until the Roman Catholic clergy became concerned and commenced discouraging their flock from attending.

Impatient to get things done and determined to get his own way, it would appear that he was also something of an egoist, a man who must have been, at

John Hamilton's father James (1771–1805) died when John was only five. His mother, Helen Pakenham, died two years later, leaving three orphan children in the care of two guardian uncles.

times, difficult both to deal with and to live with. It seems fair to add, however, that the many other sides of his personality far outweighed the negative aspects. He was clearly a very spiritual person, an intellectual and travelled widely; he was something of a linguist, having taught himself Irish and German, and had a good knowledge of Latin Greek and French. He was a competent amateur artist, and also wrote well and, fortunately for succeeding generations, he kept a whole series of detailed journals for close on 30 years which provide today's reader with a rare insight into life in rural Ireland during the nineteenth century. He was brave, not only in that he confronted threatening Orangemen and Ribbonmen on several occasions, but also in that he fearlessly visited his sick tenants – even when they were suffering from Cholera. He sometimes rendered first aid, and he also practised mesmerism, and by this hypnotic method he cured or alleviated of their illnesses a number of people. As a landlord, he was kindly and considerate, and he understood well the minds of his tenants, making him tolerant of their shortcomings. And he was, without doubt, generous to a fault.

Though now almost completely forgotten, in his day he was widely praised, and the most remarkable tribute paid to John Hamilton came from the pen of the Reverend John Doherty, parish priest of Donegal town, who knew better than most the state of the relationships between this landlord and his tenants. Father Doherty's testimony, all the more significant because he was an outspoken critic of the excesses associated with landlordism, came in the form of a letter published in the *Derry Journal* in October, 1880, when he wrote that: 'In all Ireland there never was, nor is there, a more considerate and humane landlord than the good and kind-hearted proprietor of St. Ernan's. I know the pulse of his tenants well, and I know of my own knowledge that they honour him, respect him, and love him for his personal kindliness and friendliness towards them, and for his sympathy in all their worldly fortunes and mishaps. They regard him more in the light of a friend and benefactor, like his Master 'going about doing good' – than as a landlord'.

Brownhall Cures

BROWNHALL CURE FOR CHOLERA

Castor Oil, 1 tablespoon if effectual and then a tablespoon brandy in arrowroot. If still there is an irritation or sickening give from 5-10 drops of Laudanum in cold water. If castor oil cannot be taken then 1 tablespoon tincture of rhubarb. Give drinks of cold or warm water. Hot flannels. NOT hot baths.

BROWNHALL CURE FOR A COLD

4 grains of tartare in a wine bottle of water, add a little brown sugar, a few drops of laudanum, if liked. Take 3 spoonfuls a day – at 12 o'clock, 4 o'clock and going to bed.

TWO

Young John Hamilton

John Hamilton was born in Dublin on the 8 August, 1800, the eldest son of James Hamilton, a wealthy landowner with a 20,000 acre estate in County Donegal. His family had arrived from Broomhill in Scotland in the seventeenth century and, according to John Hamilton's grandson, they were the first Scots to settle in the south of the county.

The Hamiltons were descendants of Gilbert of Hamildone in Lanarkshire. James, son of the first Lord Hamilton, whose mother was Mary, daughter of James II of Scotland, became Earl of Arran. Another son, John, became the owner of Broomhill, a large Lanarkshire estate. A branch of the family settled on the southern shore of Donegal Bay, at Murvagh early in the seventeenth century, moving a short distance inland to near Ballintra in 1690, where they named their new property Brownhall (apparently after their Broomhill estate in Scotland), which the family has continued to own ever since.

For centuries, it has been a family tradition that the eldest son in every generation is named, alternately, either John or James, a tradition which may sometimes be the cause of some confusion. Thus, the first James Hamilton at Brownhall (died 1755), was followed by John (died 1811), who was succeeded by James (died 1805), who was the father of John Hamilton – the subject of this book.

John was only five years of age when his father died (his Hamilton grandfather lived for another six years) and his mother died two years after her husband, leaving three orphaned children, John (7), Edward (5) and Catherine (2). The three children were placed under the guardianship of two uncles, Sir Edward Pakenham and the Reverend Abraham Hamilton. While with the Pakenhams, their grandmother proved to be an important influence on the young children:

> My dear good grandmother, Lady Longford, took us as her own, and her house was our own and her heart a mother's heart to us till ten years after my mother's death.

After a bout of measles, the two boys were sent to Dublin 'for a change of air' to live for a time with Sir Arthur Wellesley who was then Chief Secretary for Ireland, later to become the Duke of Wellington. Wellesley, having married John Hamilton's mother's sister, was John's uncle. Young John and his brother, for a time, enjoyed the spacious surroundings of their uncle's official residence in the Phoenix Park, Dublin, and John was afterwards to recall an apparently trivial incident which might easily have had fatal consequences for themselves and the two uncles involved.

> A curious circumstance, considering who one of the persons concerned came afterwards to be, Sir Arthur [Wellesley] and my uncle Henry Pakenham took my brother and me out to walk [in the Phoenix Park]. Evening came on – dinner time drew near, and the boys were weakly and could not run fast, so Sir Arthur took me on his back and my uncle Henry took Edward and set off running. Soon it became a race. I was a great deal the heavier and my uncle Henry, then about twenty two, was very active and left us far behind for the first couple of hundred yards. But Sir Arthur . . . began to regain his lost ground and at last came up close to his antagonist, shouting, and both put out their utmost speed and both shouted with all their lungs. The gate was to be the winning post and with a wild Hollah! Sir Arthur passed to the front and won by a few yards. But in a minute [he] was a prisoner in the custody of the guard mounted at the gate . . . who, in the dark, did not perceive who the disturbers of the peace were.

Who knows, but that the course of British and European history might have been greatly changed if the sentry had, in the dark, assumed he was threatened by an attack, and had shot dead the future victor of Waterloo.

Subsequently, all three children went to live with their grandmother, Lady Longford, at Pakenham Hall in County Westmeath. During the summer months they would stay at Langford Lodge (a name all too easily confused with Longford) near Lough Neagh with their uncle Hercules Pakenham. In fact this property had come into the Pakenham family through the marriage of the second Baron Longford to Catherine Roley, whose mother was Viscountess Langford. It was at Pakenham Hall (the name has since reverted to Tullynally Castle) that John first began to take an interest in gardening, an interest which was to remain with him for the rest of his life. He recalled later that Lady Longford was an indulgent and greatly-loved grandmother who allowed the children 'the utmost licence to enjoy the estate, climbing trees, digging pits, building piers at the lake-shore and creating their own garden'. She inculcated in the Hamilton children strong religious principles which were to have a profound influence upon each of their lives. John also recalled that his grandmother had one simple rule: 'Give no extra trouble. If you make a mess, clean it up yourselves; if you dirty a second pair of shoes, clean them yourselves.. If you want a garden, dig and plant – a summer-house, build it'. In this way all three children became active and hardy. She may well have laid the foundation of John's religious outlook, reading to the children after breakfast, passages from the Bible. As John was to write:

> The only portions we learnt by heart were the 23rd., 37th., and 100th., Psalms, the 12th. chapter of the Epistle to the Romans and the 13th. of the First Epistle to the Corinthians: a selection that gives no bad idea of our excellent teacher's religious views.

ARMAGH ROYAL SCHOOL

At the age of ten, following a family tradition, John went as a boarder to Armagh Royal School where most of the pupils, whose ages ranged from eight to nineteen years, were the sons of former pupils. 'Before going', he wrote, 'I sighed for the supposed liberty and grandeur of the school but very soon I had enough of it'. The only incident connected with the school described in any detail concerned his new-found interest in gardening:

> It was soon discovered that I was handy at gardening, and as some of the older boys were making very nice gardens I was made a fag [A schoolboy forced to do menial work for a more senior pupil] to two of them. When my brother, Edward, came to school with me the next year, he was also made a garden fag; we were given the privilege, unknown to little boys as a rule, to possess a garden, which soon was one of the nicest, although in a bad situation. A labourer, who was sometimes allotted to us at Langford Lodge for work too heavy for us, a tight little Irishman named Hughie McGrady (he used to ride postillion on needful occasions also), was sent now and then [to the school] with a basket load of moss-roses and other shrubs and flowers, his burden always increased with an Antrim cheese from the dairy, and a considerable cake from the housekeeper, which tended to our not inconsiderable popularity in our class for nearly a week each time. Hughie arrived – and he, poor fellow, preferred like a true Paddy, his heavily loaded trudge of twenty-eight miles for the young gentleman to the monotonous though less toilsome daily spade.

John Hamilton related how a school bully dug a well and charged the various gardening boys a toll for using his well to water their plants. Hamilton's plot was in a damp hollow where he had found water only two feet below the surface, so he had his own 'private' well which he kept covered by a plank and some gravel when not in use. In the evening, after dark, he used to go out to water his plants until the bully – who had become aware that Hamilton never paid his toll – saw from behind a trench the reason why. Hamilton was ordered to open his well:

which I did, then he took me and put me standing in it up to the hips, filled in the earth and fairly planted me, trampling it firm. He then took out his knife, and I really thought he was going to kill me, so great was my horror of the wretch, but he quietly and without a word cut off every blossom and bud from my poor moss-rose tree and then left me until some humane passer-by got a spade and dug me out.

John Hamilton wrote that he did not dare to complain even thought he knew the bully would have been soundly thrashed had he done so. He remained at Armagh School for five and a half years leaving at Christmas 1815, when he summed up his school experiences thus:

My progress through the school was not marked by any particular circumstances. I was reasonably diligent, tolerably clever, was never punished for my lessons, and only once subjected to birchen [A cane made from birch twigs] discipline, for bathing in the river Callen contrary to rule. I had my share of boxing, but was neither querrelsome nor scientific.

A year earlier, one of his guardians, his uncle Sir Edward Pakenham, arrived back home in Ireland after serving in the Peninsular war which had put to an end Napoleon's influence in Spain and Portugal. Young John was very pleased to see him, not only to hear about his exploits in the war, but also because his uncle promised to present him with a hunter the following year. However, shortly after this, Sir Edward told his nephew that he had received orders to proceed to America where war had broken out. He was to take the place of General Ross, the chief-in-command of British forces there. At Portsmouth, en route to America, with the responsibilities of command very much in his mind, Sir Edward managed to find time to write to the Hamilton children's other guardian, the Rev. Abraham Hamilton:

Portsmouth, 31st. October, 1814.

MY DEAR HAMILTON – I embark in an hour for America. This unexpected duty has not prevented me turning my thoughts towards the course the boys should take. . . .

He went on to say that he wanted the two boys to go to Cambridge University as soon as places could be arranged. He was anxious that they should have the advantage, as he saw it, of an English education by which 'they will be removed from the risk of forming bad acquaintance near home, by imbibing national or narrowed prejudices, and overcome a singularity of pronunciation that hereafter might be a disadvantage to them in society. . . .' He continued:

> The system of education I point out, is no doubt the most expensive, but money in such a case is well laid out, and if other means are insufficient, I am willing to turn American bear and live on my paws to give such boys the means of a gentleman's life in gentleman's education. A most kind farewell to you, my friend: Remember me to your mother, and believe me
>
> Yours much attached,
>
> E. M. PAKENHAM.

The two Hamilton boys were greatly distressed when they heard their uncle had been ordered to America. John had a premonition that they would never see him again, and when they received instructions from him to order new suits of clothes, John said: 'it is no use, for we shall have to get new black clothes before the vacation'.

Sir Edward conducted the American campaign with great personal courage and with chivalry 'to an excess' and when a peace treaty was signed on Christmas Eve 1814, the news failed to reach Sir Edward before he launched a strong but ill-advised direct frontal attack on the heavily defended New Orleans. When the British forces were repulsed with great loss, Pakenham rallied his troops, leading them in a counter attack when he was hit on the thigh and his horse was killed under him. His aide de camp re-mounted Pakenham on his own horse but he was hit again, this time mortally. Sir Edward Pakenham's leadership was subsequently criticised, though John Hamilton later wrote that 'there never lived a man on whose character such imputations could have less weight'. Pakenham's brother, Sir Hercules, was then appointed a guardian in his place; he was an invalid owing to serious injuries he had received at the key battle of Badajos in 1812, during the Peninsular War. Wellington, his brother-in-law, had ordered the capture of the fortress to prevent the Napoleonic army gaining access to Portugal. Army surgeons were about to amputate Captain Pakenham's hand when a camp follower practitioner intervened, claiming he could save it by applying *Unguentum Angelicum* which 'with exquisite torture burnt off the moribund flesh and cleansed the wound'. Anyway, the uncle's hand was saved, albeit in a shrunken state, but it had 'life enough for many years after to carve, prune trees, shoot, or hold a whip', and despite this and a serious hip injury sustained at the same time, he lived to the age of 71. The boys adored him and took every opportunity to get him to relate his many experiences abroad.

Around this time, John Hamilton began to suffer from a mysterious illness which caused severe pain and affected his vision. After several attacks, during which a number of eminent physicians failed to effect a cure, he was put under the care of a Dr. Cheyne in Dublin, and John's description of the attempted cure makes one wonder if it was worse than the disease:

> They physicked me severely, gave me a whole paper of James' Powders [an emetic] every night for thirty nights, blistered me often, bled me in the arm once a week, and in the head more frequently with many leeches, salivated me twice, made an issue in my arm, and at a last consultation they decided on burning *moxa* [a cauterising agent] on my ear. The enemy was now cowed and the patient nearly routed out of existence by the impetuous attacks of this medical storming party.

He returned to Co. Westmeath by jaunting car with the advice that he should be sent to convalesce in Madeira, though the prognosis given was that there was no hope of recovery. This news must have devastating for him, but the fact that he did recover and got what might be termed 'a second chance' may well have been one of the profound influences which was to determine the way he was to deal with his tenants when he grew up. Six or seven months later, he was well enough to travel with his brother Edward and his sister Kate to their aunt, the Duchess of Wellington 'who undertook, after Lady Longford's death, to be mother to her sisters' daughter'. The boys were taken on to Faversham in Kent and placed under the tuition of a Mr Jones who had been a tutor at St John's College, Cambridge. Not long after this, John seemed to have almost overcome his strange illness and was walking up to six miles daily; and a few months later he was running with the local foxhounds.

While his health continued to improve, his studies did not. Mr Jones 'had no idea of making us study . . . we played football, fished, shot, and amused ourselves *ad libitunt'*. Among the small group of would-be students, John Hamilton found a particular friend in Hugh Rose, a young Scot, and after discussing their mutual prospects, the two decided that they would join the army. Hugh's father agreed to send him to a military college in Germany and, leaving John behind, he travelled there in the autumn of 1817. John Hamilton pleaded with his guardian, Sir Hercules Pakenham, to send him to Germany to join his friend but he was sent – or rather brought – to the Duke of Wellington for advice as to his future career. He was by no means the only person to seek the distinguished man's advice in such a matter. Lord Stopford (from Co. Wicklow), for example, had asked the duke – on behalf of his eldest son – for a commission in the elite Guards Regiment, to which request Wellington's response was: 'Fathers all wish now to get their sons into the Guards. I went into the line and did pretty well'. The Duke's advice to young John Hamilton, equally direct, was against going to a military college but that he should to go instead to Cambridge University. 'For', as he was quoted, 'if you are worth your salt you will learn soldiering when you get your commission, and at Cambridge you will get that education both of learning and of habit which you can never get again . . . Be educated first, as if for the pulpit or the bar, and then you will have a double chance of making a first-rate soldier. I would give more than I could mention that I had a university education'.

CAMBRIDGE UNIVERSITY

So, in October, 1818, the two brothers went together to St John's College, Cambridge, where they met as undergraduates George Villiers (later Lord Clarendon, who was to be Lord Lieutenant of Ireland during the Famine); Henry Law (a brother of Lord Ellenborough); Charles Rose (subsequently he became reader of the House of Lords); John Power (subsequently Sir John of Kilfane, Co. Kilkenny); his cousin, Chambre Ponsonby, the Earl of Bessborough's son, from Pilltown, Co. Kilkenny; Augustus Stapleton, afterwards private secretary to Earl Canning, Governor General of India. Though not listed as such in his journals, E. M. Stewart, a cousin of John's, and William H. Foster, a nephew of 'Speaker' Foster, were special college friends of John Hamilton, the latter subsequently married John's sister.

He continued to suffer from occasional bouts of the earlier mysterious illness which affected his studies and certainly prevented him from sitting his first college examinations. By contrast, his brother Edward, not yet 17 and the youngest student that year, did so well that he very nearly achieved first place.

During that first year at Cambridge, John Hamilton seems to have found himself, perhaps for the first time in his life, questioning his own and other people's views of religion. He expressed repulsion at the doctrines preached at Cambridge by the Rev. Charles Simeon which were based, John thought, 'on an unworthy view of the character of the Supreme Being and this subject gave us much unrest of mind for several years'. Hamilton's own tutor gave him some moral and religious advice: 'Avoid Castle End and Barnwell after dark, and avoid Simeon'.

He strongly objected to the practice of what he called 'making chapels a punishment', a practice which, he said, 'certainly tended much to bring religion into disrepute at Cambridge'. One of the college lecturers used to visit the students during meal-times to hand out punishments: 'Mr. Hamilton, the Dean says that for being out twice after hours, two morning chapels', and then to enhance the evil, and with an expression of 'malignant joy' adding, in a hissing voice, '*Litany mornings*'. While he recorded that he read his Bible from time-to-time, religion seemed to him to be rarely spoken of and seldom considered at Cambridge, and he commented that 'whenever I gave my mind to religion I found a want of reality and of truth and, therefore, of any prospect of attaining either goodness or happiness by it'.

John Hamilton recounted an amusing anecdote about a spaniel which he was given while at Cambridge and which he named 'Sancho'.

> Sancho lived in my room contrary to college discipline which he [Sancho] very well knew. If one of the porters spied him in the court he gave chase directly, and Sancho always ran up a wrong staircase to the very top, and when the porter, puffing with exercise and wrath, was within

two or three steps of the top, brandishing his broom with fell intent, Sancho would bolt through his legs, run downstairs and be safe up in my room long before the persecutor had arrived in the court. He was fond of society and good eating, and several times when I made new acquaintances they remarked: 'Oh, that's your dog. I have known him intimately this long time, he always comes to my rooms when I have a supper, and is so agreeable that he is always welcome'. Stewart lived in lodging in Trumpington Street and always was very attentive to Mr. Sancho who, however, hated *him*, and if he condescended to accept any delicacy – he was very partial to cream ice – would lick it up growling, and with angry eyes turned up against Stewart, skulk under the sofa the moment he had done. My cousin was quite vexed at this canine enmity, and for months strove in vain to overcome it. At last I advised him to try a new plan, to detect Sancho in some fault for which the dog would know he was to be punished (this was in his educational period, later in life he was so well behaved that for years he never required even a scolding) and then to inflict the chastisement sharply, so as to impress the culprit with at least due respect for his superior. The experiment succeeded beyond expectation, and from that day Sancho actually loved him. On one occasion later we were at an inn from which we were to set out at four a.m. Stewart had gone to bed early and I had forgotten to see where his room was, but at half past three I took little Sancho along the passage and made him understand I was looking for my companion – he sniffed at each door and scratched at one which proved to be the right one. When I left Cambridge, Sancho became domiciled with me in Ireland, where he lived till the infirmities of old age overcame him in 1833.

1818 ENGLISH TOUR

One of the important aspects of John Hamilton's life was the fact that for a long period during his life he kept a series of journals in which he both recorded his views and detailed local and national events of the time. A small notebook, found recently at Brownhall, may well have been the original precursor of the whole series of ensuing journals which tell us almost all that is now known about his life and achievements as a landlord. Written while he was only 17 years of age, this notebook describes a tour which he and a student cousin undertook in 1818, which lasted for just over three weeks, during which they covered nearly 350 miles. Beginning at Windsor – about 20 miles west of London – it ended when the pair were just short of Holyhead in North Wales. John Hamilton described many of the places visited, including Windsor Castle, Eton College, Blenheim Palace and Oxford in great detail, and his observations about the scenery and the people they met are interesting and sometimes amusing. The following extracts give a flavour of his note-book's contents:

It commences with a visit to Windsor, where the pair stayed in the Swan Inn 'which is far from a dashing one'. His companion who is named here and there in the text simply as 'EMS', was one of his Stewart relations attending Cambridge at the same time. (John's paternal grandmother was Isabella Stewart, who is credited by family tradition with having been such a very determined woman that when her carriage was delayed by a trader's wagon, the rule of the road ordering traffic to keep to the left was introduced!). John recorded that they went 'to evening service in St. George's Chapel in the Castle' and described the building in great detail, commenting on 'the beautiful painted glass windows . . . the west window was to have been taken down and a modern one put up, but by good luck the artist who was to have painted it died before it was finished'. He noted that at Windsor Castle:

> From the top of the tower, there is a view of 7 different counties . . . but the terrace is shut from the public ever since the King's indisposition. . . . The most beautiful room of all is St. George's Hall where the Knights of the Garter dine, in it is Handel's own organ with a picture of Handel on this organ, the King used to play it often. . . .

After five pages of detailed descriptions of Windsor, John moved on to Eton College where he saw 'the dormitory where 60-something boys sleep, it is the dirtiest, nastiest place for a bedroom I ever saw'. He admired the College library, two stories high and 'carpeted with turkey carpet and is very comfortable for reading in'. He visited the Great Park, writing that 'it is said to be very full of game, as well it may be, for no one shoots there but the Regent and Duke of York who never bring any friends there'.

After reaching Oxford, John and his companion then hired a gig, which 'was a very ill looking jolting machine and the horse we called 'Meander', driving to Blenheim. Blenheim Palace was a royal gift to the first Duke of Marlborough; the seat of the influential Churchill family, and it was there that Sir Winston Churchill was to be born 56 years later. They admired the library with its 18,000 volumes, the Gobelin tapestries representing the great Duke's victorious battles, the paintings and the statues – all described by John in great detail despite the fact that they had 'an excerable guide who hurried us over in less than no time'. He saw, in the Titian room, '*the Loves of the Gods*' of which there are prints in Brnhall'. They walked around the park and saw, 'at a mile from the Palace, a statue of the great Duke of Marlborough holding a figure of Victory in his right hand, the trees in the park are placed as the troops were at the Battle of Blenheim'. We got some fruit from the gardener and ate a great quantity of it.

EMS swallowed a plumb stone which stuck in his gizzard for several hours'.

John and his friend then visited nearby Woodstock and went to see a Roman Villa which had recently been discovered:

> We found little interest worth the trouble of any but an antiquarian, except a nice lively little french woman who lives there to shew the villa, with whom we talked a good deal in french. She is worth going a great deal out of the way to see, or rather, hear. She is married to a English soldier in the 95 [Regiment]. I think she told us she married him *'Pour un peu de vengeance contre ses parents que veulent la Marrier a un Homme qu'elle n'aimant pas'*. After she had shown them an old bath, EMS asked if a hole there was to let the water in, she said no, *mais*, to let him out'. Her eldest son of about 4 years old talks both french and English and said as we were going *'bon soir, Monsieur'*, and after, 'goodnight, sir'.

The pair then went to Cheltenham: 'It is for a great part of the way a miserable, dreary country', but John's opinion was probably coloured by the fact that it rained heavily the whole way. They went to see 'Mr. and Lady H. Barker and sons, they had a delightful house, the same in which the King first went mad'. They then walked 11 miles to Gloucester where John thought the cathedral was not as fine as that at Ely: 'The first part you enter is the most massive Saxon architecture conceivable and very grand . . . [and] there are two very remarkable arches here of which there is a plan at the end of this book'. This was a reference to one of a number of drawings which John Hamilton made during this tour, though most of them were left unfinished and are not of the quality which he was to achieve 20 years afterwards during a tour of the continent.

They proceeded to Monmouth and Tintern Abbey where John and his friend went up a hill to:

> a view shop from which we had a most beautiful view, amazingly extensive. This place is called the Thymin, and there is a room where people may dine by payment of 6 pence but they must carry up their own dinner. Nearby is a naval temple in memory of Nelson; it is an horrid, ugly concern altogether. . . . When we got down, we bathed in the Wye and I swam down the stream which carried me along quicker than I expected and battered me against some rocks and scraped the shin off my legs by bad deal, and I could not swim up the current in the least, so I was forced to get out and run along the road about a hundred yards in my birthday suit.

John thought Tintern Abbey was 'very perfect as to walls and arches . . . a great part of the window tracery still remains. We crossed the river by a ferry boat, paying each a penny and got to Mitchell's Inn which is very tolerable and, having dined, we retired to bed'. He added a footnote: 'Mem: Not to marry a Monmouth or Glostershire wife, for their voices are very contrary to harmonious or amiable'.

The two returned to the abbey next morning where John sketched the abbey, and continued on their way to Chepstow, where they admired the castle, found the locals civil, and ate and drank heartily, quenching their thirst 'with three bottles excellent cider (or Sidor as it was spelt in our bill of Tintern) and a bottle of bottled beer'.

Next morning, they attended service in Chepstow church and walked about twelve miles to Raglan Castle where they measured a nearby elm tree 'and tho' a great part is gone, it measured 6½ lengths of my pocket handkerchief (n.b. – a large silk one), which we guessed to be about 30 feet'. And which, it might be added, suggests that his handkerchief was more than 4 ½ feet square! After three hours and 11 miles they arrived at Abergavenny where, though it was mid-day, they went to bed 'as our stock of linen was in want of washing'. Later they climbed the nearby Sugarloaf mountain, 'the highest about here, 18 hundred and something feet high', after which they walked on to Crickhowell.

The pair continued through attractive Welsh mountain scenery to Brecon, beyond which they decided that each would continue by a different route to Tregaron and John soon lost his way:

> I arrived at last at a house where a woman talked tolerable English and after some explanation, we agreed that her husband should walk with me for 4 shillings, but by some mistake she thought I said I would give 15 shillings if he would get horses, which I was very glad of, so he went into the mountains to catch his steed, and I staid learning welch from the woman and her children. They lived in a wretched house and had no light in the house, this was at ten o'clock or rather later.

Hamilton and his guide rode along mountain tracks in the dark, often having to dismount to cross rocky and boggy mountain stretches and streams, eventually reaching Tregaron at four in the morning, where he found that his friend had arrived much earlier, 'his guide understanding the way better than mine'. The two then left in the afternoon for Pontrhydefndigaid and the Devil's Bridge, passing through spectacular scenery on the way, and arrived at their destination in the dark once more. Rising at six, they went to see the Devil's Bridge and had a bathe at the falls. – 'of which the former and one of the latter I took sketches'. They headed for Machynlleth, but more than once when they enquired the way, 'we could not make the natives understand us, and we trudged sometimes in the right direction and sometimes wrong by our compass which we found of great use'. One woman whom they asked for directions 'said either nein Sasanagh or neil Sasanagh, meaning no English'.

Next morning, they hired a guide and ponies and rode almost to the top of

Pencil sketch of the Devil's Bridge, near Machynlleth in mid-Wales, drawn by John Hamilton during his walking tour from Windsor to Caernarvon when he was seventeen years of age.

Cadir Idris mountain, only having to walk the final stretch. Three days later they arrived at Beddgelert, admiring the views the even higher Snowdon on the way. While the pair were in their bedroom that evening they heard a conversation from which it appeared that:

> nine of the Inn-maids had made an excursion lately to the top of Snowdon; being romantically disposed we rather overslept ourselves next morning, and did not set out for Snowdon till past 10. We got a little boy to go with us who understood very little English indeed, also we got some milk and soda bread . . . and began our ascent. We found it much easier than expected and arrived without difficulty at the top. During our going up, the top was perfectly clear from clouds, but when we got there, it was surrounded all but on one side, so that we could see nothing. . . . The side which was not cloudy was sufficient to shew how great an height we were at. [The summit, at 3,500 feet, is higher than any other mountain in England, Ireland or Wales]. On the way up we passed a ridge of the mountain not above 6 feet wide at the top in some places, and above 300 feet high on the edge of tremendous precipices . . . the clouds covered our hair and clothes with a white dew which looked like frost. . . .

They waited for up to forty five minutes hoping in vain that the clouds would dispense, after which their little guide brought the pair down by a different route, and they continued to Caernarvon, four miles from which they were 'overtaken by a welch woman who had been in Llanberis to see her aunt, and said she had ran after us for our company being afraid to walk in the evening'.

They were glad of her company too, not least because she spoke good English and was able to tell them about Caernarvon and the road from there to Holyhead. Arriving in Caernarvon, they heard:

> a great shouting and noise which she told us was a sect (of Methodists I have heard) and we went to see them and found a Chapel, very large with a large brass chandelier in the middle. In it there were 30 or 40 people there, roaring and shouting and lifting their hands and tossing their arms about, and some of them jumping with all their might, sometimes two or three helped one another to jump. The noise of them all was horrid – the whole was like a pagan sort of worship. We saw none but girls and young women jump. [This was a reference to a sect nicknamed 'the Jumpers', who 'jumped for joy'; they were, in fact, closer to the Presbyterians, though called Calvinistic Methodists, and had been founded in North Wales in the mid-eighteenth century].

John Hamilton's account of this remarkable tour ended abruptly at this point, and it may be assumed that he and his cousin then proceeded to Holyhead and returned to Ireland.

UNIVERSITY PRIVILEGE

During John Hamilton's second year at college, he discovered that two of his friends there were about to take advantage of a university privilege which allowed a grandson of a peer ('even a peer's daughter'), if he be the eldest son and can show a lineal descent from a King of England, to take a Master of Arts degree without examination after two year's residence. Certain that he could prove this in his own case, he decided to avail of this privilege. He obtained a family pedigree certifying his lineal descent, through 19 generations, from Edward I, which allowed him to give up his college reading for what he called 'more popular studies' and then, at the end of his second year, and at age of 21, took his Master's degree without examination.

After leaving college, John Hamilton renewed his friendship with Hugh Rose who, after going to a German military college at Brunswick several years earlier, had since become an ensign in the 55th Regiment of Foot. The pair went to Boulougne to join Hugh's family there, and then moved with them to Paris. John was to recollect how much he had enjoyed this, his first visit to the continent but, as will be seen, his enjoyment was almost certainly enhanced by the presence there of one of Hugh's sisters. He returned to Ireland in August 1821 in preparation for his coming of age, when he was due to inherit both the family's vast Donegal estate and a very considerable fortune.

When Hamilton arrived in Dublin, the city was *en fete* for the royal visit of King George IV:

> There were great doings in Ireland that year and plenty of dancing in Dublin. At one of the balls at the Rotunda, Dublin, I had the honour of dancing before the king at his own particular request, addressed to myself personally. I was dancing with Miss Alexander, daughter of the Bishop of Meath, and in a quadrille, we happened to stand with our backs to a door which opened just as we began the quadrille – and in came his Majesty.
>
> Of course we moved to one side and bowed – he saw what was the case and returning our obeisance said: 'I pray you, do not let me spoil your dance, I desire that you will treat me like any other gentleman, take your places, I beg, and continue your quadrille'. After another bow, seeing he meant what he said, we obeyed and executed our *demi-queue de chat* before the august presence.

For a time he continued to be unsure what to do with his life, thinking at first he might travel around the world, and for this purpose he arranged with one of his former student friends, Henry Law, to set out on a world tour to 'acquainting ourselves with different peoples and nations, beginning in the east'. With the latter in mind, he engaged the services of a Cambridge professor to study Hindustani, but the whole project came to nothing after Law changed his mind, leaving John to reconsider his earlier intention of joining the army for a few years. Once more he turned to his uncle, for advice and assistance.

> I applied to the Duke of Wellington to put my name on the list for commissions, but he told me I would have to wait for a good while as I was particular as to the regiment [He had specified the 4th Dragoon Guards] in which I wished to get a commission.

INHERITING BROWNHALL ESTATE

In August 1821, while still awaiting news about his commission, he attained his majority and John Hamilton then inherited the Brownhall Estate along with the family fortune.

Forty-five years before John Hamilton inherited the property, Arthur Young, the Engish economist who toured Ireland in 1776, described passing through Donegal on his way to Ballyshannon, where he 'came presently to several landscapes, swelling fields cultivated with the bay flowing up among them. They want nothing but more wood, and are beautiful without it. . . . When the road leads to a full view of the Bay of Donegal, these smiling spots, above which the proud mountains rear their heads, are numerous, the hillocks of almost regular circular form – they are very pleasing from form, verdure, and the water breaking in their vales'. Three decades after John inherited the family estate, another traveller, James Frazer, wrote that: 'Leaving Ballyshannon, we pass several villas, and through a beautifully diversified country, and at six-and-half miles reach the village of Ballintra. About a mile to the right of this is Brownhall, the seat of Mr. Hamilton. Our road now runs through the undulating, fertile and closely populated country which lies between the high moorland and the flat uninteresting shore. At three miles and three-quarters from Ballintra, we reach the small village of Laghy, two miles from which, on the shore, is the island of St. Ernan's, the seat of Mr. Hamilton'.

The original Hamilton home in the area stood on a hill called Moyne, near Murvagh, possibly as early as 1590. John Hamilton's grandson, John Stewart Hamilton, was to write that he did not know when the next family house (at Brownhall) had been built but assumed that it dated from early in the eighteenth century. He recollected that a weathervane in the yard at Brownhill bore the inscription 'J.H. 1710', indicating that the old house probably dated from some time before that, and family records showed that the Brownhall property had come into the possession of the Hamilton family some 40 years earlier. While the original house still survives as a two-storey wing, the present three-storey main house, which dates from 1794, is partly the work of Robert Woodgate (who had been superintending work on Baronscourt in County Fermanagh for the Abercorn family). Woodgate probably added the porch (the only feature relieving the plain exterior), and was responsible for part of the ground floor.

Brownhall House, a plain three-storey structure, dates from 1794. Alongside it (to the right in the picture), now a wing to the main house and probably about one hundred years older, is the original two storey building.

As already mentioned, it was a matter of considerable irritation to John that part of the demesne and, in particular that part of the property where the house stood, was held under lease for twenty one years from Trinity College, Dublin. In effect, Hamilton was almost a 'middleman' in respect of that part of the estate under lease to the college, along with other notable proprietors in the county such as Lord Leitrim and Edward Conolly. Although he resented the situation, John Hamilton was only paying something like one-third of the Poor Law Valuation which, in turn, was approximately the value of the rents, thus allowing him a good profit on the land which he sub-let. Despite the fact that rents in the area at this time were low (though the college had raised them a year earlier) the Brownhall estate was yielding a gross rent not far short of £3,000 per annum:

> The rent at my grandfather's death was under 400 a year, and it was the habit with all College tenants to renew the lease every year so as to keep up the twenty-one years' term complete. The Senior Fellows of Trinity College, had the chief beneficial interest in the returns from the land, and they accepted a fine each year, for a renewal of the lease on the old terms, so that these leases, came to be considered almost as good as freehold, the profit rent being considerable and the tenure continuing from generation to generation. My grandfather enlarged the house at Brownhall upon the land held under Trinity College, though the ground within a pistol-shot was his freehold.
>
> The greater part of the county of Londonderry was held under certain companies in London on the same terms, and about the time I speak of, 1821, these companies began to look into their affairs more closely and to refuse to renew their leases, in order to get the lands into their own lands and to let them at farming value. Many of the gentry who had residences, thus lost them. College also began to raise its rents and to demand much higher fines for renewal of leases. I, therefore, through my agent, Mr. G.C. Swan, opened a negotiation for the purchase of exchange of one hundred acres about the house, so that I should not lose my time or money upon land that I might be turned out of when I came to be two or three and forty years of age. I proposed to give whatever a valuator appointed by the College should say was right, so that there should be benefit enough for the College to make it reasonable that it should sell or exchange, and I was to go to the cost of an Act of Parliament to make it lawful. The Senior Fellows were immovable. They told my agent that if it was so much to my advantage to get the land, it must be as much to their loss to give it, and after a year's negotiations the matter was dropped, as there seemed no likelihood of our coming to terms of agreement.

John Hamilton's grandson wrote the following description of Brownhall in his autobiography:

> Brownhall is a remarkably interesting old place. Like many Georgian houses, it has a large main hall with the dining room and the drawing room opening on either side. The stairway, as ornamental as you please, always rises from an area behind the hall. At Brownhall, a very long stone passageway leads to the kitchen, which formerly had an overlooking gallery. There is an Armada chest lying in the hall, it measures about 3 feet long and about 1.5 high and was probably jettisoned to lighten the Spanish ship in trying to escape this very stormy coast. Above the chest hangs a full length portrait of Lieut. General Sir Edward M. Pakenham, who was defeated by Maj. Gen, Andrew Jackson in the battle of New Orleans, two weeks after the signing of the Treaty of Ghent, ending the War of 1812.

The twenty-one year old John Hamilton set himself up in what he called his 'bachelor house' with a servant, a game-keeper, and a cook/housemaid (the gamekeepers' wife) and soon got to know some of the neighbours. He became especially friendly with the Rev. Robert Ball, vicar of the local Church of Ireland parish of Drumholm, and for some time afterwards he generally slept in the Vicarage, riding to Brownhall each morning and returning in the evening. The Rev. Ball spent his ministry in the Diocese of Raphoe, becoming a Prebendary of the cathedral there in 1820, he died eight years later and is buried at Stillorgan, Co. Dublin.

John Hamilton, writing of himself at this period, said he had been brought up with what he termed: 'Rather ultra-Protestant principles and Tory views regarding the policy of keeping the Roman Catholics from all share of political freedom, such as seats in Parliament and on the judicial bench, commissions in the army, etc., preserving what was called the Protestant ascendancy, and in all things resisting political reforms; indeed among us 'reform' and 'rebellion' were much the same. Though I did not know a single person of liberal views, I began, even when in college, to doubt both the policy and the Christianity of these ultra views'. He had also come to realise that what he called 'the faults and vices which socially prevailed in Ireland' were those of 'a conqueror and tyrant race on the one side, and those of a conquered and enslaved, or at least trampled and ill-used race on the other, and that an end ought to be put to this state of affairs'.

In this frame of mind, the new and very young proprietor immediately set about improving the property which had had lain idle for about fourteen years, putting into action both principles and the plans which had been formulating in his mind for some time, and in this respect alone he proved himself to be far ahead of the majority of landlords, most of whom spent little or nothing on improvement before the Famine. His principles included a sense of his duties as well as of his rights, which led him to demonstrate a remarkable sympathy for the very large number of poor tenants crowded on his estate – about 1,200 around Brownhall, and another 1,100 in the Finn valley further north.

> I had an intense love of the place and had long before laid out in my mind plantations and other improvements. The old plantations were mere strips along the avenues, the river and, round the lake, one or two clumps. Except one young plantation, made by my father on one of the many hills which surrounded the house; these were bare and cold looking, and the house itself was very much out of repair.

In the grounds of Brownhall there is a curious natural ravine known as the Pullins, through which the Ballintra or Pullins river flows in a deep cleft in the limestone rock, wearing it into unusual shapes and penetrating through subterranean caverns. A small notebook which has survived at Brownhall contains a hand-written copy of an article about the Pullins which appeared in *Frazer's Magizine* in 1869, part of which runs as follows:

> Running through the grounds of Major Hamilton of Brownhall is a small river which bores its way underground, from cavern to cavern, for nearly two miles. The caverns are formed in the limestone and the power of petrification possessed by the power of the water is very astonishing. Sticks and straws are soon coated and crusted over, and by degrees harden into stones. . . . The caves are some of them very beautiful and when lighted up by the aid of magnesium wire [magnesium burns with a very bright white light] the effect is more brilliant and striking, the walls sparkling as though studded with by countless diamonds. In one of them, the river makes a fine waterfall . . . plunging into an unseen depth through a cloud of mist at its feet . . . the effect is charming. . . .

In an article published in the 1947 edition of the *Journal of the Donegal Historical Society*, Hugh Deery described the Pullins in similar terms and also gave a description of an artificial lake which had been a feature of the demesne: 'At one time, there was a picturesque lake, about a mile in circumference, close to the house, and at the time . . . [John Hamilton] came to Brownhall, on attaining his majority in 1821, the lake showed signs of beginning to fill-in at the sides. John Hamilton thought to allay the silting-up process by draining the lake, and with that end in view, he blasted a bar of rock from the bed of the river where it issued from the lake, near what is known as the China Bridge. The work went no further . . . [and] the blasting of the rock finally put an end to the lake'.

The large estate embraced a multitude of townlands and places which, if fully listed, would fill several paragraphs. As usual (then and since), many of the place-names were spelt in a variety of ways, examples include Brownhall/Brown Hall, Laghey/Laghy, Muckross/Muckros, and Raroy/Rarooey. Even a limited selection of names may give some idea of the magnitude of the family's holding at the time of its fullest extent: Altilow, Archiken, Ascoby, Aughadowey, Aughadulla, Ballindolley, Ballinamore, Ballintowey, Ballintra, Ballyalla, Ballydevitt, Ballynakelly, Ballybulgin, Ballydermott, Big Park, Braddan, Clanbeorine, Clayboory, Coxtown, Drimmenny, Drimstevlin, Drineyowen, Dumsteolin, Fintown, Foyagh, Glasbolie, Glenboghill, Glenmohil, Greggstown, Heneys, The Hough, Killynard, Kingarrow, Lackdrum, Legahurry, Loughinlarkan, Loughnabraden, Maghery, Meenadowan, Meenagowlan, Meenmore, Moore Park, Muckros, Mullinasole, Murvagh, Nuasary, Poolranny, Rath, Raroy, Rock Hill, Shannagh, Tawnawilly, Tuidivin, Tullyearl, Tullynagrean, and Winter hill. One local place name, Tullygallentullywee, must qualify to be high on the list of the longest place-names in Ireland.

DEALING WITH THE TENANTS

If Brownhall Estate was in a very backward state, so also were the tenants who, however, were 'cheerful in rags, good tempered on a starving stomach'. As early as 1822, Hamilton praised the work of the local Tyrhugh Farmer's Improvement Society, formed in 1800, which promoted new farming methods and sold thornquicks for hedging (now that hedging was coming into vogue) at reduced rates, but complained that it was 'difficult to get through the conservatism of the people'. John Hamilton later recalled that when he began his own improvements; any number of men could be got for five pence a day, and pointed out that Irish coinage was then different from that in England:

> Ten penny bank tokens and five penny (called fip-penny) bits were the currency and although twenty shillings of twelve pence each, made an Irish pound, it required thirteen Irish pence to make an English shilling , and £1.1.8d. to make a British pound.

He went on to describe the primitive condition of the tenants and how he introduced new ideas and even sent some of his tenant's sons to Scotland to learn new farming methods:

> But to return to our labourers. These poor fellows, raggedly clad, came to their work with wooden spades, having iron-shod points. Indeed, iron spades would not have been usable by them, for very few had shoes, but wore on their legs stockings without feet. They were very dextrous in the use of the wooden spades, especially in setting potatoes in the lazy beds. A person not skilled in handling these implements was sure to break his spade.

> The pay was not so bad as it seems, for living was very cheap, butter four-pence or five-pence a pound, beef and mutton rather less, oats about five-pence a stone, and potatoes sometimes as low as a penny a stone of fourteen pounds.
>
> The plough was seldom used in the district, which it must be admitted was a backward one, though by no means the most backward, and when a plough was used it was a crooked stick with a second one grafted into it, to give two handles, and the point of the stick armed with a bit of iron, the cost of the implement about half a crown. The condition of agriculture may be guessed from this description, and the breed of cattle, sheep, and even pigs was a match for the tillage.
>
> Carts they had none – most of the carrying was done in creels on ponies' backs. [Arthur Young who toured Donegal in 1776, commented that there were scarcely any wheeled carts in the county]. Some superior farmers had what were called low-backed cars, a sort of platform with shafts, and under it a pair of solid block wheels. One rich man had spoke wheels, which were greatly admired. I brought over some Scotch smiths and carpenters and set them to make improved implements and carts, also sent some of my tenants' sons to Scotland to learn farming. Crowds came to see the first cart that was turned out; but though it was voted 'illegant', it was declared useless. 'For', said a sage among the spectators, 'who ever heard of a cart in this country?' and his argument seemed to weigh much with his auditors.
>
> However, a few years later the Scotchmen had at one time orders on hand for fifty carts. In course of time ploughs followed (iron ploughs were only then coming into use in Great Britain), and several very nice wooden ploughs were set going. The old fashioned ponies were not equal to the work of a plough, so these had to be changed for better steeds before the better implements could be used. A farming society was formed, having in view several objects, such as improvement in agriculture, the building of better cottages, improvement of the breed of animals, etc. This society had considerable success, though a good deal of uphill work was experienced in persuading the people to adopt new methods or new ideas. Improved cultivation is more easy to effect than improved convictions or habits in men.

Three years after he inherited Brownhall, the lands leased to the estate by Trinity College, Dublin were surveyed on behalf of the college by Thomas Noble who described something of the conditions under which the tenants lived just before John Hamilton's scheme for improvements got under way:

> 'Most of the tenants lived in claghans consisting of a great number of poor houses crowded together [Estyn Evans, 'the founder' of modern

> Irish geographical studies, defined *clachans* as 'rural clusters of small dwellings, not organised in streets, and without services such as a church or a shop'] . . . and they held land in rundale, a system prejudiced to improvements, which prevents them growing wheat, the lands not being fenced in. . . . ' Eight years earlier, in 1816, William Shaw Mason's *Parochial Survey* favourably described the inhabitants of the Donegal Bay area as 'a healthy, hardy, and long-lived race of people, many instances of longevity could be enumerated, some few exceeding even 100 years. Their dress and general appearance does not differ from that of the rest of the neighbouring counties. . . . The English language is spoken by almost all except perhaps some few in the more remote parts of the mountains; the native language is also well understood by all the Roman Catholics, and most of the Protestants speak it'.

Hamilton had succeeded to his estate at a time of great changes in agricultural practices when progressive proprietors were busy consolidating, enclosing and draining their properties. John Hamilton embarked on an ambitious 40 year plan to improve both his estate and the position of the tenants aiming, during the first five years, to double the income from rents by arranging that each farm would have about 20 acres of arable land. He was fortunate, at this early stage, in having the services of Alexander Hamilton of Coxtown (no relation), a very progressive agent who also acted for the large Conolly estate as well as for several others in the locality, and who had been actively pursuing a policy of replacing the old rundale system with 'squared' holdings. Rundale was fast disappearing as landlords tried to bring some order to the hopelessly sub-divided, sometimes microscopic tenant holdings – extreme examples of which included a Donegal tenant who had land in more than 30 different places and, in another case, a nearby half acre field which was held by 26 people. The idea behind 'squaring' was to replace the tenants' former fragments of land with a holding in a single, compact piece, properly fenced, with a house thereon, adjoining a road – a system which changed the face of much of the landscape in a remarkably short space of time. The rundale system was prevalent around Ballintra as late as 1834, but was almost eliminated from the district by 1844, after which the nearest area retaining the old system was Tawnawilly, near Barnsmore.

Though lacking any experience in running a large estate, he was, obviously, open to new methods and not without ideas of his own but, unfortunately for himself and indeed for his descendants, he tended to be impulsive and deficient in patience, which resulted in his being profligate with the family fortune which was now entirely at his disposal. The best-remembered instance of this was the new road which he built in 1824 between Rath and Lough na Darragh, running roughly east-west through part of his estate, intending to convert 2,000 acres of bog into rich land. He embarked upon this scheme without bothering

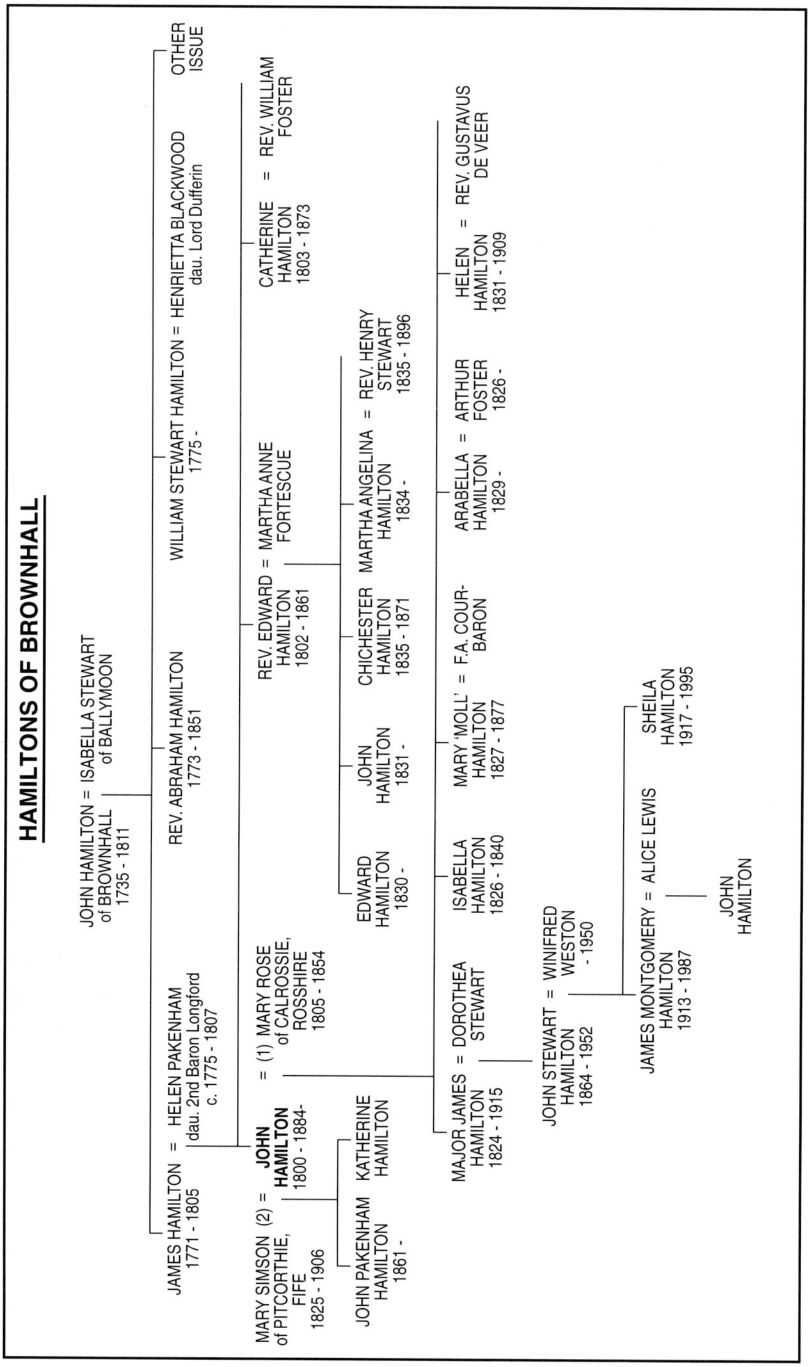

Family tree indicating the main lines of descent from John Hamilton's grandparents down through his two families.

to apply for a grant from central funds, a grant which would certainly have been forthcoming but would have involved delays and what he called 'red-tape-ism' while the application was being processed.

> I began at once a magnificent plan for improving the land and people, which in my inexperience resulted in helping largely to empty my purse. One quarter of the expenditure and half the exertion would have done more good had I been more patient, but I wanted to do everything at a gallop. Instead of laying out a road and getting it made, as others did, by the county; helping it out by my own means liberally when it was specially beneficial to my property. I said: 'I don't want the county to make roads for *me*'. – while at the same time *I* was taxed to make roads for the county, and had fully as fair a claim as other proprietors to have roads made for my estate – 'I will make my own roads and build my own bridges'.

But, even apart from forgoing financial assistance from the county, he began the work during the winter months instead of waiting for drier conditions, and made the project additionally more expensive by the means employed. It had been completed, he wrote:

> at a cost treble what it would have been had I been up to the right way to go about it, and had been patient to let the bogs and quagmires dry for a season after I had opened the drains. But I had the stones carried on horses' backs where carts could not go, and in baskets by men where horses could not go, and so had the satisfaction in September 1824, in driving my *phaeton* to Lough na darragh.
>
> My other works were carried on in the same expensive manner, but for a time a large reserve of ready money, which I had inherited on coming of age, prevented my seeing the need for a more economical mode of expenditure. My overweening anticipation of making 2000 acres of bog into rich land paying £2 an acre. The real truth was an increased rental of about £200, which did not pay one per cent of my outlay.

Writing about this period 50 years later, Hamilton recalled that when he was a young man:

> the part of my property which most interested me was the considerable extent of moor, or as it is called here, without any regard to elevation, *mountains,* which was pretty well stocked with grouse. It is a district which ought not to be populous, and its soil pays ill for cultivation; but the unhappy legislation which made leases of the value of forty-five shillings a year give a rate for the county representatives, had led my forefathers

> to encourage sub-division to such a degree that instead of five or six substantial tenants I found nearly a hundred. That they were poor I need not say, but they paid their rents duly, and were a more civilised folk than . . . could be expected.

Explaining what he meant by 'civilised' he gave an instance of how the people of that impoverished district provided education for their children:

> Their custom was, under the advice of the priest to whose communion they all belonged, to depute one or two of the most trusted among them to go into the more civilised parts and employ a teacher to come for two years, and teach all the children from four or five years old to ten or twelve years of age, generally alternately a male and female teacher so that the girls might learn to sew.
>
> The teacher lived from house to house, was well cared for, and was paid a salary in addition to board and lodging . . . . There was no school house but in summer a barn and in winter a kitchen in one of the larger cabins was used as a schoolroom. . . . The result was a greater proportion of intelligent readers and intelligible writers was to be found among these people than I think is to be found in most districts now [1871] well provided with regular schools.

In his old age, Hamilton reverted to employing an agent, Samuel Fyffe, and the following note addressed to him gives some idea of how leniently John treated his tenants:

> Some of my tenants in Killymard came on Saturday to complain that they were badly off this year and asked to me not put the rise of rent this time. You know I put off any rise this year because of the bad harvest . . . and did not let you require it from them as I had directed you. And this year I would do all I can afford to make it easier to them but I have waited long and cannot afford to all they would like – but I would say, let any tenant who is not fit to pay the rise now – let him pay the old rent and leave the rise as an arrear to be paid up in the next year or two. The tenants all spoke and behaved well, they know I have done all I could for them, and are well disposed to do their part – so I have settled to wait for the rise from any who are pinched this year.

Among the surviving family papers there are letters written to their landlord by some of John Hamilton's tenants which give some further idea of their relationship one to the other. This one was written by Hugh McGlinn of Meenadoon:

> I payed a years rent every year since I bought this place, my friend and my landlord. I trust that your honour will be kind enough to asist me at the present distress. My byre gave way where I have my catle tied, it is very stormy here at present. I have no timber nearer than Stranorlor and I have no money at present every thing is very inconvenient as you know very well and I ask the request of your kind honour to essist your poor and faithful tenant.

John Hamilton's response is recorded in a note to his agent scribbled across the letter: 'If he has paid [his rent] this year give him one pound'.

There is no record of his response to the following letter written by Neil McMonagle of Glenmohill:

> I write to let you know that I am not able to meet you [pay your rent] now and I hope you will spare me til March. I have been ill and unable to work this long time or I might have been able to settel with you but as it is I hope you will give me this little time. Please answer this note and let me know how you will deal with me.

And from Dan Sweeney of Old Kilpatrick there came a letter hinting at some obscure dispute which he hoped Hamilton would settle in his favour:

> I am sending you a year's rent which I hope you receive all right and I hope you will return me a reseat back. Your Honour, Mr. Hamilton, let me know what you are going to do with them other parties that is on the farm.

THE SEVENTEEN-YEAR-OLD BRIDE

A chance meeting with his old college friend, Hugh Rose, on the streets of Dublin in November 1822 was to prove a turning point in John Hamilton's life. Rose, still in the army, had been posted to Ireland, but was about to return to his native Scotland on three month's leave. He told John: 'You had better come with me, I sail tomorrow', and while the idea seemed attractive, John was unable to go at such short notice. He asked his friend to wait for him ten days in Dublin while he arranged his own affairs back in Donegal and Hugh agreed to this suggestion.

Hugh Rose's father was fitting-up his residence at Calrossie, near Tain in north-eastern Scotland and had, in the meantime, rented Novar House near Dingwall where the two friends arrived together less than a fortnight later. John Hamilton was to recall that the winter of 1822–23 was exceptionally severe and he described how the two passed the time shooting game:

John Hamilton was twenty two when he married the seventeen year old Mary Rose of Novar, Scotland, in May, 1823.

> [Hugh] Rose and I were equally bad shots, but we were indefatigable; prowling through the fine woods of Novar after woodcocks, which abounded, and along the sea-shore after wild fowl. Rose hated wet and did not much like cold, while I was as hardy as an Esquimaux dog, and in the duck shooting often waded through rivers among floating blocks of ice, on which occasions he generally went straight home and left me alone to pursue my game. One day on my return home I found him in the dining-room, busy roasting on a string a most miserable snipe, lean and lank, hung up by one leg. It was a 'pet' of ours which lived in a ditch on the Novar farm and afforded us nearly daily sport for many weeks. We always saw him and got a couple of shots going out and generally coming in. 'But this time', Rose remarked, 'I caught his reverence napping and having a rest on a gate I bagged him'. It was the only snipe he ever shot, so he indulged in the pleasure of roasting and eating him.

John continued his friendship with Hugh Rose for many years, and recalled that Hugh was later to ask his father for some money so that he might go abroad and make his fortune. Old Mr Rose was rather pressed financially at the time and said he could barely give his son £20. Hugh assured his father that this would be sufficient – indeed, Hugh did so well that:

> A few years after this, when another brother who had gone into business failed, Hugh sent him £2000, saying he still had his £20 to begin again upon. Hugh had gone to the West Indies, and, being clever and daring, he had undertaken perilous commissariat ventures, but always with success, conducting every convoy himself sometimes through the very midst of the enemy's ships, sometimes under the guns of the enemy's forts. He returned to Scotland at the age of twenty-nine with cash enough to buy some of his relatives' lands, who had been running a different course, and a good deal more besides with which to undertake some of the most extensive land improvements in Scotland.
>
> He married Arabella, daughter of Colonel Phipps, a very, handsome woman with a portion of £40,000. He continued to be the same energetic, generous soul till his death in his eighty-first year. His agricultural improvements were on an extensive scale. He began to introduce wheat into Eastern Ross, and was at first derided; but when I first went there, in 1822, there was a regular trade by sea in wheat to London. He later built mills and got the export to be in flour, leaving more profit in Ross-shire, for though he was a very complete citizen of the world, and patriot of Great Britain, he loved his own district especially, urged forward its advancement, and died in harness, attending a meeting at Inverness for public business. His pride was to take a friend at harvest into some of his wheat-fields, which were nearly 100 acres each, where I have seen 300 or more men and women at work reaping and binding, while he would call attention to the margin of the field inside the hedge, which exhibited an evidence of what the field had been, a border of heather being preserved to show its original produce. He changed the family name from Rose to Ross a few years before his death, consequent on succeeding through his wife to a large property.
>
> On Queen Victoria's first visit to Scotland, Mr. Rose said he regretted it was not a couple of years sooner, for he would have met her on horseback at the head of 200 plough-boys, mounted on his own plough-horses, but he had so diminished his agricultural speculations that he had hardly 100 horses on all his farms, and that would not be a sufficient force to be worthy of the occasion. It would have been a striking reception of a Monarch in days of peace and plenty.

John had spent a holiday with his friend's family in Boulougne and in Paris, as already mentioned, and was now enjoying his three-month stay with them in

Scotland. But more than the local wildfowl had caught his attention:

> On 23rd January, 1823, I proposed to Mary Rose who was aged 17 and a day, and had the joy to be accepted by my first love.

John wrote immediately to cancel his application for a commission in the army but, coincidentally, his letter crossed in the post a communication sent to him requesting a lodgement of money for a coronetcy in the 4th Dragoon Guards. However, after what he called 'the usual delays and impatience' the matter was settled and he returned to Novar, less than four months later, and the young couple were married there on the 7th May, 1823.

The young couple – their combined ages totalling just under forty years – settled at Brownhall in August 1823 – after what John called his 'wedding tour'. There is no record of where the young couple went, but 16 years after this, while travelling on the continent, John wrote without explanation that he had been to both Freiburg and Strasbourg before, a possible clue about his honeymoon. He succeeded to an estate capable of providing him with a comfortable living which at the same time sustained many hundreds of very poor tenants. These people's livelihoods if not their very lives now depended on an inexperienced young man. The unresolved problems about part of the Brownhill Estate being under a twenty-one year lease held by the Senior Fellows of Trinity College, Dublin, continued to be a cause of annoyance and of concern to John Hamilton, who did not relish the idea of being put out of his home when the lease was next due for renewal, at the age of forty two.

John Hamilton's grandmother, Isabella, with his three eldest children, James, Isabella and Mary, painted by Samuel Lover. John Hamilton's wife sold 'some useless plate' in order to pay for the picture.

THREE

The Move to St Ernan's

He began to consider the possibility of building another house for him self on some of his freehold land, and seriously began to entertain the idea of building at Lough na Darragh, a little lake situated in the Ballydermott area of his estate some miles to the east of Brownhall on the road to Pettigo. He considered reclaiming the land around it and planting trees there to make it a more beautiful place but all this came to nothing because of a dispute between two of his tenants over a another part of his property which, until then, he had never had any occasion to visit – a fortuitous happening somewhat in the same vein as the chance events which had led to his meeting his wife.

The dispute between his two tenants concerned a small island named after the local saint, St Ernan, just off the mainland on the southern side of Donegal Bay, facing Muckros Hill. It was readily accessible only at low tide or full tide; when the tide was out, the channel separating the island from the mainland was about two foot deep or less making it possible to reach it on foot; and at high tide the depth of the channel could be up to 14 feet when the island could be easily reached by boat:

> My commencement of St. Ernan's was in 1824, and was brought about owing to a dispute between two tenants who held the little island of four Irish, or six English acres. I had never seen the island as no road went near it and it lay out of sight from the tenants' houses. My cousin, T. Stewart, and I rode from Brownhall to see it and to settle the dispute. It was a beautiful harvest day in September. The view, with the tide full in and the sun shining brightly, delighted me so much that I sent the man with the boat for a spade and a cord and we marked out the foundation of a cottage, and I settled the dispute by my taking the island for myself.

(The mothers of both Thomas Stewart, mentioned above, and John Hamilton were Pakenham sisters).

Having taken possession of the island, John Hamilton then began the task of building his cottage and, two and three-quarter years after the young couple had moved into Brownhall, they re-settled in St Ernan's. His wife, Mary, had been suffering from indifferent health and, as John recorded, her health had threatened to break-down. Following the move to St. Ernan's, her persistent cough disappeared and she then became 'remarkably hardy and active', which John attributed to the invigorating sea air. Canon Maguire, in his *History of the Diocese of Raphoe* wrote that Hamilton had 'invested this honoured name with a local habitation, and rescued the saint's traditional association, as Patron, with Drumholm from hastening decay in the memories of the people, by designing his beautifully situated and well-designed summer villa on the seaside near Donegal, by the almost forgotten title of St. Ernan's'.

The house, surrounded by the sea, was subject to every wind that blew. On the day that he had first visited St. Ernan's to intervene in his tenants' dispute, he had noted that 'there was one little holly-bush on the south side of the island and one thorn bush full of honeysuckle on the north; these were the only things that grew taller than grass'. Although he was to enlarge it later, now that the original small house was completed he began to make a little garden on its south side and, in addition, he commenced planting trees to see how (or if) they would grow.

> At first I had only the island, and made a little garden close to the house to the south, and planted a few trees to see if they would live; a couple of cows occupied the chief part of our little dominion. So exposed and unsheltered was our garden that the cabbages were blown clear out of the ground, and I was obliged to fasten these plants with three hay ropes

Part of the extensive ruins of John Hamilton's corn mill at Muckros. He also built a salt works and seven schools, and is credited with building several hundred houses for his tenants.

> to pegs driven into the ground, rigging them each like a mast. The trees, however, grew beyond expectation, and I planted more in the following years. The labourers who planted them did not anticipate much success, for I overheard them one day talking together and one said: 'Boys, these wee bushes we're planting are finely sheltered by the primrosy plants growing'. 'Sure', said another, 'when they grow to be trees, won't it be the say-gulls that'll make rookeries in them!' The trees grew, and in some years' time the whole island was like a bird's nest, so bushy with thriving trees and bushes that it required more work thinning them out, than it had required in planting them.
>
> By degrees as my family increased I enlarged my cottage at St. Ernan's, becoming more and more attached to the place where my planting throve, and where especially my wife's health prospered, which had threatened to break down at Brownhall (about five miles from St. Ernan's), her chest having been severely affected before we left it. My children also prospering in the fresh sea air. I bought out the tenants in the immediate neighbourhood, and increased my demesne till at last in the famine period, 1845-50, I made my demesne extend over Raroy Hill and include about 380 acres, of which about fifty acres are plantations.

In due course, Hamilton's cottage was enlarged into a fairly substantial house, with high stone walls to give shelter to the garden, and the whole island was ringed by a ten foot high wall. On the opposite shore he built a school house, a gardener's cottage, and also a corn mill for which he diverted a stream while, at the entrance from the (now re-aligned) main Donegal – Ballyshannon road, he built a pretty gate lodge.

THE TENANT'S CAUSEWAY

Hamilton became very attached to his cottage, as it then was, but while its island location seemed so attractive at first, he soon realised that it suffered from one obvious disadvantage:

> We found it very inconvenient having no access to the land except at low water or by boat. At half tide, we could not well use either way of access; I therefore set to work to have a causeway made between the island and mainland.

John Hamilton prepared to build his planned, connecting 'mound' or causeway in the full knowledge that this would require stemming the strong tidal currents running between St Ernan's and Muckros Hill on the opposite shore. All the local experts warned him that he would not succeed; and an engineer whom he had consulted told him he would have to provide one or even two bridges in the causeway to accommodate the tidal races. Nothing daunted, Hamilton decided to go ahead with his own plan of what he called the 'mound building', determined both to achieve his goal and confound the experts.

> The channel between the point of the island and the point of Muckros Hill which projects a peninsula, is exactly a statute furlong, and the water was then fourteen feet at spring tides; it has sanded up at both sides fully five feet since the mound was made . . .
>
> This plan of bridging would have cost a large sum . . . I resolved to block it up entirely and make the water force its way and form a new channel . . . between St Ernan's and the next island to the south. To work, therefore, I set with about a hundred men with wheel barrows . . . We got on well till about three fourths of the passage was closed, coating the sloping sides with stones, round stones roughly thrown on, which from subsequent experience I prefer to paving with quarried stones on edge.

At this point, the tides running between the closing gap began to carry away the new material as quickly as it was being thrown in, and he decided to await a midsummer neap tide, when the rise of the water was slow, calculating that he could finally beat the current if he could get the work completed, at least to highwater level, during the period of one tide. At the appointed time, construction recommenced:

> We worked as for very life and kept the work above the water which rose on the north of our bank, while the sand bed to the south kept the tide out, as we knew would do so till very near high water when the tide would rise a foot or two over it, whereas if we saw its height surmounted, and one little stream begin to pass, the water would soon cut a channel through the bed of sand and relieve our embankment, which was thin and pressed by a height of water on one side.
>
> We watched earnestly as we strained every muscle to keep our start of the rising sea, but before that welcome sight came, we saw our bank begin to move, and in a few seconds, with a crash and velocity that made us giddy to look at it, our day's work was swept away and the tide poured through victorious. There was a shriek of dismay from the workers, and we looked on with heads and hands hanging down for some minutes.

Almost anyone else would have accepted defeat, or the engineer's advice to include a bridge to allow a passage for the powerful tides, but Hamilton's response was: 'We won't be beat boys. Three cheers for to-morrow, and with God's blessing we shall beat the tide and hold our ground'. When the work recommenced, a very large group of men turned up, offering their services to Hamilton free of charge. While most of them were his tenants, he was surprised to see others from neighbouring districts as well. The men decided to divide into two parties:

> One to dig the clay and fill the barrows, the other to wheel, and dig with a will they did work for a whole long summer day – making one bargain, which was that I should give neither food nor money. A drink of whisky and water once or twice in the day was all they would accept. In the evening they shouldered their spades and with three cheers for the work, would set out on their way home, sometimes a distance of fully ten miles. These good neighbours were tenants on various estates with which I had no connection, and were of all denominations and races known among us.

Hamilton was surprised early next day to hear the sound of fifes and drums, signalling:

> the arrival of a strong party from a village six miles off. They were the members of a Yeomanry Corps, and all Orangemen, fine stout fellows, but hot-blooded. They had hardly arrived when a fiddle and fife proclaimed another arrival, and I was a little dismayed when I found about an equal force on the ground from a mountainous property about seven miles off in an opposite direction, every man of them not only Roman Catholic but exactly of that class and character, most opposite to my Orange friends. In fact it was more than supposed that most of them were Ribbonmen, and their district had a very bad name for either loyalty or peaceableness.
>
> However, before I could interfere, the two parties met on the green field where our work went on. I had to cross in a boat from the island and felt rather alarmed when I saw the two parties approach each other. Just as I arrived they recognised one another, and the Orangemen perceiving the accident which brought two sets of men on the same day greeted the others with a 'Hurrah! hurrah, for the boys of Town o' Willy!' [Townawilly or Tawnawilly], which was replied to with energy: 'Hurray for the Ballydermoth boys!' Nothing could be more friendly than their bearing towards each other. It was arranged that they should that day prove whether Ballydermoth or Town o' Willy could show the best men. Ballydermoth was to dig first for two hours and Town o' Willy, to wheel [barrows]. How they did work! The object of the Ballydermoth men was to fill the barrows so full as to overload the Town o' Willy men, or so quickly as to have time to rest on their spades and cry: 'Five pounds for a Town o' Willy man to take this barrow away

St Ernan's and the causeway viewed from Muckros Hill. John Hamilton's tenants not only completed the building of the causeway in spite of several disasters but refused payment for the work.

from before me. I'm kilt waiting for one of them Town o' Willy men, where are they at all?' But the Town o' Willy men were active fellows and sometimes brought back empty barrows quicker than the Ballydermoth men could fill them, and then the cry was on their side: 'Five pounds for a Ballydermoth man to fill a barrow', and then the wheeler would sit down on his barrow and say: 'Boys, hasn't one of ye never a pipe till I take a smoke while I'm waiting for a Ballyermoth boy to fill to me?' So they worked alternately till late in the evening; neither party would be the first to stop, though many of them were sorely tired, to which it was in no small degree owing that I persuaded them at last to stop, and to give three cheers for Ballydermoth and Town o' Willy, which they did heartily, and striking up each their own tune marched off in the best of humour. Generally the men rested for an hour, the regular labourers taking their dinner and the volunteers their glass of whisky and water. When finished they grouped together, and two or three poets among them produced songs composed for the occasion, generally grotesque enough but not infrequently having touches of poetry, and still oftener of feeling. These they sang very heartily.

Just as the finishing touches to the construction work were being completed, and after a carriage had been driven across the embankment on a kind of trial run, an unexpected set-back occurred:

> One evening while the work was still progressing . . . but the mound still required strengthening with more stones on the sides, a fearful storm arose from the south-west and beat directly, upon the mound, washing down the stones off the sides, cutting into the earthwork and damaging the half-finished roadway. I was laid up with an attack of gout and could personally do nothing, and as night closed in could only look at the devastation going on. The tide fell as the darkness increased, but later in the night the moon rose, and though the wind continued to be boisterous the sky was not over-clouded. In the morning when I looked out, it seemed as if the mischief done the day, before had been a dream, for the whole mound was in a better condition than before the storm. The whole population hearing what damage was done had assembled from all the neighbourhood, and with horses and carts had worked all night by moonlight, so as to have the mound prepared to receive with repaired sides the next tide. No one ever told me he was there that night, and when I asked, I was told it must have been the 'wee folk', i.e., fairies.

Six weeks after the work on the causeway had commenced, John Hamilton's carriage was ceremoniously driven across it. After his death, a stone plaque was erected to commemorate its completion, on which the following inscription was placed:

> THIS CAUSEWAY STANDS TO COMMEMORATE THE GREAT mutual love between John Hamilton and the people of Donegal, both his tenants and others, through a time of bitter famine and pestilence. John Hamilton, not for the first or last time had stood between them and death. Knowing that his great wish was to build a road joining the island of St. Ernan's, his favourite dwelling place, with the mainland, and that owing to the Atlantic tides, he could not achieve this without expenditure far beyond his means, the people, Roman Catholic and Protestant, came in their hundreds with spade, pick and barrow to build this causeway, refusing all recompense.
>
> John Hamilton J. P., D.L. of Brownhall and St. Ernans was born in the year 1800, he succeeded his father in 1807 and died in 1884.

This was not the only occasion when the local people turned up to help Hamilton. In November, 1829, he wrote:

> May I be grateful for having my lot cast in such a part of the country. My

> neighbours are always ready to do me a good turn according to their power. Today several of carts came to help me freely in a difficult job. They belonged to tenants of 4 or 5 landlords – not above six belonged to mine . . . .

RESOLUTION TO KEEP A JOURNAL

Imbued with a sense of religious vocation, John Hamilton had begun, in 1828, to keep a regular journal, which he commenced with these words:

> O Lord, make the keeping of this journal, which I now begin, a means of drawing me unto Thee by increasing my humility, and causing me to distrust my own heart and my own strength when I find I am obliged to record so many instances of the utter insufficiency and deceitfulness of both . . .

These words set the tone for by far the greater part of the hundreds of entries which he was to write in a whole series of volumes during the following 27 years. He wrote at length, with a comparatively neat hand, about his thoughts on religion, often interspersed with extempore prayers. An early example begins:

> I thank God that I have been made so very exacting in requiring chapter and verse for every opinion I admit. This has saved me much confusion and doubt. The great advantage I can perceive to myself from the spiritual and religious conversation and communication afforded by the concourse of spiritual persons, are charity in forming opinions of others, charity and patience in hearing the opinions and speeches of others . . .

References to illnesses affecting John Hamilton himself and various members of his family occur quite often in the journals, and his descriptions of symptoms and treatments are a reminder of how frightening illnesses were at that time when medical science was still very primitive. In January of that year, John recorded that: 'Our little girl [probably Isabella, their second child] appears to have recovered from a serious illness but is still weak: The rest of the household are well again'. References to 'M' or 'Mary' can be confusing because his wife and their second daughter shared the same name, for example when he wrote four months after this: 'My M has been threatened with an illness which God has yet warded off . . . ' A few weeks later there was an entry referring to the 'not severe illness of our little Mary', after which came the following: 'Mary and her child have both been going on well'. During July, he wrote of his wife:

> My Mary has been for several days near at death's door, a violent attack of inflammation of the pleura or the coat lining the space of the lungs, came upon her on Thursday (just a week ago) and yielded only the active measures of Dr. Crawford in bleeding leeches and blistering. This was followed by a bilious fever which continued obstinate til today – it has abated this morning. . . . The prayers of the congregation of Donegal and Ballintra were offered for her, by her desire, on Sunday. She has not seen her children for 7 days, the very idea of seeing them agitates her too much for her weak state to bear.

Mary's Aunt Jane, concerned about her illness, travelled from Scotland in August, arriving after a journey 'of several hundred miles by sea and in stormy weather'. After a few weeks:

> We are just returned from a visit to Tyrcallen having gone so far to have Aunt Jane's company as we could. She is gone to Scotland – sailed today – having come to see M in her illness – and by God's blessing she has left her in such a state that we walked up the mountain of Mulloughagarry yesterday – to the top – and she was not at all tired. Hers has been a wonderful recovery, so regular, so perfect.

During the winter of 1829, all four children [Arabella had recently been born] were laid low:

> Our house is a very hospital now. Bell [Isabella] has a severe cough which we suspect to be hooping cough and, if so, Jimmy has it, for he coughs a little. Mary has still her terrible swelled and sore thumb which has defied all our efforts since March. Arabella has a most tormenting eruption over her whole body which disturbs her rest and must weaken her, though as yet she seems well. We dread the hooping cough for these two little ones.

In fact, by the following month, they had all caught the infection.

Like many other landlords, Hamilton was an officer in the local Yeomanry regiment, a body which had been set up by the government in 1796 as a kind of Local Defence Force which would be available to assist the army to cope with a Napoleonic invasion or a threatened rebellion. During the summer of 1829 he decided to resign his position:

> I must give up my Yeomen. I cannot reconcile a military with a Christian life, and though Yeomen are hardly military, yet they are liable every day to be called out, and that would not be the time to choose to leave them . . . I intend therefore to take my leave of my captaincy next parade day.

Hamilton's journal seldom mentioned his staff, so some of the exceptions are worth reproducing:

> I have been some days been [sic] occupied in arranging the removal and settlement elsewhere of one of my dependants and . . . I have done so in a way as to satisfy all. Ogilvie, my steward and gardener was quite unfit for a change beyond a garden wall and gave dissatisfaction – he has gone to a house and farm occupied by Capt. Wray to establish a nursery (Hollybank). On account of his good old mother I could not dismiss him altogether. He and his family seem most comfortably settled.
>
> Next, Mrs. Johnston, laundress, did nothing right, she goes with her family to a farmer in Tramon. T. Walker and his wife move their habitation and school into Ogilvie's home – a change much for the better. Williams takes charge of all my out of door matters as well as the gamekeeping, and being a hardy, clever man he may do well. I gave 12£ a year for his children on account of his saving me a gardener; his wife is to do our laundry 27£ a year. In all these cases I have been able to add to the comforts of everyone concerned.

Further references to his staff came in November 1829:

> Two persons who have served in the same capacity (Steward and Gardener) have filled this day with painful business. One a Scotch man [possibly Ogilvie mentioned above] lived with me two years and did not answer [suit] but he had a helpless family in whose welfare we were much interested. He was set up in business as a nursery man – by irregularity in accounts he has ruined himself in one year, going on spending without regulating expense by income and keeping no accounts. I have been obliged to take all he has and shall lose £150 at least, and several others will lose part of small sums which he owes them.
>
> The other is W., an Englishman – of very interesting character – born to better means, he was cheated out of several thousands and became a gamekeeper, in which capacity he served me for four or five years. Then finding it a needless expense, I was going to discharge him when he proposed to serve me in any capacity, and I made him as Butler. He soon became a useful and good servant, being handy, intelligent and obliging. After 2 years in the house, the confinement hurt his health and he became my general overseer in farm and garden, and promised to make a most useful servant, being ready to do anything.
>
> When gamekeeper somewhere, he had fallen under the common temptation of his place and had become fond of drink. While with me it was rarely indulged and on taking a confidential place, I thought he had seen the necessity of giving up a tasting of liqueur on any consideration.

> I had spoken strongly to him upon it, however, on Sunday he found one old companion and having begun to drink he left home and remained three days in Donegal . . .

John Hamilton's last words about this affair (he did not record what exactly happened to the man), revert – as they often did – to a religious theme but, more importantly, they are a reminder of how differently from the majority of landlords he acted towards those whose lives he controlled:

> He is now in the most wicked state of mind but I cannot keep him, I have no place for him . . . . he cannot be trusted. May God help him and guide me in my conduct towards him and may his dreadful fall warn me of my guilt in neglecting constant prayer for those over whom I am placed so that I may be enabled to place this poor man somewhere that he may not be tempted severely, and that my prayer may avail (through Jesus) for his recovery from the snare of Satan.

On the last day of the year, John Hamilton's journal ended on an optimistic note, except for one concern – marching Orangemen – a recurring theme at this time:

> I am ending this year with abounding mercies and with a hard heart and vexed spirit. My wife well, the children recovering, my friends prospering and friendly, – all is well, but tho' without there are no fightings – within there are many fears . . . . On this last day of the year, after some months perfect quietness in the neighbourhood, a rumour has arisen of an intended procession of Orangemen tomorrow.

CATHOLIC EMANCIPATION

Daniel O'Connell's name was never even once mentioned in John Hamilton's journals, despite the fact that 'the Liberator' had been campaigning for 20 years for the removal of the remaining legal discriminations against Catholics, building up an unparalleled mass movement and organising 'monster' meetings until he won a most famous election victory in Clare in 1828. Disbarred from taking the seat, his popular movement succeeded in gaining Catholic Emancipation the following year, linking Catholicism and Irish consciousness into a powerful movement which greatly worried most Protestants. While Hamilton referred to the subject of the counter-demonstrations by the Orange Lodges and the Brunswick Clubs, the following, written in February 1829, was his first journal reference to Emancipation:

Drumholm Roman Catholic church, replaced an earlier church on the same site in 1845. John Hamilton did not allude to it in his journals but almost certainly subscribed towards the cost, as did other Protestants in the area

> The political prospect of the times is indeed critical and calls for anxious prayer. All the dissenting places of worship were filled for prayer for Divine guidance to the Parliament – the day of the opening of the Session . . . The D. of W. [Duke of Wellington] proposes to give full emancipation to R. Catholics – God only knows how far this may tranquillise. While all the world is agitated by politics . . . which appear to us to threaten injury to the [Established] Church, to *the* Church, indeed, no injury *can* be made – but it appears that the *Nominal* church is about to be scourged.

Given the significance of Catholic Emancipation, and Protestant fears about its consequences, it may appear strange that it did not feature more prominently in the journals, and the following – one of only two other reference to it – occupied just three lines:

> Much bad disposition among Protestants almost everywhere. In some places they won't go to church because they take offence at Catholic Emancipation!

RIBBONMEN AND ORANGEMEN

John Hamilton's earlier references to the Ribbonmmen and the Orangemen during the construction of the causeway are quaintly amusing. On that occasion, their inter-party rivalry was, to put it mildly, uncharacteristically friendly. The grouping known as the Ribbonmen came into existence a decade or more before the period about which John Hamilton was writing when he first mentioned the organisation in connection with the building of the causeway. It was one of a number of organisations which were attempting to mobilise the growing antagonism among tenants towards a whole range of agrarian problems including such issues as the tithes, land hunger and rural poverty. Like half a dozen or more such bodies afterwards, it was necessarily a shadowy organisation – indeed the word 'Ribbonmen' tended to become a generic term covering all the similar movements active throughout this period.

Originally founded as a defensive organisation in parallel with the Defenders, the Orange Order was pledged to defend 'the King and his heirs so long as he or they support the Protestant ascendancy'. In 1813, after a force of Ribbonmen attacked an Orange Lodge at Garvagh in revenge for a previous defeat, a kind of running warfare spread across Ulster between the two organisations.

As a local magistrate, Hamilton had no liking for either organisation, seeing both parties ever-ready to deliberately bait each other, events which were a regular source of local trouble and which usually placed the police in very difficult situations trying to keep the two factions apart. Perhaps it was significant that the first journal reference to the Order in this context was written in 1829, as tensions heightened prior to and after Emancipation:

> We have been troubled in our hitherto peaceful neighbourhood by a party spirit breaking out in the most violent manner. On Easter Monday the Roman Catholics assembled to burn tar-barrels, and show some rejoicing at the grant of emancipation to their party.
>
> In Ballintra they foolishly and, I fear, set-on by evil men on their side, lighted a barrel in the street which they had promised not to do. They went out of the town to the Fair Green where they were attacked by a body of armed Protestants, the Roman Catholics being quite unarmed. One man was badly wounded by a bayonet, and the man who inflicted the wound was nearly killed by the other side with stones. The Riot Act was read out and the crowd of Roman Catholics dispersed, but many of the Protestants refused to disperse and some of my Yeomen were among the worst. They have completely driven me from their command, even had I no objection to retaining it than their conduct on this occasion. On both sides the madness of the people was and is great, but the Orange party have shown among them a cool, deliberate, bloodthirsty spirit which I could not have believed. The same spirit is *said* to exist on the Roman Catholic side; certainly not to the same degree; indeed I have not met with it at all . . . .

While the Orangemen were preparing for the 1829 'Twelfth' celebrations, the government banned their processions but, as Hamilton noted: 'a very general disposition prevailed among the Orangemen to resist the law, and many of their lower leaders stirred them up to this, assuring them there was no real law against the procession'. Sensing trouble in his own neighbourhood, he wrote to his friend Lord Enniskillen, Grand Master of the Order, who replied that he had done all he could to dissuade members from marching:

> The Orangemen resisted all our endeavours to cause them to give up their design on going in procession as usual. Their own leaders, the Duke of Cumberland and Lord Enniskillen, in vain published a declaration of their wish that such things should be given up. The Magistrates in vain used their authority. The priests of the people and of the place in vain spoke and entreated. The clergy in vain preached. They determined to walk, and in many cases I heard this determination expressed in most unchristian and blasphemous language.

But march they did, despite the fact that Hamilton had gone to a meeting of 'the masters of the Orange lodges', bringing with him letters from the Grand Master of the Order pressing the members to obey the law. As a result of his personal intervention, Hamilton managed to prevent marches in Donegal town and Ballintra from taking place: Regarding the former, he had been awakened at five o'clock in the morning by a policeman who informed him that Orangemen were assembling with arms in the town of Donegal, while horns were sounding in the mountains. More alarming was the news that Catholics were assembling in large numbers near the chapel at Barnsmore, a few miles away, apparently with confrontation in mind. Hamilton's lengthy description is worth including in some detail:

> I mounted my horse, rode to the town and found it as he told me. The Orangemen defied me to prevent their procession, saying I should have to take all the police to put down the 'rebels' at the chapel. I had sent to Mount Charles where there was a police station and a band of mounted police. I assured the Orangemen that I would, in the first place, certainly prevent their illegal procession. . . . and I had posted the few police I had in three houses commanding the town, so that any attack on one of the houses would be under the fire of the other two. I discovered the Orangemen had spread a report that their intention was to meet at Ballyshannon, eleven miles off, at ten o'clock, and had succeeded in drawing most of the magistrates and the police to Ballyshannon. The other magistrates, knowing that my wife had only just been confined, did not like to send word to St. Ernan's to call me to join them. Thus the Orangemen stole a march and they guarded the roads so that my messengers to Ballyshannon were intercepted. Towards eight o'clock I rode out to the place where the other [Catholic] party had assembled, and . . . I

counted as nearly as I could, 300 armed men with guns, drawn up in a line, with men in front acting as officers, and fully 3000 men with pikes, scythes, hooks on poles and other improvised arms.

I came back to the town . . . and told the Orangemen what I had seen but they madly refused to give up their purpose, thinking I must give into them, and use them against the others. Then as a desperate attempt, and praying to God to help me, I rode out again to the chapel at Barnsmore. The road was lined with old men, women and children of both parties, crying and wailing, expecting a bloody ending to the day. The armed party was drawn up in a field, the entrance to which was built up with a low wall about three feet high. As I leapt over this an old man, who was kneeling by it, cried out: 'God bless your soul, its all there will be of you in two minutes'.

However I rode up to the line, and a man with a fowling-piece came forward and presenting it at me asked what I wanted. I put down the muzzle of the gun with a rod I had in my hand, and said I did not know him, but was going to speak to the people who were my neighbours. Several men were now in front, all with fowling-pieces, and all strangers. The man said angrily: 'You shan't speak to one of them, take care of your life', and began to raise his gun towards me again, when a man in the ranks put out his hand and pulled him down on his back. Another man then came forward, a tall red-haired fellow, but not ill looking, and who spoke civilly. He laid his gun across my horse's neck and said: 'Sir, you can't be allowed to come here'. However, I laid my hand on his gun, and before he knew where he was, I read the Riot Act with which I was prepared and quickly appealed to the crowd . . . . 'You have the word and the advice of a tried friend, will you take it or be led by strangers to your destruction? You see I trust you, for I have come up to you without arms and without escort, to serve you and help you out of a bad case: but depend upon it, neither party shall be allowed to break the law without severe punishment'.

The people declared they would take my advice and disperse and go home as quickly as possible, and when my red-headed friend saw how matters were, he actually set himself to carry out the work effectually, and showed considerable skill in marshalling the people from each locality and getting them together. As I returned to the town I met the members of an Orange lodge who all lived close to me, though not my tenants, whom I had thought I could trust as they had individually promised me not to come out that day. 'What', I said to them, 'have you too broken your word?' 'Oh, sir', said they, 'we are glad to see you safe! – how did you escape?' 'What do you mean?' I asked. "Oh, sir, we got a message from you that your life was in danger and that you wanted us, and we determined to face 1000 muskets to bring you away safe'. I found out that the Orangemen in the town, seeing the members of this lodge faithful to their promise, had taken this way of getting them out. In Donegal I met Mr. Welch and Mr. Young, magistrates, and having communicated with them we returned towards the chapel at Barnesmore with a force of about forty police who had come up from Ballyshannon, twenty-two constabulary police, three mounted police, fourteen revenue police mounted, and their captain (Plunket). The people were dispersing as we came in view, and we rode up quite close to them. A priest who appeared to be endeavouring to keep peace, came to us to beg us not to use violence. We told him we would not, if we could avoid it, but must prepare for the worst . . .

A few of them halted rather in fear of our intentions, but . . . the dispersion of the whole was effected quietly and the peace of the district preserved, though a thousand of both parties had been armed in the morning for violence.

Meanwhile the Donegal Orangemen were not yet pacified. They were awaiting reinforcements from Ballintra, but providentially E. Conolly and my brother Edward had succeeded with a good force of police in preventing the Ballintra contingent from advancing. When we got back

Undated sketch by John Hamilton of St. Ernan's Island showing his house and the causeway built in 1824.

to Donegal after the dispersion of the Roman Catholic party, the Orangemen urged some of the magistrates, who were very hot party men, to allow them *now* to march and have a triumph, but the magistrates were too wise to countenance any such proceeding. We assembled at the hotel for consultation. While there I became very weak; it was now seven p.m. and I had been on horseback from five a.m. on a very hot day and in extreme excitement, and having just been wet through by a thundershower, had become quite chilly and nearly unconscious, when a cry was raised that the 'rebels' had deceived us, and were burning the houses of the Orangemen in Mount Charles, three miles off. This roused me, I ran down to the yard, found half a dozen mounted police, got a police horse and we galloped to Mount Charles to find it was all a lie. However this gallop warmed me thoroughly and took off any bad effects that the chill might otherwise have produced. While I was away, some Orangemen found my red-haired friend in the town. I had promised the Roman Catholic party that if they took my advice they would not be followed up or taken, and he had come in on that assurance. He did not belong to our district, but was, it seems, a noted character as a poacher and a clever rogue. I declared he could not be taken as I had given my word when I had no other means to disperse the assembly. The other magistrates thought fit to blame me for that, and said they had no doubt that 'Gibbons' came in as a spy and had his men outside the town ready to attack when people were off their guard. I did not think so, but assented to the advisableness of keeping him in custody till the next morning to see if all was quiet. At half past eight I rode home to St. Ernan's.

Here I found that my poor wife was apparently dying. She had been told that a policeman came galloping for me and that I galloped away with him, and rumours of the day's occurrences, together with the false one, which had brought out the neighbouring Orange lodge that I met on the road, of my sending for help, all these had been told her by the servants. I was obliged to send to Ballyshannon for Dr. Crawford, so urgent was the necessity. Pleurisy, along with all the bad consequences of a terror in her then state, a few days after the birth of a child, set in, and for days there was little hope of her recovery. After I went home the magistrates in Donegal committed Gibbons not to be bailed for less than £200.

I found out this next day, and bailed him at once. Everyone thought my money lost, but at the assizes several Orangemen who had again broken the law were put on their trial, coming forward to answer to their names and save their securities, but when Gibbons was called, to universal surprise, up came his red head and he gave himself up. They were all tried and found guilty. I was deputed by the rest of the grand jury to address the judge (Jebb), and to state our belief that the purpose of

> the Government would be attained by his giving the prisoners a solemn warning and a nominal punishment, as they had no doubt been deceived by bad advisers who persuaded them that the law was not against their processions. The judge agreed, they were each fined a shilling, and he gave them an excellent charge and dismissed them. Gibbons, the one Romanist among several Orangemen, remarked pretty loudly; 'Well, it is a good thing to be in good company once in a body's life!'
>
> The state of our wretched country is most alarming, the hand of God has been warning us Protestants who have had so many advantages. The Orangemen all over the north of Ireland have defied the laws of God and man, and paraded on Sunday and Monday, the 12th and 13th inst. – though forbidden by the Magistrates. In almost every case there has been blood shed.

A month later, John Hamilton related how a serious incident involving Orangemen in the nearby village of Laghey was also narrowly avoided:

> We had another deliverance from disturbance among the people yesterday. All the magistrates except myself were gone to Lifford and all the police, and I was supposed to have gone too. The Orangemen determined to make a grand affair of the return of some men of theirs who were sent for trial at Lifford – and they were to meet them and conduct them through Laghey fair, which happened that day, thinking there would be no hindrance to the battle that would have taken place. I providentially heard of this the day before and sent an express for a police force. By showing myself early at the fair and speaking to some of the Orange party, the determination to riot was allayed in a degree, and the appearance of a chief constable and half a dozen mounted men (supposed to be the forerunners of more) completely quelled all bad dispositions. Many idle men with cudgels were loitering on both sides in groups – and no business was done.

Orange processions were by no means confined to the month of July: In January of the following year, Hamilton wrote that he had been warned about a procession being arranged for New Year's Day 1830, by the Ballintra Orange Lodge, and that:

> horns were sounding all round the country to call together the Roman Catholics to oppose them. Edward [his brother] and I hastened from Brownhall where we fortunately were, and found all to be true. There was a procession and conducted so as to mark the spirit of those who joined in it. Resistance of law and provocation of their neighbours seemed to be the reigning spirit. Having taken away their music by the police,

> we succeeded in so far in dispersing them that others did not gather to attack them. The evening was disturbed only by the yelling of some drunken Orangemen, but we have reason to fear that this show of Orangeism will induce the Ribbonmen to have a parade.

The outcome of this incident was recorded, four months afterwards, when Hamilton returned from Lifford where he had gone as a witness against some of the Orangemen involved in the affair on New Years Day. 'It appeared that Edward and I had acted critically right and we were highly complimented by Judge Jebb. The men, about ten in number, were found guilty of riotous behaviour and unlawful assembly'.

Two months after this, Hamilton discovered an unexpected consequence of his actions. He noted that when he called to supervise some of his 'Sabbath Classes' (which are dealt with in the next chapter) he found attendances were down 'on account of disgust taken by the Orangemen at my opposing their party procession'.

THE BRUNSWICK CLUBS

Hamilton made a reference during July 1830 to the 'Brunswick Clubs' which had recently been formed 'for the preservation of the kingdom from the attempts of the Roman Catholic faction, any distaste for their religion is denied'. Similar to the Orange Order, which had been banned under the Unlawful Societies Act of 1825 (though Hamilton shared the commonly held view that the ban had not been rigorously enforced), the Clubs were started as a Protestant reaction to the growing challenge posed by the Catholic Association.

> In many parts of the country the Orangemen have had processions notwithstanding the proclamation of the Lord Lieutenant against them – and some blood has been shed, less than might have been expected from the recollection of last year (as far as I have heard as yet) but enough to characterise the processions.

It seems curious that John Hamilton, who had been very critical of the excesses of the Orange Order, should have shown an interest, however short-lived, in the Clubs. When a Constitutional Brunswick Club was newly formed in Donegal Town, John Hamilton presided at the inaugural meeting at which, he recorded that 'about 600 of the Yeomanry class were enrolled'. A month later he began to express reservations:

> I have been considering the propriety, or rather necessity, of addressing the Brunswickers of this Barony, and exhorting them as Christians to

> uphold the principle of peace and goodwill towards men. The Orangemen are, I fear, very unchristian and hate Popery less than they hate Papists. . . .
>
> The apathy of the professed Protestants is indeed so dreadful, and their want of charity towards their deluded countrymen so violent, that it seems to call for a judgement on the land. Clubs or combinations cannot avert it. May the Lord touch our hearts in time, and glorify Himself by causing Protestants to reform themselves and to be the means of reforming their Roman Catholic fellows.

He became increasingly concerned about being personally associated with the 'Brunswickers': 'I should be better pleased by far, meeting my neighbours at the reading meetings on Sundays; there I feel at home, but not at political meetings'. To which he then added: 'Clergy attend these political ones too much – I applaud those who refuse upon principle to attend them'. On another occasion he wrote of the Clubs that they:

> go on setting the country mad – and I fear they are all-powerful instruments in Satan's hands for leading all ranks to trusting in an arm of flesh. I have taken so active a part in them and led so many to do so that I can not now withdraw. But I pray God to enable me so to conduct myself and to show my feelings upon them as to be useful.

After deciding not to attend a meeting of the newly formed Brunswick Club at Belleek, he wrote in his journal:

> As long as there is hope of moderating the irritable feelings of the ignorant Protestants, so long I think every one who desires to support the powers that be should take an active part, and I pray God to make me useful in this way. I fear, however, that the low Orange faction will bring disgrace upon the Protestant cause and compel the Brunswickers to cast them off – if so, God knows what commotion we may expect . . .

In his final reference to the Clubs, written shortly afterwards, he reflected that 'while they were all the rage at the time, and he had lent himself heartily to their foundation', and he then added: 'I regret it'.

RENTS AND TITHES

On New Year's Day 1831, a large gathering of another kind assembled in Donegal, this time to protest about rents and tithes. No crowds assembled in the Ballintra area presumably because, as John Hamilton stated, 'I have the apparent advantage of having lowered my rents considerably before the cry for abatement'. In March, he wrote that these 'mob meetings' had:

> occasioned me to write and print a tract of advice to my tenantry, which was well received by others as well as by them, and, I believe, was a means of dissuading this district from such meetings . . . and the quiet deportment of my neighbours has obtained for them such consideration from their landlords as their conduct deserved and their necessity required.

The question of tithes arose for John Hamilton as a result of a letter written by the parish priest of Donegal to him in August, 1831 in which the priest sought a contribution towards the cost of repairs to his church. The response was somewhat tetchy but, for all that, quite astute:

> I have been considerably embarrassed by your application to me for aid towards repairs of the Roman Catholic church of this parish. I believe you asked supposing that I was desirous of befriending my neighbours of every denomination as much as is my power. But I cannot think that I should befriend anyone by seeming to approve what I conscientiously believe to be erroneous. I am a Protestant, not by birth or education but by conviction. I hold that the Roman Catholic doctrine as now held by that church errs from the true standard of faith and religion, therefore, while I love my Roman Catholic neighbours as well as my other neighbours, I cannot love their errors . . .
>
> At the same time, I acknowledge that I feel a great difficulty in refusing aid towards your place of worship while your flock are obliged by law to contribute [by the payment of rents] to the support of ours . . . . therefore from 1 November, 1831, I shall relieve all my tenants of every denomination . . . from the charge of church cess. Let them do as they will with the sum thus given to cash . . . I hope I have made myself understood and hoping that I may have many opportunities of helping my Roman Catholic neighbours consistently with my belief of the truth.
>
> I remain, your humble servant,
> JOHN HAMILTON

By way of a post-script, it should be added that Hamilton was to change his mind a decade later, donating a sum to the church in 1842.

FOUR

His Religious Thinking

John Hamilton, who once said of himself that he had been brought up 'in rather ultra-Protestant principles' also wrote that he and the family: 'were very regular church-goers, regular in private and social devotions, charitable as to giving much to feed and to educate the poor; we went to no balls or gay parties and lived a quiet but not inactive life'. Brought up in the Established Church, Hamilton began to dispute certain aspects of it – and also found fault with all the other main churches. More than any one thing, he desired that the churches would return to the simple Christianity of the early church, but he remained an Anglican – albeit a questioning one– to the end of his life. In fact, virtually everything that he thought or did was influenced by his religious outlook, and it must be equally true that his thinking was greatly influenced by some of the very significant religious developments emerging at that time.

During the late eighteenth and early nineteenth centuries, a great wave of evangelical revivalism spread through Protestant northern Europe, reaching westwards to Britain and from thence to Ireland, and this movement in the Protestant churches was paralleled by a devotional revolution in the Roman Catholic church which may have had its origins in post-revolutionary France. The Protestant revival, with leanings towards liberalism, seems to have begun in the Kingdom of Prussia. The arrival there of Moravians, heirs of the Hussites, introduced a brand of pietism and it is possible to trace this influence as it spread westwards inspiring the evangelical movement in the Anglican church, not least through the Methodist movement of John Wesley, who visited Ireland no less than 21 times, preaching 'the certainties of evangelical religion'.

The evangelical emphasis on the literal truth of the Bible and on personal faith found a ready response from many members of the main Protestant churches – especially to those in the rather staid Established church to whom the evangelical movement seemed to come as a breath of fresh air. One result of this 'Second Reformation' was the setting up of Bible-reading classes for adults and Sunday Schools for children, along with a proliferation of Bible and missionary societies – including some aiming to proselytise Catholics. On almost every visit to the capital, Hamilton made a point of attending Services in one or more of the churches with leanings towards an evangelical outlook, and he established a whole network of Bible classes and Sunday Schools in south Donegal.

His attraction towards the evangelical movement had its origins in his student days at Cambridge, where, by contrast, he also saw the opposite strand – the Tractarian movement – led by Keble, Pusey and Newman. Hamilton went to hear the latter two preach, but found their leanings towards Anglo-Catholicism (Newman, as is well known, later converted to Catholicism) personally unattractive. It was around that time that he had began to discuss religious doctrine and similar topics – not only with learned divines but with casual acquaintances. In his journals he recorded in great detail his religious thoughts and questionings and his private prayers – the latter usually seeking God's guidance when he was facing some particular problem.

Had his own bishop not turned him down, he would almost certainly have become an ordained minister of the Church of Ireland. Plainly he was hurt by that set-back but he soon became reconciled to his situation, coming to the view that he most probably would not have been happy in clerical orders anyway, while Bishop Bissett of Raphoe must have been greatly relieved that he had successfully avoided having to ordain Hamilton who would, in all probability, have been a questioning and difficult priest. In fact the set back at the hands of his bishop determined Hamilton to expand his 'Sabbath Schools' until they were attracting, in total, an attendance of over 1,000 people every week, many of whom were Catholics. It is something of a puzzle that the Roman Catholic bishop, Dr McGettigan, did not immediately intervene, fearing that Hamilton was engaging in proselytising. There may have been a reluctance to act, at least initially, against an especially benevolent landlord although this was to happen eventually.

Hamilton's criticisms of the shortcomings of the churches included, not surprisingly, criticisms of the Roman Catholic church. He took the view – shared by most Protestants at the time – that its clergy deliberately discouraged their flocks from reading the Bible, wanting to keep them 'in ignorance'. From his own writings there seems to be no evidence that Hamilton was actually openly proselytising or even using undue influence to encourage Catholics to attend his classes, but allegations had been made against other landlords that they had 'forgiven' arrears of rent to Catholic tenants on condition that their children attended one of the local Sunday or Bible schools.

Bishop Bissett's refusal to ordain John Hamilton, when it happened, caused him to think even more deeply about his own religious outlook. More than ever before he now discussed his thinking with both friends and total strangers. His decision, in 1836, to spend four years abroad in Europe was at least partly an extension of this process, providing him with an opportunity to discuss theological niceties with leading thinkers of various religions in France, Germany and Switzerland. His original plan, (though he was to change his mind) had been to spend half of his time abroad at Geneva, a city of great learning, Calvin's' adopted home, and one of the great capitals of Protestantism.

All of the foregoing is reflected in the extraordinary emphasis on religion throughout Hamilton's journals. It is quite evident from their content that what he recorded in his journals was almost certainly never intended to be read outside his immediate family circle. His religious thinking, his questioning, and his very personal prayers occupy as much as three-quarters of all the pages in his journals – an untapped seam of interest to theologians and others, all the more valuable, representing as they do, the unusually detailed religious views of a lay person at that time. This aspect of the journals conveys an almost obsessive and often repetitive interest on his part, in faith, baptism, salvation and other religious topics, but it has to be said that most people to-day would find most of it rather boring. For this reason, the journal extracts in this volume referring to religion are deliberately disproportionately small in number, but his writings point to an extremely important aspect of his life, an aspect which coloured virtually all of his thinking and how he interacted with other people – not least his tenants, whom he invariably referred to as his 'friends' and 'neighbours'.

Given his background and education and the thinking of the time, he took a remarkably fair-minded view of other religions, feeling it grossly unfair that Roman Catholics and Presbyterians had to pay tithe money to support the Established Church. However, he admitted at one point that he owed it to his wife's more cautious nature that he did not more often avail of opportunities to criticise the teachings of the other churches. Some of his views were distinctly unorthodox, including his opinion that paid clergy were inimical to simple faith, and he also disagreed with aspects of doctrine and ceremonial, feeling that not only his own, but most of the other churches too, had accumulated 'harmful accretions' resulting in a drift away from the uncomplicated ordering of the early Christian church.

BIBLE CLASSES

He opened his first weekly Bible-reading class in Donegal town one Sunday evening in 1827, by which means he hoped to bring the Bible and its Christian message to the people of the area in what he hoped would be a non-denominational way. About 60 persons attended, to whom he read 'and partly expanded upon' the first chapter of St John's Gospel. Encouraged by the response, he began a second class in Raroy on Wednesday evenings 'at Widow K's' with 55 attending there, and then started a class at Lackan on Thursdays and then another at Ballydevitt on Sunday afternoons.

He was surprised that the idea, when put into practice, seemed to be an instant success, with numbers becoming so great that some classes had to be divided into two, but even that proved insufficient when the numbers rapidly rose to 300.

> 'Well', I said hesitating, 'but what can I do with 300 people? They would make ten classes of thirty each'. 'Yes, sir', said one of the old men, 'so

> they would, and that would be a fine beginning'. It struck me they might meet in classes in each other's houses in rotation, selecting ten or twelve houses near each other to make one class, and an elderly respectable person to act as monitor in each class, and I could attend two every Sunday, and all could read the same chapters, one in the Old Testament and one in the New, according to a list which I should get printed. I proposed the idea.
>
> It was taken up, and on the spot eight or ten classes were formed in which Roman Catholics as well as Protestants united, women as well as men, but not children, and I promised to get ready before that day week a list of chapters for every Sunday. Some of them asked me to add a few hints to help in searching out the purpose and meaning of the chapters. To this I assented, and departed feeling some timidity with regard to my new position as a teacher of Divine truths. I came home, considered what chapters we should begin with, and settled on the first Psalm and the first chapter of St. Matthew's Gospel. In preparing simple notes on the portions of Scripture read to apply them spiritually to our own souls, I saw and felt for the first time the awful responsibility of teaching, professing to teach truth, and how necessary it was for a true man to ascertain for himself how much truth he knew, and to distinguish between teaching truth and searching for truth. Before the following Sunday I had my page of hints ready and all worked smoothly and well. The demand for Bibles was great . . .
>
> The weekly notes I had expanded and printed under the title of *The Sabbath Readers' Monitor*. The demand for these became large; several messengers from some distance in different directions came to ask me to send them some weekly. I said I could not afford to do so in the case of all applicants. They said they were willing to pay the cost of printing, so I agreed to extend the weekly number according to the demand.

His Sabbath Schools continued to grow and he was to remark that wherever he went at this time, whether on Sundays or weekdays, he had a 'crowd of hearers'. It was at this period that he first indicated the notion of seeking Holy Orders:

> I experienced how easy it is to lead a multitude. The people would hang upon me and, of course, I felt that gratified sense which comes from finding oneself sought out and attended to. I had to address assemblies of people on religious subjects – this was preaching – and I imagined my doing so without clerical orders was irregular, if not positively wrong, and that my not being ordained by a Bishop was probably, in part at least, the cause why I was not well contented with my own views of what I had always held as truth.

In August a new Sunday School was opened in Drinendaragh 'where alone, two dozen Bibles have been sold, four of them with marginal references', to which he added somewhat wryly, 'Oh, that more prayer had attended the giving of them out'. During the autumn of 1827, he found that on one particular Sunday 60 or 70 attended several of his Scripture classes, despite the fact that 'a fine day in the potato harvest is not apt to send such a large number to seek their God'. He obtained 'a large number of Bibles (100) with margin references at half price from the Bible Society, which Mary is going to distribute chiefly among mothers of families'. Some time after this, when he went to visit the class formed at Raneeny, he was annoyed to discover 'some jealousies have been occasioned by some women not getting them (Bibles) who declare they have as good *a right* to get them as those who obtained – how Satan turns good to evil'. He recorded that he had sold several Douay Testaments as well as two Douay Bibles to Roman Catholics 'for five and ten shillings'.

He seems to have taken some care to avoid antagonising the local Catholic clergy who were well aware of efforts being made elsewhere to proselytise (one of Hamilton's precautions being, as noted above, to distribute Douay Bibles to Catholics at his classes). The activities of the various Bible societies had been condemned by Pope Leo XII several years earlier 'for their effrontery in translating the scriptures into the vulgar language of every nation', and the Irish Catholic church had also viewed the spread of the national schools (of which there were seven on Hamilton's estate by the end if 1831) with suspicion because of the perception that they either were (or might be) used as a means of converting their children to Protestantism. Given that the schools were, notionally at least, non-denominational, it would have been little short of amazing if the Catholic Hierarchy did not view the spread of the Sunday classes with even greater distrust. Hamilton's main concern at this time was not about this but the amount of responsibility the scheme was bringing upon him as numbers continued to grow and as the demand for classes in new areas continued. Before very long he was able to record that there were 'about a thousand adults every Sabbath assembled in prayer and reading to seek God in little knots of ten to forty . . . I have also printed this year and sold most of 750,000 pages of tracts, chiefly the weekly *Sabbath Readers Moniitor'*. The continued success encouraged him to consider the possibility of beginning what he termed 'an anti-sectarian plan':

> We are Protestants, Catholics, Wesleyans, Methodists, Calvinists, Baptists, etc. but how seldom do we count it our glory to be called by His name only. It strikes me that Christians ought not only to take no other name, but ought, moreover, diligently to endeavour that no others should be applied to them.

Throughout this whole period, he found himself being drawn into considering some kind of religious vocation which caused him to write, in 1828, that 'Had I followed my own principles, I should probably have become a leader of a sect . . . '. He may have had in mind something like the Plymouth Brethren, a sect without clergy which had been founded in Dublin – despite the title – that same year. Believing that all Christians have the right to preach the Word of God and to administer the Sacraments, there was no place for clergy in their thinking. This line of thought, repudiating an ordained ministry, was remarkably close to that of John Hamilton at this particular time, and while he is known to have met members of the sect, there is no record in the journals of his attending any of their services. Later, he began to consider the notion that he might become what he called a 'Home Missionary'. He also put forward the idea of having ordained Deacons to help the ordained Ministers, adding: 'Oh that there were no differences, no jealousies between denominations of Christians and Churches! Then we might hope to see much. O God our Saviour, unite Thy people in one in Thee!'

His reasoning on religious matters veered in different directions from time to time – often as a result of having spoken to someone about his evolving thoughts. These took yet another direction when he began to consider the possibility of entering into Holy Orders for ordination as an Anglican clergyman. He seems to have been taken aback when he discussed this with his wife, her reaction representing the first hint that she disagreed with him on any matter:

> I spoke to M today about my views as to orders, she does not like them but she has no idea of my feelings on the subject or the causes of them. I have much neglected opening myself to her . . . The more I look upon my ministry among the people the more I am led to desire orders for their sake and my own, and all, I hope, for the Glory of God. If I become not an appointed regular minister I must be an irregular one.

ORDINATION SOUGHT

During his fairly frequent visits to Dublin, sometimes to re-stock with Bibles and religious tracts, or to attend meetings of one of the various missionary societies, he often made a point of attending services in the Bethesda Chapel in Dorset Street which, though built 41 years earlier, had not been licensed until 1825, a move which was seen at the time as conferring some kind of legitimacy on the evangelical movement. Regarded as the Evangelicals' 'Cathedral', this was one of a number of strongly evangelical Protestant hurches in the city which had sprung up during that revival, and it was probably through a contact made at one of these services that Hamilton had been advised to speak to a person whom he named in his journal as 'Mr. I', who lived 'at Cullenswood

[Ranelagh], near Dublin'. Hamilton combined a visit to this man with a short stay with his grandmother, Lady Longford, who was then living with various cousins at no. 8 Rutland [Parnell] Square.

> We all arrived safe from St. Ernan's after three days journey . . . My Gd. Mr [grandmother] has not been quite well and she evidently fails every time I see her. No wonder, at 85, but she still presides and carves at her table and enjoys the society of her progeny as much as any person that I know.

The 'Mr. I'. to whom Hamilton had been referred was, in fact, the Reverend Henry Irwin, a well-known evangelical Church of Ireland clergyman at this time, who was Secretary of the Hibernian Bible Society, and of whom Bishop Gregg said that no man had influenced 'a greater number of the educated, thinking and reading portion of society'. Henry Irwin, considered to be the Irish evangelical patriarch, had been appointed Minister of Sandford Chapel, which had been built two years earlier in the Ranelagh suburb of Dublin. It was named after George Sandford, Baron Mount Sandford, who had been persuaded by Robert Newenham who, living at nearby Merton House, had donated the land for the church on condition that Baron Mount Sandford put-up the money – which, in fact, he did. The new church had an independent status as a trustee church, one of a number of what came to be known as 'preaching chapels', having no parish attached at the time. Irwin's appointment would have been based on his strong commitment to evangelical ideas and to his considerable powers of oratory, and his sermons, often lasting an hour or more, attracted large congregations of people who walked and drove from the city to the new chapel every Sunday.

The Church of Ireland parish church of Drumholm (Ballintra), which lies only a short distance from the Brownhall Estate, replaced an earlier building near Murvagh at the end of the eighteenth century.

Hamilton went to Sandford Glebe to discuss his own views with the Rev. Irwin. 'as to my manner of giving up my self to the service of God'. He discovered in Irwin a man 'so kind and anxious that our conversation lasted over four hours' and Hamilton also found him very sympathetic to his own doubts and reservations. 'He has been long a minister [Irwin was then 55 years old] and says that he feels justified with having borne with what he could not like'. It later transpired that Hamilton's more confrontational personality was to make it impossible to compromise in this way.

During another visit to Dublin, occasioned by an invitation to Lord Anglesea's *levee*, he attended a religious meeting in the Chapel of the Rotunda, followed by a meeting of the Sunday School Society where he found:

> some good, some flowery, some bad, and some detestable speakers – God forgive flatterers – for they are surely the Devil's agents. I fear much injury to the cause of true religion from the false excitement and great spiritual pride which these public meetings create in the heart.

He continued to immerse himself in these activities for some time, but seemed unable to shake off the notion of ordination, and he wrote just after this 'I cannot be but in anxiety whether I am *really* called to be minister of the Gospel'. Some more of his thinking comes across here:

> I thought and prayed, consulted friends on this subject, and the result was I laid myself out to prepare for ordination. I read Greek with a master in Dublin to refresh and improve my school and College knowledge; I read theology and studied the prayer-book with an excellent elderly clergyman. This was in 1828-9. Still carrying on my classes and schools, and when at home holding several meetings among the people every week, chiefly in the evenings, in their houses which were always crowded, my dear wife advancing with me in everything, but she was the contrary of sanguine. Her temperament was excessive on the conservative side, as I was excessive on the liberal or progressive side, and to her quiet steady mind, as ballast to my sharp keel and sail, I owe it, under God, that I did not give way to the temptation often felt to proclaim the errors I saw held up as truth by others, and the truths I had been led to see but which were only partially acknowledged by others, and that in a way so mystified that their very life was lost.
>
> But these errors and truths I had but lately been made aware of, and had not sorted, sifted, considered and weighed as they required to be, and as one should do for years, before one determines how to act concerning them.

Towards the end of the 1828, Hamilton found difficulties of another kind when he had looked closely at what he called 'the Articles of Religion of the Church of England', and prayed that 'any useless parts of the Church service may be changed by God's guidance'. He repeatedly expressed the wish that the churches – all the churches – would return to what he called 'the simplicity of the Scriptural ideal', and he still had reservations about paid clergy and other matters. Given all this, it may appear rather strange that he persevered in his preparations for an Anglican ordination, a pursuit which John's uncle, the Rev. Henry Pakenham, encouraged in a brief letter. He was further encouraged following a series of discussions which he had with the Rev. Maurice Fenwick, who had become the Vicar of Hamilton's parish, Drumholm. Fenwick was described by Hamilton as 'one of the most beloved friends I ever had', a view which may have been coloured by the fact that he shared Hamilton's own tendency to 'ultra-liberalism and bold enquiry', and with whom he found he could freely discuss his various nagging doubts. The outcome of these discussions was that Maurice Fenwick:

> agreed to make me his Curate and give me a part of the parish near St. Ernan's, and, on the nomination of this curacy, his uncle, Dr. Bissett, Bishop of Raphoe, agreed to ordain me on Fenwick's assurance that I had taken my degree at Cambridge.

THE BISHOP'S REFUSAL

On these assumptions, and very probably convinced that ordination was to be a mere formality, John Hamilton then went to Raphoe where he stayed for a time with Bishop Bissett, after whose death in 1834, the Church of Ireland diocese was united with Derry. Things did not go smoothly, however, and matters reached a crises point when the bishop, referring to John's studies when at Cambridge, asked:

> 'Of course you have attended divinity lectures?' I said: 'I have not, but does that signify?' 'Nay', replied the Bishop, 'it does indeed signify, for we Bishops have agreed to be strict in requiring certificates of attendance from every candidate for orders. Bishops have discussed it together, and unless you go to the university and attend the lectures, I cannot ordain you'. 'My lord', said I, 'surely you do not expect a man with a family of young children to leave his home, or take them to Cambridge for two or three terms at least to attend such lectures. If I am not fit without it, this surely will not make me fit'. 'No, Mr. Hamilton, I *expect'.* The Bishop said calmly but decidedly: 'My young friend, I am not going to discuss the question, it is for you to settle, you know our determination, and whatever may be my feeling to you personally, I cannot break through a rule for personal feelings'.
>
> The result was, I told the Bishop I certainly would not go back to

> Cambridge in order to get him to ordain me, that in my view it would be quite wrong to do so, and if the Bishops' rule was not to ordain without that qualification, I must take it as a token that I was to go on as I had been doing without ordination, even though my addresses might be called preaching and my work be accounted an interference with the clergy. The Bishop knew very well what I had been doing, and now in the kindest manner he rose up and said: 'I have nothing to add to what I have already said, I have heard your reasons and your purpose, and' – laying his hands on me – 'may God guide you and bless your work'.

One must wonder if Bissett's stance was linked with a concern that Hamilton might have proved a difficult priest to control. John Hamilton's initial reaction was one of frustration, but after reflecting on the matter, he claimed that he was relieved rather than disappointed, concluding that he had been guided by some higher wisdom than his own, and admitting that he would have been both uncomfortable and unhappy as an ordained minister, foreseeing the possibility that he might be forced to leave the church at some future time if his own thinking 'progressed'. Shortly after this he wrote: 'My view of my own line of duty appears to me to go on *lay*, for a time at least, but qualifying as much as possible for Orders'. In a later journal entry his thoughts seemed to have evolved further:

> My views as to ordination are more and more removed from the desire of it. I do not think I could consciously enter the Ministry of the Established Church – looking on forms and Articles as I do now, but surely I may devote myself to Thee, un-ordained . . .

John continued working with his scripture classes and Sunday Schools, mentioning new ones had been formed at Tullyearl, Legahenny, Copany and Dermenadarragh. Even so, the question of ordination which had been troubling his mind for several years was not finally resolved, as various subsequent journal entries hint. In February 1829, he heard that:

> The bishop has got 800£ to build 2 chapels of ease at Drumholm – they are much wanting. The Lord does wonderfully favour this spot. There have been built within 4 miles of this spot (St. Ernan's) in 3 years – Donegal Church, Killymard Church, Donegal Methodist meeting house, Donegal Seceding Presbyterian meeting house, Raneany Presbyterian meeting house and now two chapels of ease in the adjoining parish. [Laghey – completed in 1837 – and Killymard.]

He offered to pay half the cost of a curate in Killymard, and noted in the journal: 'I have offered my own service, such as it is, and if I be rejected, my

John Hamilton warmly welcomed the Church of Ireland bishop's decision to build two chapels-of-ease in the Donegal – Ballintra area in 1837. One of these was erected at nearby Laghey (above).

walk is plain'. John did not state whether his offer of his own 'service' and of part-funding clergyman were tied together, a not unlikely possibility in view of the fact that his generous financial offer, as it turned out, was rejected by Bishop Bisset. Somewhat ruefully, John added: 'M.G. F. [the vicar] seems decidedly of opinion that I shall be more useful un-ordained: Edward (his ordained younger brother) is of the same. God's will be done'.

It may seem curious when, 16 years later, St. Brigit's Roman Catholic church at Ballintra, was completely rebuilt, John Hamilton did not mention it in his journal. Three years after Rev. Patrick Kelly was appointed Parish Priest of Drumholm (Ballintra), in 1845, he set about the construction of a large hall church to replace what the Very Rev. Canon Maguire in his *History of the Diocese of Raphoe* called 'the spacious but hideous structure that stood quite near the site of its successor'. Canon Maguire recorded that 'despite Ballintra's reputation for aggressive Orangeism the Protestants subscribed a very considerable sum' towards its erection, so it is more than likely that Hamilton, despite his silence in the matter, was among those who contributed. The family gave the parish a plot of land for a parochial house in 1867 and a plot was donated for a similar purpose at Fintown four years later.

The Catholic and Protestant Ballintra parishes are named after the former abbey of Drumholm, or Drumtomma, the ridge of Tomma, where St. Ernan, who accompanied St. Columba to Iona, had been abbot and whence his body was brought back to be buried. The parish of Drumholm, dating at least from the fifteenth century, is much older than Donegal, and the earlier Drumholm church was near Mullinacross, two miles to the west, where the only surviving part of the monastery, then thatched, was used by the local Church of Ireland congregation. Heavily planted by English and Scots following the Ulster Plantation, the 1659 census found that they had by then comprised almost a quarter of the population in the area. The old thatched church was slated in 1770 and a gallery was added, but in 1790 when there were over 400 Protestant families in the parish, a decision was made to move to a new, larger church at Ballintra. The Hamilton family contributed £100 towards it when it was opened in 1793.

John threw himself into the running of his scripture classes with renewed vigour, commencing on Sunday where he addressed a class of 60 people in Donegal; on Wednesday he went to Gregstown and then to Raroy, where 'between fifty and sixty persons were present in Widow Threlfole's house – a Roman Catholic, whose husband always had one of the Sabbath reading classes in his house – he died a year ago – and several R.C. attended'. On the following day, Thursday, he led a class at Lackan; and on Friday; one at Ligahurry, while on the next Sunday he attended a class at Ballydevitt as well as the one in Donegal town. Hamilton's 'reading classes' continued to have over 1,000 adults each Sunday, 'assembled in prayer and reading to seek God, in little knots of ten to forty – all sprung from an unpremeditated day's reading – with seven persons – eighteen months ago at a children's Sunday School'.

As will be seen, Hamilton was later to consider becoming an ordained minister of the Moravian Church which he came to admire, though nothing came of that either, after which the matter was not mentioned again.

FIVE

The 1831 Famine

The journal for 1831 began on a gloomy note: 'A year of transgression but of long suffering and of mercies has passed. O that this may not be on my part like the last!'

> Last year began with a day of anxiety, so also this year. We feared a tumultuous assembly at Donegal for the purpose of crying down rents and tithes – notices were circulated, the people were agitated – we were in anxiety – but our unworthy cry was heard – so far there has been no assembly – and the feeling of the people seems against it. I have the apparent advantage of having lowered my rents considerably before the cry rose for abatement.

Life went on, as usual in the area, and John Hamilton's journals continued to record all kinds of events, enabling the reader, a century and a half later, to visualise life as it then was. Murder was far from unknown, and the following entry describes one which occurred not far from St Ernan's in 1829:

> Jno. Little of Drimmenny and his wife were murdered on Sunday night and their servant man beaten and left for dead, and their house burned. He was known to have money, which is supposed to have been the object of the murders, but they began their work with murder as the evidence of the servant shews. The circumstantial evidence is strong against persons in custody but the inquest is not over.
>
> The bodies were interred to-day and if an horrible thing had been committed in the murder, the horror of the wake and the funeral was greater. Spirits and tobacco, light and profane talking – quarrelling, cursing and swearing were the prominent things. The murder shows how wicked some 2 or 3 persons are. The funeral shows the spirit of the people.
>
> The persons accused of the murder of the Little's have been committed upon the verdict of the inquest.

A footnote was added to this journal entry on 15 August 1831, 'Three brothers have been hanged for this murder'.

Just after this, John Hamilton made a reference to his profligate spending:

> I have nothing to ask heaven for as regards earthly prosperity. I am, however, spending quite too much, yet in all things so good in themselves, attempting to improve the land and the people, and so little on what is generally called selfish enjoyments, that I deceived myself into the sense of doing right.

John decided to move temporarily to Brownhall, staying with his brother while building work was proceeding to enlarge the house at St Ernan's:

> Yesterday we were to go to Brownhall to spend a month with E & N [John's brother and his wife] while some alterations are making here. An accident which might have been v. serious delayed us. Our dear boy fell against the castor of the tea chest and cut open his forehead for about 2 inches to the bone. It bled so much as to make him very faint and at first we could not form an opinion as to the injury, however to-day he appears quite well and M, with the two little ones [his wife with Arabella and Mary], is gone to Brownhall leaving me to follow with J & B [James and Isabella] to-morrow.

The Hamiltons were to be abroad on the continent in 1839 when, on 6 January, 'The Night of the Big Wind' was to cause an immense amount damage throughout Ireland. He was, however, present and described in some detail some very severe storms during 1829–30, one of which he called 'a hurricane and a whirlwind'. It stripped slates off roofs, windows were smashed, trees were blown over and crops destroyed or severely damaged – all in the space of half an hour. Further damage was caused by a very rapid rise in the sea-level, flooding many shore-side houses up to the tops of their doors and even demolishing some of them. He noted that although many people narrowly escaped death there had been no fatalities – though it certainly would have been otherwise if the storm had struck during the night.

Nowadays, dramatic changes in weather patterns, are usually blamed on 'global warming' resulting from the state of the Ozone Layer. Such explanations were totally unknown in the nineteenth century, and exceptional deviations in weather patterns, or even crop failures, famines and fevers were often attributed to God – or rather to God's anger at the wickedness of sinful people. This explanation surfaced again when there was unusually stormy weather early in September 1830, followed two weeks on by even more violent storms which continued to rage for more than a week, provoking a number of references to the subject:

> To-night is a most terrific storm, the house trembles and the sea is raging

> furiously. 'He rides upon the storm . . . ' Much fear is entertained for the crops. If this unprecedented stormy season now gets worse instead of better, famine stares us in the face.
>
> Sept.20. Yesterday was a dreadful storm, last night very desperate, the prospect for the provision for next year is sad. I have spoken to Ed.[his clergyman brother]. And we, again, to his assistant curate, Mr.K. on the subject of a general meeting for humiliation and prayer, seeing we have sinned as a people and are, as a people, visited by God's wrath.
>
> Sept.30. The matter spoken of in the last page has been brought to a good issue by God's blessing. In this parish and in Donegal and one place in Killymard the people assembled in districts, chiefly on Tuesday – and in a few instances on Wednesday and Thursday – in numbers from 40 to 300 at each appointed place . . . ..
>
> At Greggstown at Tuesday at 10 o'clock (the first real fine harvest day we have had) fully 300 persons attended, very many of them Roman Catholics, one man, a RC who had 7 hired reapers at work, came with his men, leaving their hooks idle for 2 hours – having prayed for the Lord's blessing . . .
>
> I pointed out the cause of our assembling, that God's voice in anger heard in the storm and threatening us with famine, called us to assemble and as a people to humble ourselves before God . . . There was appearance of much feeling in the people.

In the middle of October he wrote:

> Since our meetings near three weeks ago we have had uninterrupted fine weather! I do not believe that since this January we had two fine weeks together before – and though the sowing time and growing time was most unpromising, God's blessing on the seed sown had given a full crop for this good time of harvest.

But the stormy weather returned in mid-November, with especially severe gales doing much damage in south Donegal:

> An awful warning and visitation has been sent to us by Him who hath his way in the whirlwind and in the storm. On Saturday 20th [November] in the morning soon after day break a hurricane arose which was indeed terrible, quickly the house [he was still staying with his brother at Brownhall] was stripped of much lead and slates and many windows were blown in and trees torn up or broken across. The violence lasted only half an hour but in the time many families were rendered house-less and many lost all they had in this world, and very many were injured by the loss of corn and hay and partial injury to houses. The church roof (at Ballintra] is a wreck and the RC chapel as bad.

> But the awful part was on the coast; the tide rose many feet higher than ever had been known. Houses that were supposed to be safe from it as if they had been in the mountains were filled to the tops of the doors. The people escaped but the violence of the waves dashed in pieces the doors and windows and carried out much property and, in many cases levelled the houses completely with the ground. At Mullinasole [close to Murvagh], 2 large salt works [one was owned by him] are quite ruined, and 12 or 14 poor peoples' houses overwhelmed at Ballyweel. Just opposite St. Ernan's there are several houses down. In Donegal there are many boats wrecked in the streets. At St. Ernan's my mound parapet was covered some feet deep and on the waters subsiding was found levelled the entire length (630 feet). All my timber for roofing a part of my house was floated off (20 logs and much small timber) and hundreds of rabbits from the warren on the opposite side of the channel were picked up at St. Ernans and the neighbouring shores. One of the tenants had 7 stacks of corn carried out of his haggard and part of it cast ashore about a quarter of mile off and part carried out to sea.
>
> The rise of the water was so rapid that there was hardly time for the people to escape out of their houses. If it had been in the night, the loss of life would, as far as man could judge, have been very great . . . . The people, as far as I have had opportunity of conversing with them, seem to be full of awe and to acknowledge the warning voice in this dispensation.

Following-up on the theme that the hurricane-like weather was a warning from God, he wrote:

> Yesterday and to-day I met some of my neighbours by appointment to return thanks to the Lord who had heard our prayers in September. Tho' the season (except 3 weeks in which the harvest was saved) was most unfavourable, still there is a good sufficiency of provisions spared in the country and well saved. At Gregstown yesterday forenoon about 180 met, about half the number that had met to pray for fine weather . . . . At Ballydevitt about the same number came, and many R. Catholics, and all were very attentive. . . . To-day I met from 80 to 100 at the Lord's house in Aughadoey Mtn.

On 2 November, the diary reads: 'Edward has been this evening blessed with a son. N [Edward's wife, Martha Anne, was known by the family as Nanny] and her first born are, thank God, very well, and she had very little suffering'. They were to have four children, Edward, John, Martha Angelina and Chichester. John commented that the new baby was his grandmother's seventh great grandchild; 'our 4, K's 2 and Eds.1'.

During 1830, Hamilton had set-down what he called 'the manner of my spending a day':

> Weekday: Rise at 8. God awakens me (though disinclined) to private prayers. Family reading, exposition and prayer at 9. Teaching J [James] after breakfast. Reading and prayer with M for three-quarter hour at 11. Visiting sick, or ignorant, or giving out meal to poor for 2 to 6 hours from 12 o'clock. Family reading and prayer at 10pm. Social reading for one hour – and prayer til half past 12 or 1. And at some time during this last space, prayer with M.

The simple life-style of the Hamiltons was also to be seen in their attitude to money – even long before their financial position forced them to cut-back on expenditure. Several years earlier, Hamilton had written:

> Lover, the miniature painter, began the picture of grandmother and our three children – it will be expensive but I think not only pretty and interesting but useful. Mary has agreed to transform some useless plate into the picture – why not some more into a school or into some other really useful thing or, indeed, why keep any useless plate or anything useless?

This reference to Samuel Lover (1797-1868), probably better-known as a novelist and playwright, serves as a reminder that he was a many talented man, being also an accomplished musician (he even wrote a comic opera) as well as a painter who had been exhibiting since 1826.

FAMINE STRIKES

The cataclysmic years 1845-1850 have all but erased the memory of the earlier famines which were a regular occurrence before that awful event. Famines had occurred in 1739, 1763, 1785, 1800, 1807, 1816, 1821, and 1826, and now during the period 1829-1831 there was further deprivation in many parts of Ireland, not least in the heavily populated districts in County Donegal. Some people blamed the unusually stormy weather for being the cause of a the appearance of a disease which rotted the 1831 potato crop, which in turn precipitated a serious scarcity of provisions with the inevitable result that prices of provisions rose too. John Hamilton was involved in organising a subscription fund launched locally and the money raised was used to assist many of the poorest people with cheap food in the short term, but the outlook was distinctly unpromising.

Hamilton commented in his journal on the fact that the scarcity of food had caused hundreds of local families to take to the roads begging for assistance. He mooted the idea of fasting by those families not affected by the problem in order to make more food available for the very needy. He commented in a footnote that 'the cottagers and small farmers contributed largely on the plan proposed here'. During the month of April, he implemented his scheme of fasting, commencing in his own household where, by giving up one meal in the week for a period of five months, the food saved was then given to the local poor.

> This urged me to boldness with the gentry, and having sent round a proposal for subscriptions to employ the poor and provide provisions, the result has already been a fund of about £1,100 to be spent in employing the poor.
>
> A loan of 200£ is raised and put at my disposal (to be repaid by me), as treasurer, to import potatoes. I applied to Government to facilitate my endeavour to do this quickly and at the least expense. The answer by return of post was: 'We have brought a cargo of potatoes (123 tons) at three pounds a ton, we give them to you at two pounds a ton, and send them free of expense to your coast'.

In June, John Hamilton returned to the subject of the famine and recorded the steps he had taken to raise money for provisions for the poor:

> Last year in a time of famine, I had 1,000£ to my credit in the Bank which I worked upon and brought in a supply of meal and employed hundreds of poor whom I saw starving. While the need was, I kept on the expenditure, and was warned that if another season of want should come, I should have no means to give help. I did not expect two seasons of want in succession and partly from this cause and partly because I did not like to give up what I began, while there was need, and partly from opposition, and partly from natural recklessness, I spent all I could muster, saying if God sends another year of distress, he can provide for it. If faith in his providential care had any share in leading me to open my hand last year lavishly, it had but little spare for when I saw the distress this year, and looked at my exhausted treasury and exhausted credit too (for I have been building myself an house [the house at St. Ernan's was still being extended] which I had begun before the famine commenced, and could not stop without too serious a loss, besides throwing very many, directly and indirectly, out of work. When then I saw how matters stood I would gladly have fled from the suffering I anticipated among my neighbours . . . .
>
> Thousands of small farmers who had consumed their deficient crops before the usual time were driven to market for food. The supply was deficient and many of those who had food, to their shame (and ours who have not tried to teach them better) used every extortion.

I called on my few rich neighbours who met and resolved to subscribe for importing provisions and ultimately placed about 150£ in my hands which, with 50£ of my own, formed a fund for importing provisions for a district reaching from hence to the north of Rutland on this coast, containing 7 or 8 large parishes, and I imagine 70,000 inhabitants – of whom fully half are in distress, and a multitude in a destitute state.

By the Lord Lieutenants' aid and bounty I (to whom sole management of the fund has been given) have imported four cargoes of potatoes, value about 700£, besides 200£ freight, which have been sold at about 500£, and yet without much diminution of our funds. These arrived in time to seed the ground and there is the best crop growing that ever was known here, and the season has been most favourable. So great is the distress now that at Donegal above 1,000 persons came on our sale day last week to buy provisions, potatoes in quantities not above four stone. And this is the best end of our District.

Last year I was much out among the poor and always attended to the sale and distribution of provisions, but this year I could not, being a close prisoner to the bedside of my dear wife now for near three months . . . . [Their fifth and last child had been born in March.]

Now the famine is at its worst. The government bounty is done. My own means are nought, there being no rents to signify this year and my bank credit being overloaded. To-night I got letters praying me for God's sake to send help to thousands who are famishing – the calls upon my little and diminished funds are enough for one of several thousand pounds, and each subscriber grumbling at getting so small a share when, in fact two thirds of the capital invested in helping them is provided by me at my own cost and risk – besides the government aid. These things concurred in making me despair of going or doing anything except for my own tenantry to whom I am bound. But to-night brought a letter from Lord Roden [He was Auditor General of the Exchequer in Ireland and M.P. for Dundalk, and lived at Tollymore Park, Co. Down], who had seen a letter from me about our distress, enclosing £50. And another from a Relief Association in Dublin with £200 for our aid.

There was still great 'want' in the area and Hamilton's means to do anything further were, by his own account, almost exhausted. He was grateful that many strangers had been sending aid – in contrast to many of the landlords who were contributing 'so little as to be a mockery of charity'. A few weeks later he added:

The poor have received relief to a wonderful amount. Along the W. coast of Donegal I am sure 15,000£ worth of provisions must have been sent, of this at least 12,000 by strangers. My own opinion is that the

> landlords who could relieve their tenantry are the recipients of these alms, as they are saved the expense first, and then enabled to get their rents which otherwise they might seek from dead tenantry and waste farms.

Conditions for those living all around Brownhall and St. Ernan's were bad enough, but the situation further north in Hamilton's Fintown estate was even worse. Patrick McKye, a national school teacher in the nearby Glenties area, sent a 'memorial' to the Lord Lieutenant on behalf of the 9,000 tenants of West Tullaghobegley, describing the awful situation in which people there lived. Itemising what they owned between them, he listed: 'One cart, one plough, sixteen harrows, thirty two rakes, eight saddles, twenty shovels, seven table forks, twenty seven geese, eight turkeys, a single wheel car, not a pig, not a clock, and not a pair of boots, and no fruit trees, nor crops of turnips, parsnips, carrots or clover'. He added that: 'None of them, either married or unmarried women, can afford more than one shift . . . nor can many afford a second bed, but whole families of sons and daughters of mature age indiscriminately lying together with their parents, and all in the bare buff. Their beds are straw – green or dried rushes or mountain bent [grass], their bed-clothes are either coarse sheets or no sheets, and ragged filthy blankets . . . '

AN EMIGRATION STORY

Emigration had been established as a way of life – especially among the poor – often prompted by what might be called the frequent minor famines before the Great Famine. Hamilton described how he helped some members of his tenant's families to emigrate to America, and added a touching story about the repayment of a loan:

> Before the failure of the potato crop in 1845 and in the following years, there was a considerable flow of emigration to America, but few well-to-do people went there. It was chiefly young men and sons and daughters of poor families. It often happened that means were raised with great difficulty for one of a numerous family to pay a passage to America; and on such and similar pleas I was often asked to lend the price of a passage to be repaid by the emigrant. I frequently lent the required sum, then only from £3 to 4. They left in small sailing ships from every little port, and with very inadequate arrangements for their welfare.
>
> Contrary to what might perhaps be expected, these poor emigrants generally sent me back within a year the sum lent. The exceptions, I am ashamed to say, were the very persons of whom I had felt most secure, decidedly of a class looked upon as more respectable; while the poorer

and less esteemed absolutely never failed me, and this latter class was very numerous, and consisted for the most part of persons over whose families or relatives here I had no power, as they were tenants or cottiers on other landowners' estates. Among these was a very large and poor family. The eldest daughter was sent for by a relative who had emigrated some time before, and who paid her passage to New York. She dreaded going alone, and succeeded in getting a loan from me sufficient to pay a brother's passage. The loan was duly repaid within a year. The next year, the same family, hearing of situations for two more of their number, borrowed the greater part of two passages, which again was repaid within the promised time.

Not long after this, another brother borrowed the price of his passage to New York. A year passed, no repayment came; and a second year likewise. In the course of the third year his brother came and brought the money, about 3 10s. I asked if his brother had sent anything to help his old mother, or to assist another to go to New York. He said he had not – 'not a farthing'. 'Where is your brother now?' I asked. 'I don't know where he is, it is so long since he wrote' and saying this he suddenly stopped and coloured. 'Why' said I, 'how long is it since you heard from him?' He stammered, hesitated, and said he did not know. 'Is it more than a month?' 'O yes'. 'Is it three?' No answer.

'Six months?' Still silent. 'Is it a year?' 'No, sir, it is not a year'. 'Come now, tell me how long it is'. 'Well, sir, I got the letter in November'. 'And this is September! How is this? Why did you not bring me the money as soon as you got it?' He coloured, and said confusedly, 'I couldn't come with it sooner'. 'Nonsense!' said I; 'you could not come four or five miles! Now I see what it is: you have used the money your brother sent to repay his debt, and have traded upon it in some way. Had you lost your speculation how would it have been? Your brother would have been supposed by me to have broken faith and neglected his promise. Is it not so?' 'No, sir, I would never let my brother's promise to you be broken'. 'Then how is it? Why were you so long in fulfilling it?' 'I could not help it'. The poor fellow was greatly confused; but his flushed cheek changed to pale when I said: 'Now you did not intend, I see, to be quite dishonest, as you have at last brought me the money; but you have not spoken the truth. Have you your brother's letter? Was that it out of which you took the bank notes?' 'Yes, sir'. 'Let me see it'. 'I can't show it, sir'. 'Why not, if what you say is true?' 'No, sir, I can't; I can't show it'. 'Well, then, I must think it would make you appear more of a rogue than I thought you to be. You may go, but you are the first of your family that has given me reason to suspect your truth or honesty'. He turned and went slowly, and as I thought sullenly. I stood for a minute and watched him. He stopped, took the letter out of his pocket, opened

> it and looked at it; then turning round and seeing me still there he came back slowly, and thrust the letter into my hand saying, 'There, you can read it, sir. I would never let you see it only I know he couldn't bear that you'd think me a rogue or a liar; he'd rather you would know *all* than that'. The letter was as follows: 'Dear Brother, – I suppose you all thought me dead when you were so long without hearing from me. I was very near it. I met with an accident and broke some of my bones before I was three months in America, and I have been in the hospital ever since. They say I shall be months yet before I am fit to work. I was hoping to send you some help before this time, but you see how it is. The greatest burden on my mind is the money Mr. Hamilton lent me to pay my passage. It ought to be paid long ago. So, brother, as soon as you have set the potatoes on mother's little place, go some way where money is to be earned, and get as much as will pay the gentleman, and take it to him, but don't let him know a word but that I sent it, as I made a promise to do'.

DOUBTS ABOUT BAPTISM

During April 1831, John was in a contemplative and self-critical mood:

> I differ from most men in temperament and in my idea of pleasure. I love not wine and therefore am sober. I love not money, therefore liberal or lavish. I love not sitting still, therefore I stir myself. I have tried a hobby of gay and worldly pleasure and found it not to my taste, not satisfactory. I tried more quiet stirring – farming – improving land – improving outward condition of tenantry and I found it not sufficient, and I have made a hobby of religion!
>
> It is true I am convinced that this is the only pursuit which can satisfy and that if it were followed with a single eye to the glory of God, then there would indeed be great reward, not for such work but in it. I have learned to know more what religion is, and to wish to be truly religious, but to deny myself I will not be barred – my will is yet my God.

The Hamiltons' fifth child had been (as already noted) born at the end of March, after which John's wife had been severely ill. 'My dear wife has been very ill since I last wrote here and is this day getting up for the first time since our little Helen was born'. A month after this reference, he wrote:

> My dear wife is still in bed and not making any apparent progress towards recovery though she is spared any great degree of pain. Now she is tried, and now she finds the blessing which attended the severe sickness

> which followed her confinement in 1829. Then her hope was tried. [Arabella, their fourth child, was born in July of that year.]

Just after this he noted that: 'This night [May 7] completes eight years since my God gave me my dear wife. Then I thought my cup ran over. Now my wife is in her bed of pain and long continued sickness and is brought very low'. At the end of May, his wife's illness was further complicated by Rheumatic pains:

> Mary has suffered much from Rheumatic pain, so severe as to make her cry out sometimes for hours together. Though this is not an actual part of the illness which has long afflicted her, yet it both weakens by its irritation and the wakefulness it causes at night, and it retards her recovery and lowers her spirits.

Two months after Helen was born, John wrote: 'Our little baby is not yet christened', but this had less to do with the mother's health than with John's doctrinal doubts. 'I can not consent to the form or the doctrines which seem to be set forth in the form. I cannot believe that the child being sprinkled is regenerate. I know I was not so when I was sprinkled and the thanksgiving for my regeneration was a farce and I do think it is generally so'. His view at this time was that the baptism of infants had no scriptural support and therefore the ceremony should be retained 'for those [adults] who have believed'.

John was annoyed when he discovered his doctor had, while he himself had been absent, and without Mary's knowledge, vaccinated the baby. Not long after this, he wrote:

> My wife has had an unusual freedom from pain now for three days together and her progress in strength is good. She could yesterday stand up stoutly. . . . With regard to our infant, the subject of Baptism is still heavy on my mind. [These words are followed by no less than ten journal pages of personal reflection on infant baptism, concluding with a prayer for guidance].

Mary, though better, continued to be unwell, prompting John to write in October: 'Our dear children are all, by God's blessing, well and the affliction of our poor M is diminished and her general health much improved . . . ' But, in July of the following year, an entry in his journal records that: 'My Mary now gradually gains strength and her prospect of recovery is good' and, at the end of the month, she was just able to walk a little'. Though John did not say so, it seems likely that Mary's health was not improved by his continued refusal to allow the baby Helen to be baptised: 'We have come to no satisfactory conclusion about the Baptism of our little Helen. My views against it are stronger and stronger'.

He continued to agonise on the subject of baptism, and in August, the journal hints for the first time that Mary was very concerned that young Helen had not yet been baptised. John visited an uncle and aunt who were spending a few days at Tyrcallen Estate near Stranorlar where, seeing a book lying on a chair, he picked it up and found it to be a book which contained a sermon by Bishop Heber [a noted hymn-writer and religious author] on infant baptism, but in John's view, 'it proved nothing'. During that same month, Mary went to church for the first time since her illness where she 'gave thanks for her recovery'. John and Mary discussed baptism with his brother Edward and later, when they returned home to St Ernan's, they continued the discussion with each other 'but without coming to any agreement. She intends to have her child baptised and is still so weak in body that the distress occasioned by our not agreeing has shaken her very much.– I am truly tried now . . . My conviction is stronger and stronger'. In the Spring of 1832, Hamilton seemed, at last, to be reconsidering his position on infant baptism, or at least trying to reconcile his own views with Mary's concerns. He took the view, convoluted as it was, that baptism 'divested from the un-scriptural attributes with which that form invests, it may be reasonable and not un-scriptural, but agreeable to the general spirit of scripture, while not positively supported by precept or ordinance . . . ' This particular entry continued in a similar vein for the next four pages of the journal. However, on 29 August, despite his convictions and misgivings and, at last, in deference to Mary's anxiety and the effect it had been having on her, the journal recorded that:

> Our little Helen was baptised on Sunday. I suffered Mary (who was so anxious that I could not resist her desire) to take her child, yet I am not at all sure she is rightly convinced of the propriety of Ch. of E. Baptism or of infant. She says she feels that God would have her to bring her child to him but I do think superstition and prejudice are at the root . . . One thing that puzzled me in speaking to Edward on Baptism is cleared up in me: he insisted much on the *spirit*, and not strictly on the *letter*, being what we should adhere to.

After staying with his brother at Brownhall for five months, John and his family returned, late in the autumn, to St Ernan's where work had been proceeding on renovation and extension. He had hardly settled back in his own house when news came concerning local protests about rents which prompted Hamilton to print and distribute a tract on the theme:

> In some things I have been urged to activity for my neighbours. The endeavour to stir them up to mob meetings against rents and tithes occasioned me to write and print a tract of advice to my tenantry which was well received by others as well as by them, and was, I believe, a means of

> dissuading this district from such meetings, which has been a great blessing, for no good ever follows mob law, and the quiet deportment of my neighbours has procured for them such consideration from their landlords as their conduct deserved and their necessity required. There is unusual want of money and provisions among us this year; hundreds of families are out of their homes begging through the country and the distress must encrease before harvest, the seed of which is yet unsown.

It was at this time that John Hamilton began to notice that all was not going well in his religious classes:

> At the quarterly meeting of reading classes many were found very deficient in numbers and some totally given up. I believe I spread too far, and neither could superintend nor find assistance in superintending all the outlying classes, however, many Bibles were spread among the people and their attention wakened. That is good . . .

He noted in the journal that for four weeks in succession he had held 'meetings for his neighbours' at Greggstown, where he had to erect a temporary structure to shelter those attending, because the numbers were:

> too great for any house there to contain them . . . . Our chapel has been poles and ladders laid on large stones in an open place sheltered from the winds on three sides – and God has provided each time a roof in a serene sky. Much attention has been shown to the demeanour of every denomination who attend and I trust that making it a regular place of assembly on Sunday evenings may be made useful to many. At Muckros Female Sunday School the attendance continues good and my class of 19 girls from 12 to 18 or 19 years old are growing in good knowledge – some of them appear to know and feel the love of Jesus, and to love him who has so loved them.

At the end of October, John's journal recorded that he had just returned from a week's tour visiting relations and friends in Dublin, Ardbraccan and Collon. His sister, married to the Rev. William Foster, lived at Collon:

> In Dublin I found our old Grandmother (now near 86) so well as to be about the house and occasionally to walk in the streets . . . [He took the opportunity to go to a service in a meeting house in Abbey Street frequented by his cousin, David Stewart.] At Collon I saw my dear sister and brother[in law] well, but our communications have been so few that I did not enjoy my visit as I should otherwise have done – or as I did with my dear and kind uncle H.P. [the Rev. Henry Pakenham] at Ardbraccan.

THE MORAVIAN BROTHERHOOD

During October 1831, John went with his wife and son to Tyrcallen, which they had briefly visited three months earlier and where they now intended to stay for two days, but ended up staying for a fortnight because Mary became unwell. He did not explain the reason for going to this estate near Stranorlar, where the Marquess of Conyngham (another benevolent Donegal landlord) had built a shooting lodge thirty years earlier, but perhaps he simply wished to see what was considered at the time one of the finest planted demesnes in the county. Anyway, while there, John decided to visit the Moravian settlement at Grace Hill, Co. Antrim.

A lesser-known Protestant religion, the Morvian Brethren originated in what are now the Czech provinces of Bohemia and Moravia, indirectly founded by followers of the reformer Jan Huss, who had broken with Rome before Martin Luther. Accused of heresy, Huss refused to recant and was burnt at the stake. The ancient Protestant Episcopal Church of Moravia, after the country came under the rule of the strongly Catholic Hapsburgs, were persecuted almost to extinction, most of the survivors fleeing initially to Silesia and Saxony (now part of western Poland and eastern Germany). Many of their members later dispersed westwards across Europe, settling mainly in Germany, Holland and Switzerland. Others went to America, and some to England from where several groups settled in Ireland.

John Hamilton paid several visits to their settlement at Grace Hill in County Antrim and the fact that he later visited Moravian groups in several parts of England, as well as several continental settlements during his European tour is an indication of how impressed he was by their simple piety and the emphasis they placed upon a personal religion and the active participation of the laity. The Moravian emphasis on the lay office, and the fact that the Brethren did not regard their ordained clergy as a privileged group would also have appealed strongly to him at this time. He arrived at Grace Hill without advance notice, finding there the Rev. Thomas Mallalieu, Minister of the settlement from 1824 to 1836. Hamilton referred to their hymn singing, for which they were noted, the first Moravian hymn book dating from 1501. The Moravian church at Grace Hill, built in 1765, is still active, surrounded by the original school buildings and the settlement village, all built with local cut stone in stark contrast with the whitewashed cottages which originally surrounded the village. Intended to be a self-contained and self-supporting community, it was based on the pattern of those already founded in central Europe:

> I have just returned from a visit to the Moravian settlement at Grace Hill, Co. Antrim. I went un-introduced to Mr. Mallalieu, the pastor . . . My journey was not undertaken for mere curiosity, it was undertaken with a desire to know how the rules and forms of the *Unitas* had worked, and

Gracehill village, Co. Antrim, the principal Moravian settlement in Ireland, dates from 1765 John Hamilton's son, James, attended the school there for several years.

how their tenets stood . . . They adopt much of the Church of England Articles and their liturgy is in many points similar. In their Services there is a very great deal of singing, more than I found pleasant, for it seemed strange to me to sing confession and prayer . . .

On Monday, Mr. Harke, assistant pastor, showed me about the place and I visited some of the poorer people, tradesmen, etc., in their houses. The congregation, chiefly in the village, consists of about 700 persons old and young. There is an estate between 200 and 300 acres belonging to the brethren. A square is surrounded on three sides by their public buildings, church, ministers' houses, academy, ladies school, inn, day-school, and in four short streets the people live.

Their houses looked less remarkably tidy than I had expected, but in decency and comfort, they are fair, far before any of their class I have seen in Ireland. They hold two or three acres of land and a house . . . every one has a cow, and though none make much money all are comfortable and seem happy. There is a house where the single sisters may go and live and support themselves by their work, under one or two matrons. About 50 now live there, and there was a similar establishment for single brothers, but so few chose to avail themselves of it that it is discon-

> tinued. There is also a widows' house supported by a legacy. In the ministers' houses where we were staying everything was neat, no affectation of simplicity, nor any affectation of style beyond their very limited means, which are small beyond credibility to us who are used to small livings of £300 to £400 a year, and moderate ones of £600 or £700.

Hamilton thought 'a multiplying of such settlements' would be a good idea, though he could not imagine the Moravians accepting a situation where their ministers would be appointed by 'Lord This or the Duke of That'. In fact, this visit to the Moravians showed that Hamilton had not, even at this stage, entirely got out of his system some kind of desire for ordination. He actually suggested to the Rev. Mr Harke that he was well disposed to the idea of becoming a Moravian minister, a suggestion that was not, however, taken-up by Harke and nothing came of it.

Old Recipes from Brownhall Kitchen

COXTOWN SODA SCONES

Rub 3 oz. of butter into 2 lbs. of flour, ½ oz. of Soda, ¼ of Tartaric Acid and a little Salt, well blended together. Make into a soft dough with Buttermilk. Cut into 8 scones. Prod them at the top with a fork and bake in a moderately quick oven. The soda to be lightweight.

DRUMHOLM BREAKFAST BREAD

Mix a teaspoon of baking powder in 1 lb. of flour dry. Then wet with a teacup full of new milk warmed and 1½ oz. of butter melted in the milk. Then add whites of two eggs well beaten, when all is well mixed divide into four little loaves and bake for half an hour.

LAGHEY CAKE

6 oz. butter, 6 oz. moist sugar, 6 oz. currents, a handful of plums or sultanas, spice to taste. 1 lb. flour, 2 eggs, essence of lemon, about ½ pint of milk, ¼ oz. soda.

Beat the batter to a cream, add the sugar and spice, with currents and plums, the flour with the soda through it, add by degrees. Whisk the eggs, a little essence of lemon through them, or lemon peel chopped finely. Sufficient milk to make it the consistency of cakes in general. Add some of the milk to the eggs and when mixed with the cake, if not wet through add a little more milk. Beat the cake for about 5 minutes and put in a tin lined with buttered paper, and bake about 2 hours in a moderate oven.

SIX

'Financially Cramped'

John Hamilton went to Dublin in November 1831 to arrange for the family to stay there for six months. He found his grandmother, now nearly 87, in good health. However, when he returned to Donegal, his plans had 'gone awry, and it seems unlikely we can go'. John made the best of the change of plans, noting that Cholera had broken out in England 'so it will probably be soon in Ireland, and our place then would be at home and, besides, a town is the worst place to go while infection is rife. It threatens to be an awful scourge here, a dense, ill-fed population is a bad subject for the disease. . . .'

Cholera is usually associated with poor hygiene and takes the form of acute diarrhoea; even the mention of the name struck horror at a time when both its cause and means of treating it were poorly understood. During the week after the previous entry, John heard that 21 cases of Cholera had been reported in Sunderland, 'seventeen fatal and the rest hopeless'. However, no Cholera epidemic reached the county that year (although it did so in 1832, the year after the first dispensary was established in Donegal – pre-dating the workhouse there by 11 years).

On the last day of the year, John's wife was still far from well and they were both anxious about 'a reoccurrence of our poor little Mary's illness'. His closing remark in the 1831 journal was: 'In all my children there is in our image too visibly a heart disinclined to God, but I do hope I see a growing conviction that God is their friend'.

During January 1832, the journal recorded that 'Wednesday is appointed for a day of solemn fasting and humiliation for this Nation, in consequence of the visitation of Cholera' but the subject was not mentioned again until the following June when news came from Dublin that it had broken out there and some 200 people had been infected and almost 100 had died. It was also rampant throughout central and southern parts, but so far Ulster had been the least affected province with only two outbreaks, one at Bundoran where 17 had died, from where it had spread to Ballyshannon. There were wild rumours that 10,000 of the 12,000 inhabitants of Sligo had fled and that some 1,600 died, but Hamilton made no further reference to the epidemic that year.

However, early in the New Year of 1833, cholera broke out once more in County Donegal, with 11 cases and two deaths in Ballintra, as well as further cases in Donegal town. Hamilton wrote on 17 January: 'By God's blessing we have begun a new year and in doing so we have been awfully called up to consider our ways' adding that he had 'seen death more frequently within these past few days than ever before, having occasion to act both as doctor and minister in several cases'. This was a reference to the fact that he had been going into houses where cholera had struck, demonstrating yet another side to his character.

> My Sabbath was a busy one . . . beside the bed of death. Three whom I saw and tried to help, died, and I think a fourth, who was then cured but who by imprudence relapsed, and will die . . . I have not felt the smallest nervous tremour in attending those sick; nevertheless, I avoid every unnecessary contact, for I am not blind to risk, though fearless of it . . . My dear wife, with tears she prays that I may not needlessly risk myself, nor faithlessly shrink from my duty. The poor deluded people of Donegal. . . . set themselves against those who are stirring to aid them. They burnt a barn yesterday which was prepared for the widow and orphans of some who died of cholera.

This epidemic appeared to cease as abruptly as it had begun, but six weeks later there was a new outbreak – apparently affecting a single cottage – where a child and her aunt died and the child's father was thought to be dying. Hamilton had been laid-up with a painful swollen leg (his doctor told him it was flying gout) and the news of this latest outbreak reached him on the first day he was up and about. No one from the Board of Health would go to the house, though a nurse did, so he went himself, finding the unfortunate man in the last stage of cholera:

> his wife lying helpless having had a child a few hours before . . . and as soon as the nurse tender had dressed the child she fled, and no one had been in the house to help them since dawn. This at one o'clock p.m. Their poor little children, six and eight years old, and the infant were in the house. I gave the man what might be useful and repeated the dose frequently, but could get no one to attend him or her, though Roman Catholics. I searched all the neighbourhood and offered [a] large [sum] to pay for a nurse. At length at evening we got one and I was permitted to return home, but the man died shortly after I left. The woman did not take the infection, nor has there since [at that time of writing] been a case of cholera in Donegal. . . .

In 1834, cholera broke out once more, this time at Trimmon, only four miles from Brownhall, and John rode out with his brother Edward to find that two persons had already been buried and several persons were very ill:

> . . . one of the two infected houses (each having only one room) was empty, and the sick were lying among straw and filth in the other. I tried to get help to clean out and prepare the empty one but in vain and at length succeeded in doing it alone, assisted only by a little boy, son of the sick woman, about 10 years old, and I got the sick into tolerable comfort but left them in appearance dying. I have not heard from them to-day (Sunday) but yesterday my comrade in the work, the poor boy, was so ill as to be expected to die. Why not I? The idea is very terrible to me – not that I have the least fear of death, but I do fear leaving my poor M. in the world . . . .

Not surprisingly, his wife continued to be concerned about her husband going into infected cottages:

> I spent yesterday and to-day chiefly ministering to them but my poor wife is so nervous about my sick that I do not know if I can do so any more. She seems to think I care less for her and my children than for those to whom I have no tie, because I unhesitatingly leave this society to attend to the sick and declare my readiness to be called hence in that duty and to leave them to the Father of the fatherless and the God of the widow. O my dear wife might know how she is a widow indeed whose husband is dead while he liveth, who is not ready to lose his life and trust his dear dearest ones to God as well as his own body and soul. . . .

About 30 people died in Donegal town, and more in the surrounding areas, during this epidemic. Hamilton himself became ill ten days later and thought, at first, that he had contracted the fever. 'As I lay disordered in stomach and bowels, and deadly cold notwithstanding many active means to produce heat, I felt it right to look cholera in the face'. However it was not cholera, and the subject ceased to feature in the journals. Hamilton did not even mention – when it happened – that Mary's father died of the disease in 1846; we only know of this because his young daughter Moll kept a diary for a short time and it included an entry: 'Heard of dear Grandpapa's death from Cholera on Wednesday morning, September 3rd. at Inverness'.

ENCOURAGING THE TENANTS

Hamilton regularly communicated with his widely scattered tenants by letters which he would get specially printed. When he wrote them in January 1832, he must have been feeling discouraged by the meagre results of his work on their behalf:

> Is it of any real use or profit to you to receive attention and kindness from me, and do you find any advantage from the expense of money and trouble which I lay out among you?
>
> My dear friends, let me see you endeavour to live more like Christians, make the best of what you have got; making bad use of little is not the way to get more of God's good gifts. Try to make your houses more comfortable and decent; let your women exert themselves to keep the house clean, and the clothes of the family mended, a torn garment is a disgrace but a patched one is an honour. Stir yourselves and I am ready to forget how little encouragement you have given me. I am ready to advise, encourage and help you to be more comfortable and respectable, and to live more like Christians.
>
> Do not tell me it is of no use. By continuing to be dirty, ragged and miserable, I cannot help you . . . I have determined to begin with a number of premiums for those who shall improve most . . . The list of premiums . . . is published among you. Do not fear because you are poor or weak and cannot do much. *Do your best.* I will consider as fairly as I can what each ought to do, and the premiums will be given accordingly.

He then outlined a detailed plan to encourage his tenants to improve their own circumstances:

> To have your houses as they ought to be, there should be a space at least six feet wide, if possible, all round the house, so fenced that neither cow nor pig could come into it, and this space should be gravelled or paved, and sloped so that the wet should run off from the foundation of the house.
>
> The pig-sty and the house for geese or ducks should be outside the fence around the house, and they should never be fed inside the space which is gravelled or paved.
>
> No dung-hill should touch the house on any account, nor be in front of it, nor under a door or window.
>
> The floor of the house should be level and higher than the ground outside. The windows must open, and never be stuffed with rags, or hay, or such things. The inside should be kept white – with great pains to make the chimney take away all the smoke. Potatoes should never be stored in the house.
>
> Let your farm be well worked, make good fences *and keep them good* particularly those planted with thorns. Keep your family busy and do not let them leave their clothes in rags.

Hamilton then ended his exhortation with an assurance to the tenants, that if

TO THE

Tenants on the Estate of St. Ernan's.

St. Ernan's, September, 1880.

My Dear Friends,

I have been looking over several old letters to you, which I have had printed and handed to all my tenants at different times in the last 40 years, which is only a part of the time we have known one another. I have copied out some parts of these letters, and I now send them to you, because I see that things are spoken in our neighbourhood that might make it seem as if all tenants were oppressed and all landlords oppressors.

In an address to the Right Honourable Mr. Childers, in Donegal, the Tenants are made to say :—" *We are tenants at will, that is, the landlords at will can and have enormously rack-rented our farms, on which they never expended a shilling in improvements, but have, on the contrary, confiscated our improvements, and destroyed our Tenant-Right and the Ulster Custom by an arbitr... and unjust increase of rent,*" and more to th...

I send ...

... of renting it

... a long term of years.

I cannot conclude this letter without saying that I quite agree with the good friend who told you all at a meeting in Donegal, not long ago, the unwelcome truth, that the worst landlords were not so hard on the Tenants as they were upon each other. For I know that if a Tenant lets a field or two to a neighbour, he will extort a far higher rent than any proprietor of an estate would think of asking.

But these, my friends, are not questions between you and me. I don't want to rack-rent you, much less to turn out any tenant who has a mind to stay ; and less still do I wish to hinder any one who may have to leave, from getting the fullest value for his Tenant-right ; and as I have all good will towards you all, I have confidence in your good will towards your old friend and landlord,

JOHN HAMILTON.

Part of one of John Hamilton's letters which he printed and circulated to his tenants. If Hamilton was not unusual in corresponding regularly with his tenants, he must surely have been unique in addressing them – as he usually did – as his 'Dear Neighbours' or 'Dear Friends".

they did not understand anything in the letter, they were to come to him and he would be 'always ready to explain and advise'.

John Hamilton made a reference in his journal to the Kildare Place Society Schools, which were run by an organisation founded in 1811, composed mainly of members of the Church of Ireland and the Society of Friends. It was the first large-scale attempt to bring primary education to Irish children, a pioneering venture considerably ahead of anything comparable in Europe, but it was to run into difficulties because its curriculum included the teaching of the scriptures. The society claimed that this was done 'without comment' and it felt – rightly or wrongly – this was fair to all denominations. Two decades after this, deeply uneasy about proselytising, the Roman Catholic bishops intervened and in 1831 – the year Hamilton wrote the following note – primary education came largely under the control of a new body, the National Commissioners of Education.

> I am much busied about the schools and the break-up of the Kildare Place Society Schools by the withdrawing of the government grant of £2500 a year, because the whole Word of God, without note or comment, was read in them – and has upset the education of the poor. I have seven schools on my land, not all or nearly all filled with my own tenantry, but the chief care has fallen on me and now will, I fear, be quite cast on me, which must lead to the closing of some of them.

Although he was appointed High Sheriff in County Donegal in 1826 and a Commissioner of the Peace in 1846, Hamilton did not take any active part in politics, and was careful about being identified with any factions, as witnessed by his resignation from the Yeomanry and the Brunswick Clubs and his distancing of himself from the Orange Order. Uneasy about an offer now being made of being appointed Deputy Lieutenant for the County of Donegal, he decided to turn it down.

> I have been tried this week with a temptation to worldly pursuits by an appointment of Deputy Lieutenant of this county. I had gone out of the sphere of political and magisterial influence and become *nobody*. This appointment at once offered me the opportunity of stepping into an influential place among the gentry of the county of the Kingdom, but I thank God that I had no inclination for it and declined it by return of post.

His initial rejection of the offer was not accepted and, some time after, he scribbled a note across the journal page to the effect that, finding the title 'merely a name' he had decided to accept it.

FINANCIALLY EMBARRASSED

Hamilton was a man of many parts, and his skills appeared to include an ability to render first aid:

> John Farrell fell to-day off a cart of hay and dislocated his shoulder, it was supposed to be broken but in comparing it with Graham's medicine book I found it was not broken, and by following the instructions there laid down, I succeeded in putting it into its place an hour after the hurt.

The Hamiltons had a visit from a Mr Enright, who seems to have been a Bible-class inspector, probably from the Hibernian Bible Society. He inspected a few of the classes and 'gave an account of his scripture reading classes at Delgany'. At the same time, John Hamilton made his second reference to numbers at some of the classes having 'grievously fallen off' during his enforced absences caused by Mary's illness, and he resolved to re-establish the ones which had failed.

Shortly after this, John recorded news about his clergyman brother: 'Edward's family is encreased by another son and Nanny is again out and well'. The death of an infant nephew prompted John to list 'the extraordinary number of children born to those within a degree of cousins in these last few years, and among which this was the first death':

> There are in my Uncle Longford's house – 10; Dr. Hercules Pakenham's –6; Dr. Henry Pakenham's – 4; My house – 5; Edward's – 2; Kitty Foster's [his sister] – 3; E. Conolly's – 7; Louisa Rollards – 8; H. Hares – 1; Sarah Law – 1; F. Townsend's – 1; besides E. Evans, F. White, J. Pakenham, A. Stewart, R. Pakenham, and others that do not occur at this moment, amounting in all to about three score.

During the Spring of 1832, Hamilton was again expressing concern about his financial situation, mainly brought on by his almost reckless expenditure, although there is little evidence of his spending in his journals:

> With regard to expenditure, I feel this sorely. On looking over my affairs which are inexcusably tho' not irretrievably embarrassed, I find that, conforming modestly to the ways of the world, and struggling to pay what I owe, and to keep up the charities which I have supported, we cannot live on less that 1,000£ a year, clear of all estate expenses and interest of debt. From this deduct 100£ a year allowed for childrens' expenses, and about 50£ for uncharged charities, and it leaves a household expenditure of above 800£ a year, while I am cramped in every endeavour to do good by my limited means!

> I believe that generally (but not always) it is right for one circumstanced as I am, to have a good, comfortable roomy house, wherein to rear my family, study Thy word, preserve books etc. which may conduce to useful knowledge, wherein I may exercise Christian hospitality towards my friends and strangers, and it is right to have such furniture as is needful for comfort – especially of invalids, and to provide such diet as shall be fit for all ages and constitutions in my house.
>
> But the danger is, in spending on my house (to make it like the world) seems above what is needful which might house the houseless. . . .

No doubt it was a combination of these concerns that prompted him to make a proposition to his brother Edward that they might consider 'dwelling together, having but one establishment, both to have more opportunity of provoking each other to love and to good works, and of helping each other in spiritual things, but also to diminish our expenditure and enable us to devote a larger portion to God's more immediate service. . . '. While he saw many advantages in the plan, it seems likely that Edward – or even the two wives – were not enthusiastic about the notion of the two families (with five and two children respectively) living under the one roof. 'I suspect', John wrote 'it will not come to pass'.

Another cause for concern was exercising Hamilton's mind at this time: 'I have had much anxiety about our boy James; the close attention I am obliged to pay to M. prevents the possibility of attending to him'. This was not the first occasion – nor the last – that a reference was made to James's behaviour. Whatever the actual cause his anxiety, he resolved to send his son to Grace Hill School which he had visited 'and liked much' in the previous Autumn. The records at Grace Hill show that James was admitted to the Moravian School on the 7 July, 1832, where he was placed 'in the care of Mr. and Mrs Hawke'.

Mary's health continued to be a cause for concern but by mid-August she was at last well enough to accompany her husband on an extensive tour around the country, starting with their Conyngham friends near Stranorlar, where they stayed for a week. They moved on to Coleraine and travelled from there to Grace Hill in order to visit young James, where they stayed for a further week. It seems quite likely that John availed of this opportunity to discuss his thinking with the Rev Mr. Mallelieu, and to enquire further about the Moravians, including the location of their other settlements both in England and on the continent. From Grace Hill the family travelled to Langford Lodge, also in County Antrim, of which John had fond childhood memories, and where he found all his maternal relations in good health, though John himself was suffering from boils. The couple then went to Rostrevor where they were so 'taken with the beauty of this place and the kind of society which may be enjoyed here that I think it is probable we may take a house for a year or two' – though nothing came of this. The tour continued to Ardee where John paid another visit to his cousin at Red House, from where they travelled the short distance to Ardbraccan Glebe, staying with John's uncle for a fortnight, after which they went to Dublin to visit relations and friends before returning to St Ernan's at the end of November.

DUBLIN, DELGANY AND DERBY

During March1833, John decided to travel with his son to Delgany, County Wicklow. There is no explanation in the journal as to why this destination was chosen though he did record, a year earlier, that a Mr Enright of the Hibernian Bible Society had been there. On the way, the pair stopped briefly in Dublin where they found all their relations well and Hamilton mentioned that:

> On Sunday, I heard Mr. H. Irwin in Sandford Chapel on the parable of the Kingdom likened to seed which a man took and sowed [this was his second attendance there], and in the evening at the Moravian church, Bishop street [The stained glass windows of this church were later removed to Grace Hill].
>
> On Monday, went to Delgany. The situation of Delgany village and parish is quite delightful, sloping from the mountain Sugarloaf down to the sea, both picturesque and civilised. The village is small and straggling, on uneven ground, it contains several pretty cottages belonging to the gentry, a good glebe house, and a neat, roomy church which, with its spire, completes the view.

John and his son returned to Dublin and joined the extended family circle at John's grandmother's house. Now in her 89th year, she entertained her children and grandchildren to the number of twenty-two. One of the objects of this visit was to obtain a governess for the younger Hamilton children but John had also made the decision to return with the whole family to Delgany, where he had arranged to rent a house, Glencarrick, 'sufficient for us and some friends whenever they may come to us' During their subsequent stay in Delgany there were staff problems:

> We have had a sad, melancholy affair in our house since we came here – our housekeeper . . . we discovered was in the habit of drinking (not, that I know of it, to intoxication), and of sending out those under her for whiskey. She is gone, to our great discomfort, and our man servant must go too.

One of the visitors who came to Glencarrick was a Henry Newman from

Bandon 'who spoke about Irish society so as to give me hopes that, through them, something might be done for the poor in Fintown, that is a thorn in my conscience – I am an Absentee to it, almost as bad as those who do not live in Ireland at all'. Part of the Hamilton estate was situated some 20 miles north of Brownhall in the Finn valley which, judging from this reference and the very few other allusions to it in the journals, was not often visited by John Hamilton (though it was frequently visited by James when he grew older). Despite Hamilton's self-reproving remark, he was praised by the local newspaper for his work of consolidation, enclosure and drainage on the 8,000 acre Fintown estate, less than one tenth of which was cultivated prior to the implementation of his improvement scheme. Hoping thereby to double the rents, much was achieved by 1848, including the introduction of green crops and corn, which caused other local proprietors to view him as a good example to follow.

While staying at Delgany, he travelled to Glanmore Castle, near Ashford, about ten miles away, to meet a Mr Synge, and although Hamilton did not elaborate, he spent several days in his company. The explanation for this visit becomes clear when it is realised that John Synge, who was the grandfather of the playwright John Millington Synge, was a committed evangelist and one of the founding members of the Plymouth Brethren sect. John Synge had some other interests in common with Hamilton. He was a keen landscape gardener and had laid out drives and paths through his demesne which included the scenic Devil's Glen, and it is not difficult to imagine them strolling through Synge's demesne viewing the waterfall from the various built-up vantage points, and discussing religious topics while sitting in the tea-house recently completed by his second wife. John Synge's first wife, who had died three years earlier, was an Isabella Hamilton who, though from County Donegal, was not related to John Hamilton. Perhaps the most significant connection between the two men was that Synge had spent four years on the continent in pursuit of his religious interests, and this may well have prompted Hamilton to do the same four years later

It was shortly after this that John got word his grandmother was unwell and he hastened to Dublin where he found 'all hope of recovery gone'. She rallied for two days and then 'ceased to take notice of us and got very rapidly lower . . . before she departed quietly without a sigh or movement, she was 88 years old in January'. The next journal entry was written two weeks later when Mary was, once again ill, but there is no record in the journal of the grandmothers' funeral.

Back again in Donegal, John Hamilton planned to visit England, but Mary's continued ill health forced him to abandon the idea until mid-September when he sailed with a Miss Markworth from Kingstown:

> and after a rough passage landed little after 6 the next morning at Liverpool. Miss M not very sick and self not even squeamish. We left Liverpool

at 7, crossed the river to Birkenhead where the coach set out, in which we had taken places, and reached Birmingham [a distance of some 100 miles] that night, and searched town for lodgings this evening after the easiest journey for its length I ever made. Nothing remarkable having occurred except the Lord's remarkable kindness to us in our goings out and comings in. We found Miss Markworth here, to her sisters' great delight, and we had happy communion in the word of the Lord and in prayer and in praise.

I have not been in London since my marriage – not since I loved the world and the things of the world. It gives me more pain than I anticipated approaching the places of which all my reminiscences are guilty. . . .

After adding that he had yet to begin a search for governess for his daughters and a tutor for James he reminisced: 'I have not been far from my dear wife since our marriage, nor as long absent as I propose (if God will) now to be. I feel very dreary yet not cast down'. John Hamilton spent only a week in London, moving thence to Derby.

THOUGHTS ON SCHOOLING

While in London he had taken the opportunity to visit a Moravian clergyman who was probably responsible for advising him to travel to Derby to assess the Moravian Settlement at Ochbrook, 'chiefly to see the boys school conducted by Mr Connor'. He found the situation 'pretty and healthy' and the school itself 'in nice order' catering for fifty boys.

> Mr and Mrs Connor showed all brotherly kindness and Moravian courtesy. I took share of their dinner at 1 o'clock. How pleasant to be asked to dine – not to feast. I propose, if God will, to go to Manchester in the morning where Miss Uppleby resides, whom I hope to get for a governess to help Mary. Also I intend to visit the Moravian settlement and school at Fairfield [near Manchester], where my inclination is much bent to settle James (and ourselves too), for a time.

John Hamilton was continuing to have some difficulty in determining what to do about James's education. Having originally decided on a private tutor, he subsequently found the Moravian school at Grace Hill a more attractive proposition for his son, but less than a year on, James was again being tutored at home. After returning to Donegal, he mentioned he had also gone to see the Rev Haldane Stewart in Liverpool, who seems to have convinced him that young James would find a better all-round education at the Fairfield Moravian school, and having made up his mind to follow this course, he also decided that: 'for a change of scene and air for my dear M., I intend to go to the neighbourhood of Liverpool for this winter'. The whole scheme was dropped because, as he expressed it, 'the Lord has, for the present, closed the door which seemed to have been open for our boy's education and in doing so has given us new trials and new mercies'. A subsequent journal entry, written during a visit to Dublin explains what actually happened:

> While I was at St. Ernan's last week preparing for our moving to Liverpool, I heard that our boy had got the measles. This of course, stops our voyage, for tho' he has recovered well, the others have to go through it and, except [young] Mary, they have not yet taken it decidedly, though I think they all have it. We were very anxious about poor little Mary – her being so great a sufferer for, between 4 and 5 years, made it likely she would be a bad subject for measles, especially as her eyes are often very bad. She took it a few days ago and she has had the disorder, so far, as lightly as possible. Her acquaintance with her Lord has been a great support. She got me yesterday and the day before to read to her 'the story of the little girl whose Papa prayed for her' (Jairus' daughter) and of the little girl whose Mamma prayed for her' (The Canaanitish woman's daughter).

The set-back resulted in the comment: 'It seems remarkable that when Edward [his brother] and I had both settled to pass the winter in England for our wives' health, our intentions are frustrated, in his case by his own illness of a doubtful and painful nature (one says pleurisy, and another gout). Nanny [Edward's wife] and his children have joined him at Brownhall where he had gone, like me, to prepare for the winters' absence. . . '. This was followed by an enigmatic entry, hinting at some disagreement between him and his brother or, more probably, with his sister-in-law: 'May God grant to us (Edwards' house and mine) that if we do pass another winter in close neighbourhood, it may be more to edification and much more to our Lord's glory – who has signally and repeatedly reminded us to consider our ways – and to consider His ways!'

If one is to judge by the journals, Mary seems at first to have been fully supportive of almost everything which her husband said or did, but hints here and there suggest that John and Mary, did not *always* see eye-to-eye in various matters, and there were several instances mentioned in the journal, including the recent disagreement over Helen's baptism, indicating that Mary had a mind of her own, at least in some matters. It may have been her frustration over the lengthy baptismal argument that made her now openly disagree with some of his religious ideas which, given the important part religion played in his life, must have been deeply unsettling for him. He confided some of his thoughts about this to his journal: 'I fear she thinks my unworldly ideas nonsense', he wrote, after which he added a prayer: 'O God, enable me before I go hence, to witness to those dear, dear to me that it is not nonsense'. His mind must have been in considerable turmoil, perhaps all the more so as there seem to have been only a few such incidents – incidents that were more than off-set by the frequent journal references to the couple praying together. He closed this entry with the words: 'I have hitherto in my selfishness shown more deference to her feelings than to Thy command. O how unfaithful, how unkind to her! Can I possibly thus benefit her? No, I may thus see peace where there is none. O God, my God, her God, help and guide me and make me faithful to my dear wife's soul, though I grieve her at first. Amen, Amen'. All this led to the following entry:

> M, as usual, obliges me to consider over and over again the doctrines which God's word teaches and which are contrary to some orthodox dogmas. I am often impatient with her when I see a ray of light . . . and when I think it fully and clearly proved, and she does not see it, or shuns to look at a doctrine contradicting to whatever she has before viewed. But all is well ordered. If I had a wife new-fangled or she had a husband what I may call old fangled, we should both be badly off. She would be apt to receive no food – and I should be apt to digest mine too little, and neither would be sufficiently nourished.

Already beginning to feel the pinch, financially, Hamilton considered how he might continue to assist his poor tenants after he had seen their plight during February 1834:

> In visiting my poor sick neighbours, I see great want, which to a certain degree at least may be relieved by my superfluities. I mean superfluities to a Christian and I can enjoy a meal or enjoy an evening's reading when our comforts are the shearing and flesh of the poor man's lamb. My silver fork would feed a poor family for a fortnight, perhaps a month, and I cannot say: 'In the name of Jesus I will enjoy this' when I should not like to see Jesus beside me . . .

He returned to this topic again:

> Matters have led to our being without footman or gardener, and I intend not to fill their places; our coachman will become a garden servant, and thus save me from keeping two expensive servants. My carriage horses too must go to market. Their place also remains vacant. My dear wife has also joined me in parting with superfluous ornaments of gold and jewels. These have been sold and brought as much as will make a nice girls' school. I added to her sacrifice of ornaments a diamond ring of my mother's, not doubting but that if the spirit of my dear mother can see and be interested in earthly matters, she must rejoice to see that that which could have only ministered to vanity is turned to God's service.

Hamilton discussed religious topics with a Scots' clergyman in July 1834,'chiefly on denominations in the church and upon lay preaching, and I have been led in it to see some erroneous notions commonly current. We disagreed much on the necessity of belonging to some Church or denomination of Christians. I agreed as to a Church, but totally dissented as to a denomination, and argued that what we call churches are miscalled so . . . '. One is left to wonder what exactly was said that caused him to write a long dissertation about what precisely constituted a 'Church' or a 'denomination'. After several more pages on the subject, he ended with the comment : 'I have been made aware of the want of expression of love in my manner in addressing others on the subjects of their souls' salvation and their Lord's glory' It would appear that John Hamilton, a man with very strong opinions, was meeting with dogged disagreements on several fronts and did not much like it.

It will be remembered that the first time John Hamilton met his future wife was when he visited her family then staying at Boulogne in 1821. In September 1834, the couple returned there to be with her family – presumably there on a holiday – once more. 'We had a prosperous journey, everything was ordered even for our pleasure. We left my dear son at Mr. Ostrehan's in Glo'stershire, 20 miles from Cheltenham and have every reason to like the family with whom we have been led to place him'. This signalled yet another about-turn in Hamilton's thinking on his son's education:

> In our journey of 1300 miles and 4 crossings of the sea we were preserved in health and safety, only being delayed a couple of days by Mary's not feeling it prudent to go on. But the very day we returned home I was attacked with a complaint like Cholerene which for between 2 and 3 weeks has kept me in a state in which I could not have travelled at all.

During the final few days of 1834, John Hamilton returned to Gloucester to bring James home from school to Donegal, arriving back on New Year's Day. That same evening he was 'attacked by gout in the foot which, though a light attack, was sufficient to be a cause of thankfulness that, as in my journey in Summer, so now I had been brought home before the least affliction was laid upon me'. Immediately after his return, he took the family to Brownhall to stay with Edward's family because of his disappointment over the recently appointed governess from whom so much had been expected:

> We want Miss Uppleby's removing from St.Ernan's before going there ourselves. She has made an unadvised, unhallowed engagement with one who no one imagines can make her happy, and is persuaded that we are all her enemies because we would prevent her by persuasion from, that we can not go home while she remains. . . .

Long afterwards, Hamilton added a pencilled footnote in the margin of this journal page stating that the woman died after a life of much suffering 20 years later and that his wife 'loved her very much and they were of late years sisters indeed'.

The first entry for 1835 was written at the Moravian settlement at Grace Hill where John stayed for a few days. He was, once again, unhappy with James's education, and had decided to bring him back for a second time to the Grace Hill school which he had been attending two years earlier. The reason for removing him from the school in the first place was not stated but may be explained by his remark at this point that 'there is some improvement in the religious exercises of the School . . . and from the temper and disposition of the Moravians I think there is reason to expect further improvement'. While at Grace Hill, Hamilton attended a service at their church, and considering how much of his own time was devoted to religious discourse, it seems slightly ironic that he added the comment: 'I am rather weary with the length of services in the chapel, having been there in all about 8 hours'. One might also wonder what exactly prompted the remark which followed this:

> Some to whom I opened my mind have denounced me as a heretic and, mistaking private conversations when I have had no opportunity of clearing up the matter, they have led many, I fear, to believe that I deny the Salvation which is in Jesus only because I take a different view of it from theirs.

The fact that he was on friendly terms with most of the local Protestant clergy in Donegal and that he continued to attend Services at and to support Drumholm parish church, did not inhibit him from continuing his criticisms of aspects of the Church of Ireland and the other mainstream churches:

> I am much perplexed as to my duty with regards to the established church, as it is called. My decided view of it being that it is a Society (not a Church) in which there are some – and I hope many – churches. But I hold that a connection with the Establishment does in no way imply membership even in the visible Church of Christ . . . and many of the ministers of the Establishment do not seem to be Christ's people . . . but I cannot act upon my feelings until I am more certain that they are well founded . . .

This entry, in the same way as others like it, continued in the same vein for many pages, ending with a prayer asking for 'deliverance from doubts in matters of faith, and from perplexity in matters of action'.

Not for the first time, Hamilton was disappointed by some reaction – or the lack of action – on the part of his tenants, when he wrote at the beginning of 1836:

> Though utterly defective in the sight of God, yet I know my tenants have no right to complain of me as a Landlord. My error has been on the tenant side. It is indeed a vexation to have my endeavours frustrated by the very people I would serve, whose souls I love. But this does not excuse my laziness tho' in a great degree it accounts for it.

THE POOR LAWS

A system of Poor Law relief was introduced in 1838 dividing Ireland into 130 unions – each with a workhouse – and sub-dividing it into 2,050 electoral divisions. The Donegal Union comprised of the town along with Dunkineely, Mountcharles, Laghey and Pettigo. When he first wrote about it, John Hamilton along with like-minded landlords, felt strongly that the system as devised could not properly meet the special and very deplorable condition of the destitute poor. He, and many of those like him, took the view that it was folly to place the estates of resident proprietors who were already doing their best to assist their tenants in the same poor law divisions as the neglected estates – especially those of absentee landlords who were doing nothing to help their tenants. As Hamilton pointed out over and over again in letters and pamphlets, neglected estates inevitably became 'veritable pauper warrens':

> the poor peasants imitating too faithfully the careless spirit shown by those who, from their station, means and education, one would suppose to show some conscientiousness in discharging the duties of the station which God had given them.

The plan for the new Poor Law Act was that the landlord would pay a Poor Rate on holdings rated at four pounds and under, and half the Poor Rate on all holdings over four pounds. Before the Bill had been enacted and indeed subsequently too, Hamilton argued that instead of electoral divisions, the sub-divisions should consist of single estates, as otherwise the improving proprietor, by his very improvements, paid an increased rate as a premium for the neglect and injury to his neighbour's tenants who were placed in the same electoral division. Whether or not it would have been practicable for the government to deal separately with each individual landed estate is open to question, but it is not difficult to see the systematic benefits that might have accrued – especially as it should have encouraged landlords to both improve their own estates and the positions of their tenants.

Hamilton wrote a long letter in May 1836 to Lord Morpeth, the Chief Secretary for Ireland, pointing out that, throughout his 15 years at his Donegal estate, he had endeavoured to improve the condition of his tenants. He wrote that he had 'very little society in the upper ranks' for the simple reason that most of the proprietors in his area were absentee, landlords, the condition of whose tenants was, in many cases, one of sheer misery. Having personally expended large sums to improve conditions for his own tenants, he viewed with concern the proposed legislation designed to benefit the poor if this resulted in 'the charge of providing for a multiplied population of a neighbouring neglected estate . . . being additionally saddled upon me'. Hamilton's long and very detailed letter to the Chief Secretary, containing various suggestions relating to the Poor Law and giving a good indication of his own considered thinking about these matters, ended with the following proposal:

> That in making a legal provision for the poor, a great enhancement of the benefit to them, and a great saving of expense would accrue from the introduction of a plan which might easily be drawn out, of admitting any proprietor to redeem his property out of the general mass, he bearing the expense, if requisite, of making his estate a distinct district like a parish in England; the paupers belonging to which he should be bound to provide for, exactly as if it were a parish, giving any neglected pauper a power of redress at Quarter Sessions, or in such a way as should be thought expedient, and if neglect of the paupers could be proved, then the estate to merge again in the district to which it originally belonged and, if thought advisable, a recognisance estreated. This would give a premium upon the *prevention* of pauperism. A landlord with a good agent would be enabled and encouraged to keep up a spirit and means of independence upon his estate, while an oppressive proprietor could not exercise cruelty in driving away the paupers unprovided for. . . . My idea of the working of the plan is this:
>
> Suppose a Poor Law passed taxing me as a proprietor with sixty pounds a year, and my tenantry with thirty pounds. I get my estate separated, and under my own or my agents' superintendance raise a voluntary – or perhaps legally compulsory – fund to the same amount as the tax would be, and expend it, or a part of it, or more than it, as the case may require, in providing for the paupers in such a way as to diminish the pauperism. Though at first in some cases it might be a weight on the proprietor, it might soon afford a sinking fund, which ought to be invested in some safe way, being the joint property of landlord and tenants, in the hands of a committee of trust. The interest of this should be used for aiding emigration, support of widows, children's apprentice fees, or such other things as the landlord and tenants should agree upon and register as their mutual agreement, and perhaps also for a poor strangers' fund to be administered by a committee or trustees.
>
> I am, my lord, your obedient servant,
>
> JOHN HAMILTON.

SEVEN

Continental Tour

It was during March, 1836 that Hamilton began to consider the possibility of going abroad for several years, even though he felt that Divine intervention had forced him to abandon a number of travel plans on several earlier occasions:

> I can not help feeling how God has formerly prevented me leaving home when I had settled on it more than once. Thrice I had actually hired houses, in Dublin, at Rostrevor, in Liverpool, and every time some thing unexpected occurred to send me home again, something out of my own control entirely. Still, I can not see that such close sticking at home can be good for my own mind or spirit – or for dear Mary's – or for my children's benefit.

The notion of a lengthy continental tour was temporarily postponed, partly because of the intervention of yet another spell of illness which prevented him from going outdoors. While still recovering, disturbing news came to him about a further falling off in attendance's at a number of his Sunday Schools and adult Bible classes, a situation which he initially felt was the fault of the teachers though he later placed some of the blame on himself for not closely supervising them.

As the months went by, John Hamilton began to lay plans for his European tour, proposing to bring with him his wife and the five children (aged from just under five to thirteen), along with a companion maid and a governess. Characteristically, at least some – if not most – of the driving force behind the idea was his desire to broaden and strengthen his religious faith through his proposed meeting with others of various religions:

> My present purpose is, if God willeth, to leave home with my family. I have been too confined here, having only once since 1821 been absent for six months together, and never absent as to do more than visit two or three near relatives, so that since my marriage in 1823 I have not rubbed with the world. And now that the time approaches in which my children, if spared alive, will be entering upon it, I find it needful to go and see the world, not to recreate in its gaieties, they are, thank God, not my

> desire at all, but to seek some association with strangers, especially those who love the Lord. Our present purpose is to go to Geneva for two years, where I hope I may receive benefit from intercourse with Christian strangers. I hope and believe that my Saviour's glory is my object. I hate leaving home, is not for pleasure in the ordinary sense that I would go, but for duty, hoping that pleasure in many things may be associated with it. If I were to stay home I *must* do something among my neighbours and something organised, for the disorganised work I have been going on with is often useless . . .

The three months or more preceding the actual departure continued to be a very restless period for John Hamilton, but he viewed the notion of a continental tour as a partial solution to some of his problems. This was at a time when travelling was often extremely uncomfortable and sometimes dangerous, but he was already a well-travelled man and not only made frequent visits to Dublin and to other parts of Ireland, but regularly crossed and re-crossed the Irish Sea to visit various parts of Britain. On one occasion he had travelled from Donegal to Cheltenham and back in the middle of winter, a journey which took him six days each way, to bring his son home during school holidays.

Many of Hamilton's longer journeys were undertaken in order to discuss his own religious thinking with various divines, and there can be no doubt that the opportunity to meet continental scholars and theologians was the principle reason for his decision to set out for Europe in August, 1836, intending to spend four years there, leaving his huge estate and his many tenants in the hands of an agent. During his long absence, he communicated with the tenants from time-to-time by means of printed letters, several of which carried descriptions of the manners, customs and agricultural practices of the countries which he was visiting. He seemed satisfied that neither his estate nor the tenants would suffer because of his absence and noted, on his return, that 'while I was absent from this country, I did not – in the four years that I was away – draw fifty pounds a year form Ireland but continued to spend what belonged to my home'.

One can only wonder at the reaction of his wife to his decision to leave home for such a long period, and if Mary voiced opposition, or had reservations about the idea, this is not recorded in his journals. During the four years, as they travelled thousands of miles almost entirely by boat and by horse and carriage, all the members of the family were ill at various times, sometimes seriously so and on a number of occasions two or more were ill at the same time. It remains a matter of some regret that he recorded very little detail of his experiences in Europe during the first three years of the tour, but as soon as he arrived in Switzerland he began to write detailed descriptions about the scenery and of his experiences there.

ARRIVAL IN GERMANY

After travelling across England and through parts of France and Belgium, the family settled first in the small German town of Nieuwied-an-Rhein, near Koblenz, where they lived for almost a year. It may seem surprising that Hamilton decided to stay for so long in this little-known small town, but the reason, though not mentioned by him, lay in the fact that, when the Moravians began to disperse westwards from Silesia, Neuwied was chosen as one of their first settlements. Also at Neuwied, as in many of the cities and towns where the Hamiltons stayed, they found a resident 'colony' of English people, with some of whom they made friends. John's friendships soon led to his assembling an English 'congregation' to whom he ministered each Sunday. Having noted that many of the local labouring men slept late on Sunday and that, 'after a poor meal in a cold room', they then spent the day in some inn, he felt encouraged to study the German language in order to minister to them too. It will be remembered that he had already been learning Irish for the same purpose, and as soon as he felt sufficiently proficient to express himself in German, he then commenced evangelical work among these people too.

> They naturally become much out of spirits in the evening and wander out, then finding the street cold and seeing dozens of drinking houses with the doors open where they can sit in a warm place for a couple of hours, they will drink and play a batz or two; and no friendly door is open for Christ's sake where they can be warm and quiet for an hour or two.
>
> Churches are cold, and these poor are miserably clad and ashamed to go there, and having generally none of that knowledge of God in Christ which constrains to worship with others, they do not dream of entering the only place of worship which is open in the evening where also, as most of the persons attending are such as have made some advance in Christian knowledge, the whole service and sermon are not suited to these poor ignorant men's wants. Reflecting on these things with prayer, it struck me that if a large room were provided and these poor wanderers invited to come, and treated with a good cup of hot coffee, etc., after an hour's reading and application of the Scriptures with prayer, and then, during the meal a useful conversation being kept up, it might be a blessed means of preventing much crime and of winning souls to the Lord. Accordingly I went to a man who knows the poor well, the master of the Oratoire Infant School, M. Velsel, and consulted him. We found a room, and M. Velsel and the wife of the proprietor of the house, a poor but Christian woman, undertook to arrange the repast and yesterday (Sunday) we had our first meeting; about forty men and women, very poor, attended. Some were notorious frequenters of the drinking houses. They

> were very quiet and attentive. I read Matthew chapter ii. and spoke to them of the Saviour as well as I could, and God gave me utterance much more than I could have expected in a strange tongue. All the people seemed highly pleased, and we had reason to thank God for more than we could have thought. It was a very striking meeting, some of the poor people very squalid and wretched looking.

A few weeks after this, Hamilton was able to write that:

> Three of our Sunday meetings have gone by and I trust, with blessing. The very off-scouring of the population were among those present. Two meetings at the little Oratoire and one at Lavanchi's in the Rue de la Halle. I find I am reasonably well understood when I address myself with all my heart and soul to these poor neglected souls.

A DAUGHTER'S JOURNAL

Although John Hamilton's journal gives little descriptive detail during the first part of the tour (apart from his efforts at evangelising), luckily this is more than compensated for by a diary kept by his ten year old daughter Mary, known to the family as 'Moll'. The neat handwriting may look rather more like that of an adult (possibly her governess) than that of a child, but whatever about that, there can be no doubt that the *wording* comes across clearly as that of a bright and very observant child, and it is not difficult to picture her looking wide-eyed at all the strange sights so far removed from the familiar scenes which she had witnessed in her very small world at home in Donegal – often prompting her to write that such and such a thing 'was the first that we had ever seen'. Only one volume of the two originally written has survived, the second went to America and returned to Ireland only to disappear again. However regrettable this loss, the fact remains that Moll's surviving journal fills a gap in the tour narrative, covering as it does the family's first 18 months abroad, and by a happy chance it was from that period onwards that John Hamilton's own journals suddenly began to describe the rest of the tour in greater detail.

Mary (or 'Moll' to avoid confusion with her mother after whom she was named), began her narrative: 'We left Brownhall and St. Ernans. and all our dear friends on the 8th August, Monday'. Her first detailed description – written at Derry where the family was due to sail to Glasgow – gives a good indication of what was to follow:

> We came to Derry crossing the pretty white wooden bridge in the evening and walked on the ramparts, a thick wall goes all round the town and on it is a broad gravelled walk, and on it there is the Pillar of General Walker

> who defended Derry when James 2nd besieged it. The ramparts were not at all like what I expected them to be but were broader and more hilly, I saw cannons there for the first time.

The family boarded a ship which called at Campbletown and Greenock before arriving in Glasgow, from where the family reached Edinburgh the following evening. Moll commented on the food there, writing that 'we got everything good to eat in Mamma's country'. A two-day journey by ship brought the family to London and the impression made by this large city on a young child comes across clearly in her journal where she recorded visiting the Colliseum and the zoo, and being brought to Regent Street in the evening 'to see the lamps all lighted'.

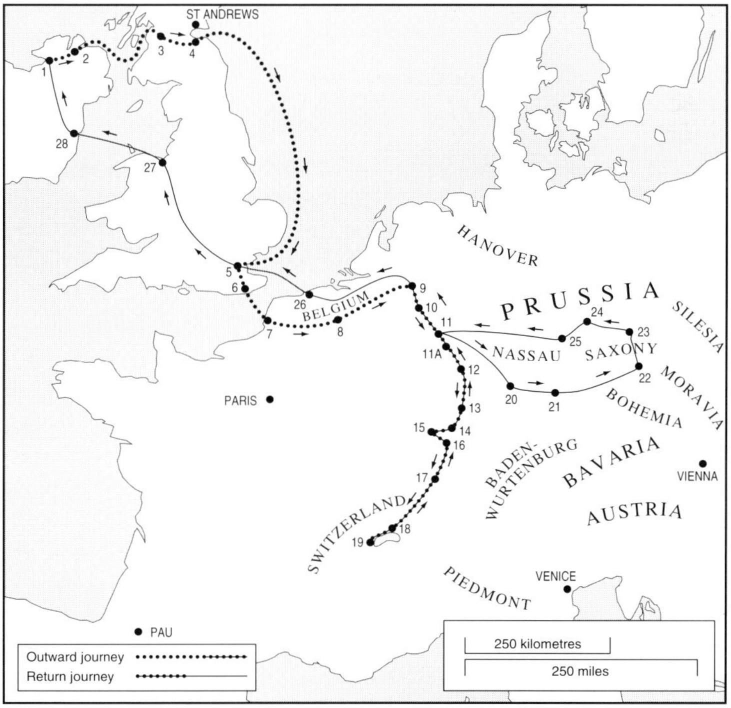

Key to Numbers: 1 Donegal; 2 Derry; 3 Glasgow; 4 Edinburgh; 5 London; 6 Dover; 7 Boulogne; 8 Brussels; 9 Aachen; 10 Cologne; 11 Nieuwied; 11a Koblenz; 12 Mainz; 13 Carlsruhe; 14 Baden-Baden; 15 Strasbourg; 16 Freiburg; 17 Basle; 18 Lausanne; 19 Geneva; 20 Würtzburg; 21. Nurnberg; 22 Prague; 23 Dresden; 24 Leipzig; 25 Weimar; 26 Ostende; 27 Liverpool; 28 Dublin.

Map showing the route followed by the Hamilton family during their continental tour which lasted more than four years.

The Hamiltons travelled by coach to Dover, and after a four-hour sea-crossing to Boulogne, they went to the Custom House but, 'they did not search us or any thing about us except Miss Bagot's basket, and Rebecca's'. Miss Bagot was a governess and Rebecca McClearn, aged 23 and from Raphoe, seems to have been a companion maid. A feature of the family's tour of the continent, was the large number of English people encountered, many of them apparently residing there, and it is interesting to learn the ease with which they were able to find one another when travelling from place to place. The first of these encounters concerned some of their Rose relations living at Boulogne. (It will be recalled that John Hamilton was first introduced to his future wife's family in Boulogne some 15 years earlier).

Moll thought the old town was 'a dirty little place, full of mud houses' but she liked the upper town with its ramparts 'like the walls round Derry, but I liked the walls here the best'. They went in a donkey gig 'to see Buonaparte's pillar which he built in remembrance of conquering England though he never did this!' [It is said that this *Colonne de la Grand Armee* marks the spot where the Emperor decided to turn east to attack Austria.]

After a brief stay there, the family set out in a *Diligence* which Moll described as 'very queer, but . . . they are far snugger to sleep in than the English coaches, and there is plenty of room in them', and they reached Lille that evening. The most striking feature of the town, as far as Moll was concerned, was the number of dog carts there and the town's ramparts. She also admired the horses, 'the finest horses that I ever saw, very, very fat and strong, for they drew carts that would have frightened the nice little horses of Ireland'. The Hamiltons continued their travels through the flat country of north-eastern France and into Belgium [which had only achieved its independence seven years earlier]. Arriving in Brussels, Moll was impressed by the sight of the trees in a park 'shot through in the Battle of 1830 – they were all painted over where they were wounded'. Further on, they saw the battlefield of Waterloo, the scene of triumph for the family's famous relation only 23 years earlier, where 'there is a large mound and on it is a lion made of the cannon that was used in the battle, and under it lies the bones of many of the people who were killed in the battle. We all saw it except Helen who was asleep'.

PRUSSIA

The Hamiltons changed coaches at Namur, and after Liege they crossed the border and 'we did not drive far in Prussia before we came to Aachen (which is also called 'Aix')'. On their arrival there, settling into a hotel, Moll wrote that on the beds there 'were sort of silk sheets all wadded, and they were very warm and snug. The beds here are very small, and Mamma and Papa had hard work to squeeze into them'.

I must now tell about the hot springs and Baths. The water bubbles up out of the ground, hot. Papa drinks the Spa every day out of a lion's mouth and bathes in the hot water every day but not at the same place that he drinks at. The Baths are good for gout and Papa takes what they call a Douche every afternoon and sometimes a common warm bath, to put away his gout. Mamma has taken 3 Baths, and intends to take more as she likes them very much. Bell and I took a bath one day and intend to take it again if Mamma lets us. The one we were in was Marble. The Spa has a very disagreeable taste.

John Hamilton left the family for a few days to go on to Frankfurt 'to see where we should take up our winter quarters'. While he was away, a Mr Fortescue called to see the family on his way home from Switzerland and after that 'Captain Wellesley came and staid for 5 days and Papa came home in time to have a day's quarters of him'. Moll wrote that she greatly regretted leaving Aachen when the family set out for Cologne:

in two coaches, two horses to each, We saw nothing of Köln, as they call it here, because we arrived late in the evg. and left early in the morning. This was the first place where we met with the funny edderdown quilts [duvets] – they were almost the size of the top of a small square table, and very light . . . In the morning I got up very early as the Steam Boat sailed at 7 . . . we liked being in this Steam Boat for it was only going up the river Rhine . . . We saw a bridge made of boats fixed together, and boards laid across them, it was a curious bridge, and the first we had ever seen.

As the family continued up-river, Moll noted the first the vineyards as they came into view, remarking on the very cold weather (it was now November). They disembarked at the small town of Neuwied-am-Rhein, about fifteen miles down-stream of Koblenz, which John had chosen in preference to Frankfurt – not least because, as already noted, there was a Moravian settlement there.

We went to the inn of the Moravians at Neuwied, and staid there nearly a week while we were considering whether we should stay here for the winter. We found a nice quiet place and Papa had a letter of introduction to Mr. Merian, the head of the Moravian Schools, who was very civil, and helped Papa to look for a house for us.

One thing we liked Neuwied for was the Palace Garden which is open for everyone to walk in . . . From the garden we have a very pretty view of the Rhine which flows close by, and a range of hills in which there is a gap through which the river runs. And as it is a gap, it reminds us of Barnsmore [which, of course, was visible from St. Ernan's]. The

> town is very regular and the streets clean and wide. Close to the inn is the Moravian Church, Papa and Mama and Miss Bagot went to it, and Bell and I hope to get to it soon as we are learning the Litany which is used there in German. At the inn we were obliged to talk german as the servants understood no french or English.

Moll described the riverside meadows where she and her sisters were allowed to play, and the flood banks built to protect the town, but despite the latter, large parts of Neuwied were flooded during that December. Just before Christmas, a German mistress, Mrs Unger, was secured to teach the two older girls, and Rebecca 'had a german master every day'. The family enjoyed walking, but the short days largely curtailed these exercises. However, on one occasion the family went for 'a long walk to an iron foundry, a few miles from this, where we saw the iron was first pounding, then pounded, then we saw the cannons, cannon balls etc. that had been made out of the ore, but we could not see it making – for there was *Eingang Forbidden Entrance* on the door'. They continued this walk as far as a 'swinging bridge across the river Wied. Papa said it was like the famous Menai Bridge in North Wales only much smaller'. [Her father was to make a similar comparison with a bridge near Freiburg]. They also walked down-river to 'the flying bridge' across the Rhine at Andernach where 'some of the stones placed for a fence along the river, Papa said, were like those found in the Giants' Causeway in Ireland. Some of these had eight sides and some four, and looked as though they had been chiselled'.

Moll thought that the whole family liked Neuwied ever better than Aachen, commenting that 'there are a great many Moravians here and they have a nice church, and a school for boys and one for girls. They are mostly at one end of the town, and another corner of the town is chiefly inhabited by Jews, and most of the churches are Protestant'.

> The Prince of Neuwied is quite a young man, His father died last year and his uncles live with him . . . . The two uncles are very fond of shooting, they take some of the english gentlemen with them to shoot but not Papa yet . . . . The prince gets all the game and sells it.

She described how, on Christmas Eve, the family went to the Moravian church where they did not understand much of the Service but they liked the singing of hymns and the musical accompaniment of the organ 'and plenty of fiddles'. The Moravians were, in fact, especially noted for their hymn singing and may well have been at least indirectly responsible for the prominent part this subsequently played in most Protestant church services. After the service, all the children 'had cakes and tea handed to them, and at the end, each has a lighted wax taper, half a yd. long and as thick as one's little finger – it looks very pretty – and when they were going out, they blew them all out'. She continued:

> When we returned to our house, Madam Harborne [the owner of the house] sent to ask us to go to her room [she was unwell], and when we sat down we saw a table covered with beautiful cakes, and in the middle was the 'German Tree', which is the top of a young fir tree rather more than a yard long, this was in a little stand with moss all round it, and a nice little tiny house in the stand and 3 sheep in it. On the branches of the this tree were hung all kinds of little cakes, and very pretty little figures of men, cats, horses, wine-glass, harps and I don't know what all, but they were all made of cake and very good to eat.

What Moll was describing was the forerunner of the Christmas Tree, an old German tradition which was introduced into the British Isles several decades later by Prince Albert of Saxe-Coburg, the consort of Queen Victoria. Frau Harborne had also made heart shaped cakes covered with glazed white sugar, inscribed in letters of 'raised sugar' with the name of each individual member of the Hamilton family, and she invited them to take the cakes upstairs to their own apartment.

On New Year's Day 1838, the Hamilton children were given presents both by their parents and by the Harborne's. The weather continued extremely cold and the deep snow meant that for a time horse-drawn sledges were used, the horses having bells affixed to their collars 'to warn people to get out of the way, for they went so silently'. Moll wrote that, on her mother's birthday, the Harbornes baked a cake which awaited the family at breakfast time, 'and on it the german words, done with sugar, *God Preserve her yet long for the good of her Children'*.

NASSAU

The first mention that young James had been left behind in Ireland was only made at this point when Moll wrote that her father travelled back to London where James had been taken by his uncle, Abraham Hamilton.

John Hamilton, along with James, was delayed rejoining the family, partly because they stayed in Paris for a week 'so that they might see grand mamma and all our aunts there, but G. Papa was not there', a reference to the Rose family. When the Hamiltons were again reunited, John and Mary walked with James to Ems where they 'took rooms' for a week, and the rest of the family followed, along with Miss Bagot and Rebecca, in a carriage which 'was like a basket made into the shape of a boat with four seats in it, and nine of us in it and the Driver crammed into it'. On the way, they crossed the boundary between Prussia and Nassau, Moll noting that: 'in Prussia all the palings along the chief roads, and all the signposts, and all the turn pikes and the *Schlagbaume* [large bars at the turnpikes] are painted with black and white stripes, and in Nassau they are all striped orange and blue. We should be stupid if we did not know this'. The family enjoyed their short stay at Ems after which they returned to Neuwied by boat where:

> We came to our house and found them all in great distress, for Mrs Harborne our landlady had died a few hours after we had set out to go to Ems. She had been ill ever since we came to the house, but we had often gone to her room to see and sit with her, and she has been very kind to us.

With the onset of summer, the weather became very hot – uncomfortably so for the Hamiltons, prompting the mother to make all the children go to bed for two hours at mid-day, but allowing them to stay up longer in the evenings. One evening, when the family set out for their usual after sunset walk in the cool of the evening:

> We staid up very late to see the fire flies in the Palace Gardens, they looked like very small little flying stars moving about among the trees, we had great fun trying to catch them, and we brought some home to shew to Rebecca, who was quite frightened at them, and thought they wd. burn the house.

During July, John's uncles, Abraham and William Hamilton, who were on a tour of France and Switzerland, called to see the family, 'it seemed very queer to see them here'. Other people whom they met included Mr. and Mrs. Wilson from Delgany, Co. Wicklow. During this month, John had an attack of gout which not only confined him indoors but also curbed the activities of the rest of the family. A doctor recommended him to take the waters at Wiesbaden, so the whole family travelled there, staying for five weeks 'which did Papa much good'. John and Mary travelled on two occasions from Wiesbaden to Frankfurt to visit Hugh Pakenham and his wife who were residing there.

Moll mentioned several times that her father made sketches of some of the views they saw during their walks and drives, and several of his sketch books have survived showing him to have been quite a competent amateur artist. On one of the 'sketching' walks, going to the nearby castle of Mont Repos, they entered a thick forest and Moll wrote that 'we wandered on til I thought we were quite lost, and that we must sleep in the woods, and make beds of the leaves' – showing that she must have become acquainted with the German folk-tale about *Hänsel and Gretel*. When they found their way to the old palace of Mon Repos they thought it 'not very pretty, but the woods around it are' and it was situated in meadows 'quite lilac with autumnal crocusses growing wild, as plentiful as daisies'.

Though Moll's journal did not record the fact, the family must have returned once more to Neuwied, where James was now boarding at the Moravian school, coming home to the family each Sunday. Moll wrote of this: 'I did not like his going away, but when he came every Sunday we were very glad to see him'. On one of the family walks during their stay there, they went:

> to a pretty place called Altwied. There is there an old Castle, standing on a hill, close by the pretty river Wiedbach, and high wooded hills all round it, there is a wee old fashioned village close to the Castle which was fortified. Papa took a sketch of it while we sat down under the big rocks, and Jemmy climbed up all about the rocks, and he larked like a monkey – he had to get down.

WURTEMBURG

When the Hamiltons left Neuwied at the beginning of November, they travelled 'to Mayence' [Mainz], where they slept overnight before continuing to Mannheim. 'It was desperately ugly all the way', wrote Moll, and they arrived that evening in Heidelburg. It rained all next day, and Moll noted that, 'Helen [now eight] slept almost the whole way, and Mamma tumbled asleep too, and Bell slept at a great rate, and Reb [Rebecca] too, but I wd. not go asleep, for I was not sleepy, and I wanted to see what sort of a country it was that I might write it in my journal'. It was dark and very late by the time they reached Heilbronn where they stayed overnight, and they were back on the road by nine o'clock the following morning, driving along by the banks of the Neckar river, 'not near so pretty as the Rhine', through Ludwigsburg to Stuttgart. It was now early December and when they awoke next morning, everywhere around them was covered with snow. Two days later they moved from temporary accommodation in an inn to rooms which John had secured:

> There was always great fun and fuss when we settled in a new house, altering the quarters, making of the beds, for they cram several straw wedges, like queer shaped cushions about the bed, and make the bed in such a shape that one must nearly sit in bed instead of lying . Mamma always upsets the bed the first thing she does when we come to a new lodging . . . . Mamma had to go to the Market and buy pots and pans and kettles and cans – and Potatoes or, as they are here, *Kartoffeln* – and we like our own dinners better than the ones we got from the Restaurant.

A new school was found for James who started there two weeks before Christmas, and Moll wrote that Stuttgart was the dirtiest town she was ever in, the abundance of mud along with snow made the family stay indoors for some time, and the journal mentions that Isabelle was limping because of chilblains.

Christmas came and went after which, Moll wrote, 'James was going back [to school] to Stettin', but this must have been a locality nearby, not the city hundreds of miles away on the Baltic. When John got rheumatism in his back and knee, he blamed it on the dampness of Stuttgart so the family moved to Ludwigsburg once more – just one day before heavy snow fell again, making travelling impossible for some time:

> In a few days the windows were so frozen we had to cut the ice away to open the windows that we might open or shut the Shutters which are in this country always outside. The snow continued almost constantly til towards the end of March'

According to Moll, the house where the family was staying was:

> built by one of the royal Dukes, and the ceilings were very pretty, some of them covered with gold, one ceiling had beautiful wreaths of sticking-out gilt roses and other flowers, and the doors and windows were a great deal of gilt about them, but the best of all was there was a grand play-room close to the drawing room, it was very large and high and there we cd. run about and skip (for we had skipping ropes) when we cd. not get out in winter.

During April, John Hamilton had an attack of 'Ereysepelas' [Erysipelas, an inflammatory disease], affecting his face which 'was all tied up' and, because he was convinced it had something to do with the house, the family moved a few streets away to a new lodging, where they soon had a visitor:

> About this time Capt. Wellesley came here from Neuwied where he had been staying for the winter, his brother lives at Stuttgart and ... he often came to stay a day or two with us . . . . While Capt. W. was with us, on Papa and Mamma's marriage day, we all went to see the Palace . . . . It was very grand even at the outside and it was a great deal prettier than we thought it wd. have been, and Capt. W. who had seen the Stuttgart Palace said that this one was much grander.

The immense Baroque castle of Ludwigsburg, built more than a hundred years earlier by one of the Dukes who wished to create his own 'Palace of Versailles', is situated in a beautiful park with patterned flower-beds and arbours:

> We first went up a grand stair case with bronze figures as large as life and then into a long picture gallery in which were great pictures of all the Dukes and Duchesses of Wirtentburg [which] has not long been a Kingdom, it was Buonapart made it into a Kingdom, the present King is the

> 2nd King . . . . There was a dandy bedroom for the King which was several rooms away from the Queen's . . . . her curtains satin and his crimson satin, the beds however looked very uncomfortable and dreadfully short. One room had been fitted up by the late Queen for her brother, the Duke of Clarence, afterwards William 4th of England. One room amused us very much, it was all lined with looking glasses, walls and ceiling, doors and all, and we saw ourselves in every direction . . .

Moll remarked that there were no English people at Ludwigsburg, but she and her sisters played with some local children from the family Klett, while Rebecca also had some friends, including the 'family where there were little meetings every Sunday' – one of Moll's rare references to the informal Bible meetings which occupied much of her fathers' attention. James was now back with the family, on holidays from his boarding school, and Moll wrote in her journal that 'poor Bell got a swelled knee, and we had to get the doctor, and she was made to lie in bed for many weeks, but the knee did not pain her at all, and she was not sick'. This was the first intimation in Moll's little book that there was something wrong with Isabella, her elder sister with whom she was very close. When John's face got better, he went with his wife and young Moll to see James's school during its anniversary celebrations, attending a Service in the boys chapel. Moll, who had been learning German, wrote that she was 'able to understand it a great deal, and they sang my favourite hymn, *Nun danket alle Gott'*, [Now thank we all our God]. A month after this, the family was to have moved on, but several of the children, including Moll were unwell in addition to Bella, whose knee had not improved despite her enforced confinement to bed. When they finally left, Moll was sorry to lose her German friends and 'as we drove along we were thinking of all the people of Ludwigsburg and of it too, wondering if we would ever see it again'.

BADEN AND THE BLACK FOREST

On the following day, they arrived at Karlsruhe, the capital of Baden, which Moll described as 'a nice, neat, clean, small town . . . curiously built in the shape of a wheel – the travelling did not hurt Bell or Papa but rather did them good'. After a few days there, they went on to Baden-Baden. The family would have liked to have stayed at Karlsruhe but there was no spa there 'and we wanted this for Papa, Bell and Helen'. Lodgings were secured at Baden with some difficulty 'as it was just the bathing season', and while the family was still unpacking 'who should drive up to us but Mrs Pollard who had just come a week before, we were very glad to see her'. The Hamiltons had met the Pollards while they were staying at Neuwied.

> We soon settled ourselves in, and an old Doctor came to see Bell, who ordered baths for her, and let her walk about a little, but her knee did not get better . . . . Then Dr. Ludwig, the Stuttgart Dr. came to see her, and all the Drs. said it must be lanced, and another Dr. came to do this. Her knee then got much better, but her ankle became bad, and had to be lanced too.

Because John was troubled with rheumatic attacks, the family was confined to short walks. Moll went with her father to the spa 'but it was not much fun as the Wiesbaden Spa for it was in a nasty part of the town'. With the onset of the cooler autumn days, father, mother and Moll went for three day excursion into the nearby Black Forest which Moll described in detail. They passed 'the Eherstein Schloss, [Ebersteinburg Castle] with views of the Mourg [Murg] valley below'. This was a very hilly route for horse-drawn traffic, with many steep inclines through tortuous defiles as the road followed the river. Reaching Gernsbach, they changed coaches because the first one had been damaged on one of the steep hills. The second coach was 'a common wooden drag' but with a pair of strong grey horses and a 'dandy post boy with large black boots half way up his thighs, a bright yellow jacket with scarlet facings, and the post boy's queer brass horn slung around his shoulder and waist by a thick coloured cord . . . and to make him quite perfect, ear rings in his ears'.

They continued through the northern Black Forest, rising higher until they had wide views across the Schwartzwald hills and, crossing back again into Würtenburg. 'Fortunately it was a very nice day, like an irish day with a showery looking sky', and Moll noticed a church 'with a queer steeple covered with painted tiles of all sorts of colours and forming little patterns'. Descending into a valley she saw 'the people were busy making their second crop of hay, and most of the women had on their broad straw hats'. The Hamiltons stopped for dinner in 'the very pretty little town of Neuenburg where they changed horses before going on, Moll commenting that the scenery seemed to improve with every step. A long steep hill brought them to the village of Calw, where there was a Moravian settlement (though this was not mentioned) and where: 'the queer post boy got off and let the horses get up as they chose – a steep precipice was on one side of us, but the post boy did not mind this, tho' we did'. During the final, long steep descent to the village the post-boy led the horses and they saw lightning flashes but got to an inn before it rained. They continued next day to Wilbar 'a small town or a large village with a straight, narrow street'. Moll did not like this place and was glad that they were 'not amongst the hundreds of english that were crowded there this summer'. Driving along the valley they saw 'in some of the woods the ground was quite red with cranberries, and Papa and Mamma said this was like where Mamma lived in Scotland in Rosshire . . . We met a great cart of wood, for I ought to tell they cut a great quantity of wood in this forest, their houses are built of it and are very neat.

After Besenfeld they found that their road had rejoined the Murg river which had accompanied them at the outset of their trip into the Black Forest, passing 'a tiny, tiny church where, they told us, children were baptised and catechised, and sometimes they preached there'. Going down one steep hill, they were tempted to ask the post boy to go slower but 'the Germans don't like to be interfered with and they generally take their own way at all events'. They passed so many pretty places that John decided he would have to return there again with James in order to sketch some of the scenes.

They stopped overnight at Glasshutte, and walked to the glass works which gave its name to the place:

> We went into it and there we saw great furnaces, I had never seen such a place before, and was very glad to see the different things they used in making glass. The man . . . brought us near one of the furnaces to take out some of the melted glass with a long pipe, but the fire was so bright we could scarcely look at it . . . . We saw window glass in large tubes, before it was heated and cut flat, and I thought it very queer when the man said they wd. heat it next day and cut it open with large scissors.

The little party was delayed next morning until noon by a dense fog and heavy rain, but before long they arrived back in open country out of the forests, with vineyards and fields once more, near Gernsbach, where they completed a circle of about 100 or more miles in the three days. After watching people sending wood down the river, they continued on towards Baden-Baden, Moll commenting on the fog – which had persisted all day– 'and often we had the clouds quite underneath us, while it was quite clear where we were driving, I had never seen fog like this before, and thought it very queer'. Back at Baden, Moll 'had a gt. deal to tell sisters and Jemmy – we found them all well when we got back'.

At this point there were no more pages left in Moll's little notebook, though as already mentioned she went on to keep a second journal, since lost, describing most of the rest of the family's tour abroad with details not included in her father's journals. Someone who saw it nearly 50 years ago, noted that Moll referred in it to the death of the family's 24 year old travelling companion Rebecca McClearn. Rebecca's death occurred just after the above narrative, in December 1838, during the short gap between Moll's two books; the cause of her death is not known, but her body was taken to Karlsruhe for burial 'in a foreign land', as her tombstone records. It seems curious that John Hamilton's own journal did not mention anything of this until several years afterwards when he described her simply as 'a faithful servant and beloved sister in the Lord'.

So we now return to John's narrative, commencing at the point where the family travelled on from Baden to Switzerland. It was only after arriving in

John Hamilton's drawing of the graveyard at Carlsruhe where Rebecca McClearn, who died while travelling with the family as a companion, was buried in 1839. Her tombstone is to the right in the sketch.

Switzerland that he began to describe the family's travels in any detail, commencing with a journal entry written in the following May, in which he wrote a summary of the journey to Geneva:

> On the 3rd of this month I arrived here with my wife and children, intending, please God, to pass the summer here, and hoping to find spiritual and bodily advantage from the climate and society. The weather has been favourable on the whole during our 12 days journey from Carlsruhe on which we visited the cathedrals of Strasbourg and Freyburg in Briesgau [Freiburg in the Briesgau region, to distinguish it from the various other places of the same name], both of which I had seen before [perhaps a reference to his 'wedding journey'], but was still more astonished with that at Strasbourg and delighted with that at Freyburg.

He remarked on the bridge by which they crossed the Rhine at Breisgau, which was 'above 900 feet in span and 170 feet high. It looks too light to bear any weight, indeed I should think it will not last at all like our bridge at Bangor' [a reference to Telford's suspension bridge across the Menai Straits in North Wales, built 13 years earlier].

After visiting a number of English people at Strasbourg and Freiburg, the family had moved to Baden-Baden for a further brief stay because 'Miss N. stirred me up to try to do something for Baden-Baden in the way of sending a French missionary'. The suggestion was that a missionary would be secured by Hamilton when he arrived at the Calvinist city of Geneva. En route, they reached the Swiss frontier at Basle on Sunday, 28 April where, uncharacteristically, the family did not attend church, 'M. being seriously unwell'. His wife was, however, well enough on the following morning for the family to set-out through Solure [Solothurn], Bern and Lausanne to Geneva, a distance of some 150 miles, reaching the latter four days later. Of the route, Hamilton wrote:

> The view of the Bernese Alps was very splendid as we approached Bern, and from the terrace and the top of the cathedral we enjoyed a very splendid prospect. But little H [Helen] alarmed me by the appearance of disease on this journey, and the Dr. here does not think it at all dangerous and she and all our dear children are in good general health though dear B[Bella] has not walked now for a year.

The frequent references to members of the family being ill during this long tour poses a question about the stress and discomfort of travelling, especially in bad weather. All the Hamilton illnesses except one were followed by good recoveries, the exception being that of Isabella, whom the father usually called Bella, or Bell. Bella's illness remains something of a mystery – firstly because she had been ailing for so long before her father made any reference to it, and secondly because the precise nature of her illness was never explained even though it got progressively worse.

AT GENEVA

Before they had left Donegal, John Hamilton had planned on staying in Geneva for two of the four years they expected to be abroad, but because they had stayed much longer in Germany than originally intended, the family only arrived in the city late in the first half of their third year. No doubt the city of Geneva had acted as a magnet to Hamilton because of its strong Protestant connections dating back to 1530 – even pre-dating John Calvin, one of the leading Protestant Reformers. Calvin made his home there, and it was also where he organised his Reformed Church, of which the Presbyterian church is a branch. Ruskin called the city 'the centre of thought and teaching' because of its many notable citizens and the large numbers of scholars, men of letters and divines who stayed there, and there can be little doubt that Hamilton originally envisaged his stay in this city as one of the highlights of his ambitious tour.

Arriving there early in May, he immediately looked for a suitable house in the outskirts of the city, proposing to stay there until the following spring. The house which John Hamilton rented was situated at the foot of Mount Saleve, a long ridge rising to over 4,000 feet south of the city, the summit of which actually lies just across the border in France. He drew a sketch of the view from the garden, and described the house as being:

> under the Mt. of Saleves, about 2 miles from its base, looking eastward up the valley of the Arve with a pyramidical mountain before us and, in the distance, the ever-snowy mountains of the Alps. From our house we do not see Mt. Blanc but from the neighbourhood he, too, is visible . . . . We have got a nice airy situation at Vallon, about 1½ miles from the Porte de Rive near Chenes. Houses here are very dear and generally seem to be got up rather expensively which we would not desire. However we found one rather Rattletrappish house with room enough, and old fashioned furniture, that is quiet and shady that the children can live out of doors, which is the main point for a summer residence. Mr. Lauterburg [a tutor] is to join us in about a fortnight to work with James.

John thought that 'on the whole the lake disappointed us, although some views in the neighbourhood taking in portion of the lake are truly fine, and to persons not used to fine sheets of water I can well understand this lake appearing most beautiful'. He had earlier mentioned that as they first approached Geneva: 'Mont Blanc came out of his mist, the day was thundery as it has been every day since we left Basle, and the other mountains were in dark shadow, while upon Mt. Blanc a dazzling sunshine shone and gave us our first view of this King of European mountains to the greatest possible advantage'. His repeated references to Mont Blanc indicates something of the fascination it held for him, though he was not aware that a peak in the distant Caucasus was the real European king. John thought the whole area was perfectly delightful and, while he described the rented house itself as middling, he was pleased that there was 'nice gravel for the children's play, and places for them to hoke and poke about to their heart's content'.

It was only a few days before John Hamilton wrote that 'he longed for more intercourse with the Christians of this neighbourhood'. He was suffering

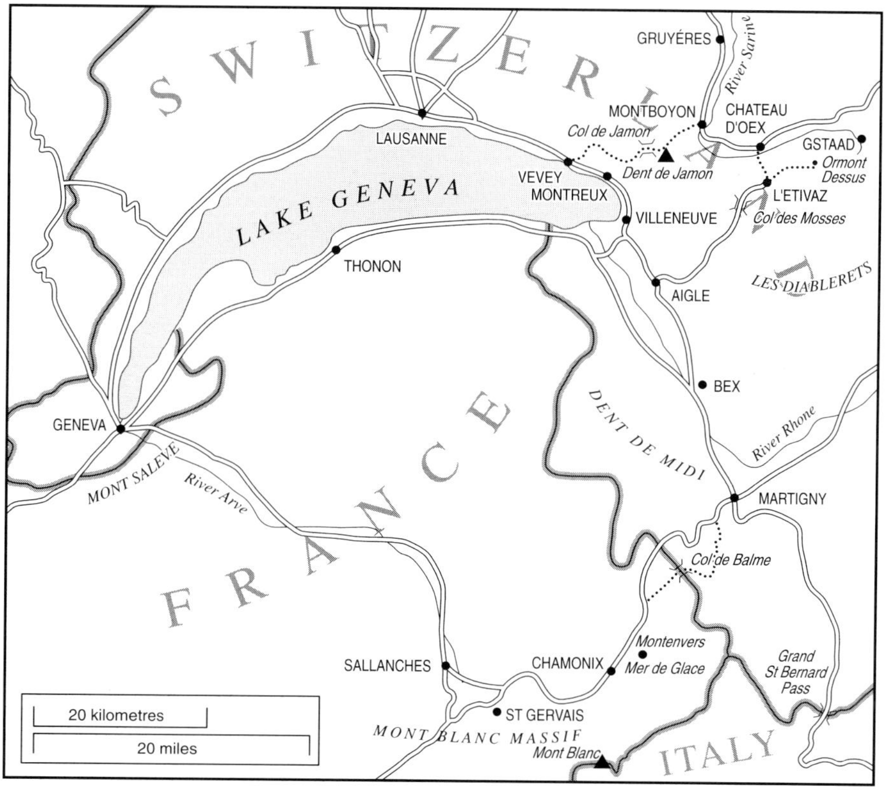

Map of the area around Lake Geneva showing the location of the two places when the Hamiltons stayed while there – Geneva and Vevey. John Hamilton completed three extensive walks while there, from Vevey to Chateau D'Oex over the Col de Jamon, from Aigle to the high alpine valley of Ormont Dessus, and from Martigny to Chamonix across the Col de Balme.

from a rash, as was his son, and he supposed it was because both of them drank from a mountain spring while walking on the nearby Mount Saleve. As soon as he had recovered, he wasted no time in seeking out some of the leading theologians – Calvinist, Catholic, Lutheran, Methodist, Moravian and others, living in the city. One such was a Pastor Malan:

> Soon after arriving in Geneva I visited Malan. Hofacker had warned me to prepare for a sifting and to buckle on my armour before I went to him. I therefore made the *less* preparation wishing to have my *ordinary* resources put to the test and not to meet the expected sifting by any extraordinary resources.

The extract which follows actually occupies about one and a half pages of Hamilton's journal but is only a fraction of the whole entry. Even in its abbreviated form, most people to-day would probably find his convoluted arguments too concerned with theological detail (almost like arguing how many angels could stand on the head of a pin), and seemingly at odds with his often expressed view that the Christian denominations should shake off their accumulation of baggage and return to a simple Christianity. The following lines may give some idea of the complexities of his thinking at this time:

> I found M [Malan] a person agreeing with me and with whom I could agree on a great many matters of the deepest importance, particularly as to what salvation is, what faith is, what religion is, what truth is. On some points he took me up hastily and set me down as wrong, though what I hold was precisely what he, at great length, explained to me to be his own views. We soon, however, began to differ, and though I saw where our difference had it source, I found I preferred letting him find it out by degrees, as thus the whole of our views might come out more, and I might receive more benefit from him than if I barely stated that I saw the root of our own difference to be, that I believed the promises of God to their fullest extent towards men, although some things which God has said, and much that we see, are not easy to reconcile (in our minds) with the fulfilment of the promises and the full manifestation of the Almighty's love towards all men. However, he soon came to the point and when I explained that I would preach the Gospel to all men, as addressed to all, as concerning all, as intended for all, he then protested that this was wrong, for we had previously searched out the question whether any that God intended or willed to be saved could ultimately be lost, and were agreed that the Gospel is not an offer but a declaration. . . .

However, though Hamilton strongly disagreed with the Pastor on many points, this long entry (albeit only part of the whole) closed with the sentence: 'He invited me most heartily to the Sacrament in his church next day which I partook with great joy'. Hamilton then recorded that though he was keen to discuss religious matters with others in the neighbourhood, but he shrank from it because:

> I know I must begin to battle with them, and dread it. I have no doubt about the great truth on which I stand as opposed to them. But I fear what? That the truth be put to shame? NO that is impossible, but that I may be put to shame. Oh yes, self, self, self – there, there alone is my bane. O Lord, do thou bend me, and of Thy mercy, cut off my enemies, this enemy of selfishness especially, and make me a holy and devoted subject and soldier of the cross . . .

He continued to attend services at M. Malan's church in Geneva for more than a month, commenting on the ministers' various sermons and recording that he, himself, had been invited to preach there on one occasion, and he continued to avail of every opportunity to discuss religious matters:

> This day I was again hospitably asked to dine and meet several good people at Mrs Valoney's. I had mentioned to several persons that I met that my great desire was to visit the interior of some of the quiet parishes of the canton, and this day I heard the sister of Madame Valoney say she was to accompany her relative M. Olivier, a dissenting minister to whom I had been introduced, to visit some of his flock scattered through several mountain parishes, and to end an excursion of several days at the parish of a cousin where there was to be a re-union of the believing souls of 2 or 3 parishes on a mountain convenient for the inhabitants to assemble, who at this season are scattered in chalets with their herds among the very tops of the mountains.

IN THE BERNESE OBERLAND

So, a few days later Hamilton set out on this excursion which, in fact, proved to be a very energetic series of long-distance walks among the mountains of the Bernese Oberland. After leaving the family in Geneva, he travelled to Vevey near the far end of Lake Geneva, where he stayed with Madame Valoney, a Mrs Chenon Churchill, and her niece. He set off the following morning with the two latter women and the Rev. Mr Olivier. He wrote a note to his wife to reassure her that, although he was 'imperfectly recovered from an attack of lumbago', she need not be afraid of him 'being over-walked, for I was in company with a clergyman in delicate health, and two ladies'. Hamilton explained in his Journal that M. Olivier had, as a young man, gone to Canada as a missionary to the Indians:

> but he found it advisable to stop among the French Canadians, finding them sadly in want of someone to proclaim the truth of the Gospel among them, but two American winters ruined his constitution which, it seems, was peculiarly ill-suited to bear the tremendous changes of temperature there, and he was obliged to return with a body much weakened, but eager in the cause of Truth as it is in Jesus. He is now minister of a dissenting church at Lausanne.
>
> The government pays the pastors of all other denominations, Protestant and Catholic, but the dissenters think it right to keep free from receiving all payment which is compulsory, or which shall bring the church under the influence of the state, and so while they willingly pay the taxes imposed upon them by the state, they also support their own minister and church and, I believe, very sufficiently.
>
> The pastors in general are reasonably well-off, few rich, none (ought to be) poor actually, but all comfortably provided for, so I was told in all hands, and what I saw agreed with this. There was an air of comfort with simplicity for the Cure's I visited, but it was the simplicity of a gentleman's house. The younger men are sent to the poorer and mountainous parishes; as they advance in years, they are moved into those where the income is larger, the climate better, and the toil less. The revival of religion

From the Col de Jaman (upper left in the above photograph), which Hamilton and his companions crossed during an energetic hike through the Bernese Oberland, the party also ascended the impressively steep Dent (Tooth) de Jamon, seen to the right of the picture.

> in this Canton has been chiefly among the young clergy, and thus the mountain valleys have had an advantage, and I understand that, in general, the Gospel has its followers more in proportion there than in the plains and cities.

The party set out from Vevey at 4 a.m., and the purpose of the very early start was that they hoped to cross a mountain pass known as the Col de Jaman in order to reach the small town of Chateau d'Oex in the next valley by evening. Byron had crossed over the same pass a couple of decades earlier and described it as 'beautiful as a dream'. The distance involved was about 27 miles, first through the villas around Clarens overlooking Vevey, and much of the rest of the way along rough tracks and involving a long and fairly stiff climb of more than 4,500 feet to the gap.

> We wandered quietly along towards the mountains going behind Clarens and Montreux and, ascending tolerably rapidly, here and there we stopped where we found convenient stones or blocks to sit on in the shade, and we read the word of God together and worshipped the Lord in the midst of beauties and glories of his creation.

When, after eight hours walking, they reached the col, 'a pretty, high pass between two mountain peaks', an area which Hamilton described as 'this beauteous natural flower garden', they saw the impressive and strangely tooth-shaped Jaman mountain (its summit is over 6,100 feet high) immediately to their right and rising so steeply that its slopes seemed in parts to be almost vertical. Despite the long journey which still lay ahead of them:

> the Dent du Jamon [Dent de Jaman] attracted the attention and excited the desire of the ladies to get to the top. It seemed a most insuperable Rock rising to a great height above us, however . . . after half an hour's climbing we came to a wilderness of rocks tumbled about in all directions. The way among them was difficult to find, but more difficult to pursue when found, for the uneven surface was concealed by the leaves of innumerable flowers which grew here. It truly was worth the pains of the ascent if only to see these flowers. Martigon lilies, yellow and white Aconites, yellow Foxglove and a multitude of others of every size and hue, from four feet high to an inch, and from snow white to deep scarlet. There were some Rhododendrons but not in bloom . . .

These Rhododendrons were actually the Alpine Alpenrose, and he was unlucky to just miss, by a few weeks, seeing them in bloom; and had he been there a little earlier in the year, he should have seen a stunning display of acres of wild narcissi for which the area is famous.

John Hamilton's sketch of the view from the terrace of the house which he rented for the family's sojourn at Geneva. Though there was a fine view of the Alps, he regretted that Mont Blanc was not visable from the house.

> We then began the proper ascent of the Dent, steep enough it was, and not free from danger. Mr. O. and I were loaded with our own packs containing a rich store of raiments, and each had a ladies basket to carry with a similar store for them. These we were fain to leave under a rock a few hundred yards from the very point.
>
> When we attained our object we were indeed paid for our pains. Lake Leman [Lake Geneva] lay at our feet, the lake of Neuchatel was in the distance and altogether the alpine scene was glorious. It was also very clear and warm so we could safely enjoy the view [which on a clear day extends as far as the Jura mountains lying along the French border, over fifty miles away] for a long time.

After surveying the view, they then made the steep descent back to the col where:

> on a pasture near the root of the tooth [the Dent de Jaman] was a herd of a couple of hundred cows with their bells, which added much to the magic of the scene. On going down we made a digression to the top of the valley below us, to get some *petit lait* in a chalet, and descended a valley full of rocks and stones in admirable disorder, and at the foot of most splendid precipices many of the stones were of such size that one or two enormous pines stood upon them in most curious and picturesque attitudes. It was wonderful to see how the roots, after consuming the nutriment of the little soil on the top of the stone, had crept down like great cables at the sides of the stones and fastened themselves in the ground beside. Were it not for this, I think many of these stones must have been upset from the towering height of the trees growing upon them.
>
> After a few hours descent, we came to a road and soon after passing a fine gorge we arrived at a poor little inn where we were right glad to halt at 9 o'clock in the evening, having made a pretty beginning of our ramble by doing 10 leagues – and such leagues – the first day.

John Hamilton's estimate of the distance seems to have been exaggerated as the distance from Vevey to the first village after descending the other side of the col, Montbovon, is about 20 miles. Even allowing for the very energetic diversion to the summit of the Dent, the mileage covered was hardly the 35 which he claimed, which is not to say that it very probably felt like that! Next day, they covered the remaining seven or eight miles to Chateau d'Oex, which today is an attractive minor resort beautifully situated in a pleasant valley. The castle, prominently situated on a hill above the town, and which gave the place its name had, long before Hamilton's party arrived, been replaced by the church which Hamilton visited.

A beautiful walk along the Sarine [river] brought us with freshened appetites to Chateau d'Oex. The scenery was in many places splendid along the river and some bridges very picturesque, the river sometimes working and toiling through limestone rocks welling at each side like the Pullins at Brownhall, and then raging along more huge blocks of stone which incumbered its course.

In the afternoon we called upon the Pasteur of Chateau d'Oex, Mr. Beaup, who with Madam and another lady and a gentleman received us kindly and hospitably, soon covered their board with excellent fare and made our meal more delightful by profitable conversation. Mr. O [Olivier] then went to visit some families of dissenters and Mr. B. and his family took us to the church where there is a fine view of the beautiful valley, and beautiful indeed it is, shut in by mountains, some covered with pines, some green to their peaks, with pastures dotted with chalets and herds of cattle, and some covered with enormous peaks of rock while the Sarine flows winding along the middle of the valley, which is one of the widest and most populous in this part of the country.

Mr. B. and his company accompanied us a couple of miles towards L'Etang [l'Etivaz], a valley which branches out of that of the Sarine, opening into a narrow gorge with high banks mixed of precipices and pines and overhung by high mountains.

Here Mr. O. rejoined us and we pursued our path, the only entrance to the parish of L'Etang, and practicable for miles only by mules or pedestrians. An excellent desert of [wild] raspberries was ready for us on either side of the path, this fruit was both very plentiful and remarkably fine growing as underwood under the pine forest.

The valley opens after passing the gorge but it is still much shut in. The parsonage and church stand together in the middle of the parish, among a few peasants' houses of which more are scattered at short distances, but most of the inhabitants are at this season in the chalets on the higher pastures and the houses in general are quite shut up.

In this valley is a sulphurous spring [Les Bains de l'Etivaz] and a simple kind of inn and bath house is erected there where we put up for the night and though the bathing accommodation was of the rudest, some of us enjoyed as a great luxury a bath after our long walk. The whole establishment proved as rude as the bath department. Even here we found in its way that the bathing place was a peasants' Baden-Baden, and where God had given healing waters, men had made a place of *rendez-vous* to dishonour that God.

The next day being Sunday, preparations were being made for all sorts of amusements for the company expected. Targets were erected and a wooden stag prepared which was to be shot at while sliding down an inclined plane. Many peasants sat up all night gambling in the room

> under that which our lady companions slept, and the whole place early on Sunday presented so sad an appearance that we were glad to fly to the farther end of the valley where a meeting of truly happy peasantry waited for us. Several walked along with us and I had much interesting conversation with them.
>
> In a peasants' house we had a small but profitable meeting. Mr. O. read and commented upon a portion of the Scripture and asked me to say a few words to the people which I did in my poor French which, however, their desire to understand made, by God's help, tolerably intelligible, as I found by subsequent conversation with them. I tried to stir up the converted to do something especially for the children and suggested Sunday Schools to them . . .

John Hamilton left the company for a while to sit on a rock in the glen 'where I was most delightfully solitary'. Later, there was another 'meeting' after which some of the peasants asked their visitors to stay, offering to prepare beds for them but 'M. Olivier's plans did not admit of this so, having returned to the inn, we paid our bill and took our baggage and returned our march to the Plaine de la Mosses, a high grassy plain surrounded by high peaks of Alps'. The Col des Mosses, where the party stayed in the Hotel de Combellaz, is a now

Chateau d'Oex lies in the same alpine valley as Gruyères. The photograph was taken from the church which was built on the site of the old castle from where, as John Hamilton wrote 'there is a fine view of the beautiful valley'.

popular winter ski resort. Hamilton found the accommodation excellent, but recorded that 'the cold was intense after sunset', adding that where the hotel stood, it was higher than the summit of Mont Saleve, the ridge behind the rented house back at Geneva. His observation about the respective altitudes of the two places was correct, Les Mosses, at 4,750 feet, being 460 feet higher than Mont Saleve.

After staying for two days, Hamilton parted with his companions who intended continuing 'over a difficult mountain . . . to which I found myself quite inadequate', and set-out to return to Geneva:

> I went by a tolerable path down to the village of [Le] Sepey, where a magnificent road was laid down a most beautiful valley to Aigle. The scene going down is almost perfection. The glorious Pic due Midi, or Dents due Midi, is right opposite the opening of the deep ravine along whose sides the road creeps in zig zags cut in the rock or raised on masonry; a torrent rages many hundred feet below.
>
> On my way down, feeling both sore and solitary, I spied one carriage toiling up the zig zags far below me and after half an hour meeting it, I was delighted to find it full of acquaintances, Madam Chenod Churchill, Miss Chenod, etc., who were going to Ormond Dessus [the nearby high Ormont Dessous valley] to be present at the planned re-union . . . They . . . continued the route to Sepey in the carriage and thence, as the road is as yet made no farther, they went on foot to Ormond.

Hamilton, who was recovering from lumbago, had been accompanied for most of this long journey by a clergyman whose health had been rendered delicate by the privations of several Canadian winters, as well as by two women -aunt and niece– then completed this extremely energetic circular mountain tour of the Bernese Alps by walking alone down to the floor of the Rhone valley where, at Aigle, he took a coach to Villeneuve at the eastern end of Lake Geneva, and boarded a steamer to Geneva situated at the lake's furthest end.

Accompanied by a Mr Lake, Hamilton set-off a few days later, this time determined to retrace his steps but continuing to the Ormont Dessous valley 'in the high mountains' to rejoin the others at the reunion. At Aigle he found a coach to take him up the long steep road to Le Sepey, 'in the rain', from where he walked to Ormont 'in the mud', taking two full days to complete the journey. His former travelling companions were already there and next day they all went together up the valley, ascending for two hours to a little cluster of chalets where the 're-union' was due to be held:

> The valley, even with the disadvantage of a gloomy and sometimes drizzling day, was very beautiful, and the numbers of wooden houses – chiefly for hay – quite astonishing. The hills about the church are covered with

> good looking peasant houses among trees of most beautiful foliage, and the side turned to the north is clothed almost to the river with pines.
>
> On ascending the valley towards its upper end where it loses itself in the mountains, we approached the glacier of the Diablerets, but could only see the lower parts on account of the clouds. The precipices and rocks were very magnificent on the opposite side as we climbed up the pasturable side to the south. At our highest elevation it was piercing cold and some snow was mixed with the drizzle.
>
> Very few persons came, and those were such as had seen us going up, for no one thought the minister would come in such unfavourable weather. We had a little meeting in a poor chalet as these high up ones all are. M. Hostache read and explained a Psalm with much feeling and clearness, and the peasants entertained us with a true alpine feast, having kindled a great fire in one corner of the chalet, they put a tub of glorious cream on one side with a tub of hot milk on the other with a vessel full of curds. Each was armed with a curious shaped wooden spoon and, seated on one-legged milking stools, or blocks of wood, we began a valourous attack upon the fare before us. We had a most picturesque romantic and stomach-satisfying meal and enjoyed it most exceedingly. The peasants too were not a little aroused, especially at the English who upset themselves off their one-legged stools. Not being used to the spoons with the crooked handles growing out of the side, often daubed more of the butter-like cream upon their noses than they succeeded on introducing into their gaping mouths.

After staying over-night, the whole party decided to travel down from the mountains to Bex, returning by the good road to Aigle which Hamilton had walked alone a few days earlier, rather than, as originally intended, over a mountain pass. Before they had trudged the entire '5 league route', the skies cleared and the journey was completed by moonlight.

CHAMONIX AND MONT BLANC

Towards the end of August, John Hamilton set-out yet again to the eastern end of Lake Geneva, accompanied by the same Mr. Lake, while young James went ahead, separately, with his tutor Mr Lauterbourg. The plan was that they would all meet-up at Martigny, but when John arrived there 'after a splendid drive', he discovered that his son and the tutor had decided to proceed to Chamonix, over several high passes across the French border about twenty-five miles away.

> Accordingly, we got a little provender to prepare for the walk, and with a guide and a mule to carry our packs . . . we faced the mountains. The

> day was hot and the ascent tolerably severe to the Col de Balme, the highest point to be passed, nothing very interesting on the way. Larch forests began on these mountains, but not fine trees.
>
> The whole way was on the dreary style and the only incident that enlivened our route was near being an awkward accident. Not far from the Col de Balme the path was very steep, an ugly ravine to the right with a steep bank to the left allowed no choice of way. I saw that the path was exceedingly greasy . . . and though I had good experience of the mule's astonishing security of foot on rough rocks among loose stones – even in very steep places – I did not think it could possibly keep its feet here, but as we were scrambling up a very steep place, I could neither halt nor dismount, so I drew my feet out of the stirrups and prepared for a catastrophe.
>
> As I foresaw, down came the poor beast on its nose, after 2 or 3 desperate attempts to dig its toes into the hard yet slippery soil, I half sprang, half threw myself off up towards the bank to the left and clamboured out of the way. The mule, relieved of my weight, after five or six times using its nose for a fifth leg, contrived to get to the top of the slippery place. We passed several ladies on mules with parties crossing the mountain in the opposite direction to us; they were bolder than I . . . .

The explanation for Hamilton's choice of this much more difficult route, when there was an easier alternative way slightly further north, lay with his continued fascination with Mont Blanc. The track at the summit of the col is more than 7,300 feet high from where, had he enjoyed clear weather, he would have had a panoramic view of the whole of the Mont Blanc *massif* as he commenced the descent towards Chamonix.

> The great object of the ascent to the Col de Balme we lost, Mont Blanc being quite be-clouded, we therefore chose the un-picturesque inside of a little kind of inn on the ridge, and having lighted a fire, for the cold was intense and the windows (Aug 23) half blocked up with snow, we produced a little shoulder of mutton, and having procured bread, butter and a bottle of wine we roughed it very smoothly. And being refreshed, troubled the mule very little in the descent to Chamonix where we arrived about 7.

When they reached Chamonix, the father found no sign of James and his tutor, although he did meet many acquaintances at the three inns there. The Hotel de Londres where they stayed was, like the others, completely full of visitors.

The next day the party went to see one of the great sights in the area, the Mer de Glace, and in order to reach it they travelled to Montenvers [which is spelt Montannet in the journal] to view what he called 'the Sea of Ice'. This is the largest of Mont Blanc's glaciers, almost nine miles long but it was even longer when Hamilton saw it. He described the glacier as 'curious and pleasant', adding:

> The Sea of Ice is like an arm of the sea, tossed by winds and suddenly frozen while the waves ran high. It is very curious indeed, it is a glacier, or sort of ice river, descending from the snows of Mont Blanc quite down to the cultivated part of the valley.

Hamilton found 'the crowds of tourists there made it a poor contrast with some of the wilder places previously visited', a reminder that even in the 1830s, Chamonix was already a popular international resort, attracting about 10,000 visitors each year. It was much favoured by the English who were influenced, in the first place, by the poets Byron, Ruskin, Shelley and Wordsworth, all of whom visited the area. Among the English were also many of the earliest Alpine climbers and, while the first ascent to the summit of Mont Blanc had been made by two local men just over 50 years before John Hamilton saw it, the third successful ascent was made by an Englishman. The first successful ascent by a woman (whose party included a dog) was made just three years before Hamilton's arrival there.

With still no sign of young James and the tutor, Hamilton left instructions for them and then:

> went in a *Char a Cote* to the Bains de St Gervais. The road was covered with parties of tourists in *Chars* going and coming. If the valley of Chamonix had disappointed me, the entrance of the valley from this side made amends. It is truly fine, the [river] Arve rolling and raging along a rocky bed in the valley narrowed by the approach of the mountains upon both sides and clothed with good larch forests. The whole drive to St Gervais is exceedingly beautiful and the Glacier de Bossons very curious and fine, part of it advancing very far upon the valley and consisting of brilliant white and pinnacle-shaped rocks of ice.
>
> Having ascended the valley of the Arve till opposite a branch valley in which the Baths of St. Gervais are situated, we crossed the flat [plain] between the mountain bases which here is unproductive and sandy but covered with bushes, chiefly Buckthorn and Barberries, the berries of both in luxuriant abundance and brilliant orange and red and very gay.

St. Gervais les Bains-Le Fayet, to give its full title, which lies about twelve miles west of Chamonix, is internationally famous for its very large *Etablissment des Bains* and its thermal springs, situated in lovely wooded park-land. The doctor referred to here by Hamilton was Aloysius-Francoise de May, proprietor from

1839–1880.

> At St. Gervais we found a great hotel and bathing establishment, the property of a doctor, which are frequented by people with skin ailments as well as liver and kidney disorders. We were well housed and I had a bath of the warm sulphury water. The situation is lovely and the establishment seemed good and I was told by an acquaintance that it really is so, which he knew, having spent 3 weeks there with his family.

On the following morning Hamilton and his friend walked a few miles further on to Salanches to take a *Diligence* to Geneva where there was still no sign of James and the tutor, though a letter sent by his son a week earlier from Martigny awaited him. The party had considered continuing with a further tour into the mountains but, with no sign of an improvement in the weather, Hamilton turned back to Geneva the next day, travelling by steamer, where he was greatly relieved to find that Mr Lauterburg and James had arrived back just before him. Just a day or two later, James developed Scarlet Fever, prompting his father to express thanks to God that the fever had not developed earlier while the boy was hiking in the mountains far from the rest of the family. The Hamiltons continued to live quietly in Geneva, John spending as much time as possible discussing his religious views with clergy of various denominations and with casual acquaintances alike:

> To-day a Mr. Stuart, brother of Lord Castlestuart, called here, a brother in Christ. He and his wife, sister to Lord Powerscourt, are staying in Geneva, he wishes to set going a meeting among a few English to read and preach the scriptures with prayer.

Around this time, Hamilton got word from Donegal that his brother, the Rev. Edward Hamilton, 'has had some tossings and knockings about in a very unpleasant matter which is also calculated to injure the parish and his usefulness', but he did not elaborate about this in the journal. At about the same time, he also heard the alarming news that his sister was 'at death's door', though she was to make a good recovery.

VEVEY AND LAUSANNE

Having brought the family on an extensive tour of Germany and Switzerland, John suddenly proposed to bring them to the far south of France, to the Pyrenees, instead of staying in Geneva until the following Spring. This further change of plan was, however, thwarted by the slow recovery from his recent illness of young James and, more significantly, by the illness which had been afflicting Isabella for about a year but which, curiously, had previously been mentioned only briefly in his journal:

> Our plan had been to go to Pau in September, as we find the air and climate so far from the Atlantic so dry and exerting that we think it has done harm to the children. However, James, having taken the scarletina, prevented this plan, and though he is well now, still we should not like to coop him up in a carriage with the others for a journey of 500 miles or upwards. So we settled . . . to remain in these parts and I made a tour from Geneva to Vevey and there see about houses and fix upon one here, to which we came two days ago, all safe and well.

So the whole family travelled eastwards along Lake Geneva towards Lausanne and Vevey, but because of the eldest daughter's illness, 'part of us came in a steam boat and part by carriage on dear Bella's account, for it would be so difficult and dangerous to get her out of the steamer on to the little boat which takes the passengers to land, for she can as yet use one foot and go a little about on crutches'. This was the first definate indication in the journal of how this un-named illness was affecting the 14 year old child, and that it was causing some real concern.

The Hamiltons then settled near Vevey, which had the added attraction for John of being close to Lausanne, a city of learning which, like Geneva, had strong associations with Calvin and some of the other Propestant Reformers, and also a place which attracted large numbers of English, prompting Victor Hugo to describe Vevey as 'white, clean, English and comfortable'. Among the English who stayed in the area were Byron, who toured extensively in this region, as did Edward Gibbons, who finished his *Decline and Fall* locally, and Charles Dickens who commenced writing *Dombey and Son* while sojourning there:

> The house we got (the first floor) is a two storey house outside the town below it, and quite close to it, called St. Luce, belonging to the Marquise de la Roche Jaquelin, and the ground floor is occupied by the Marquise de la Tour due Pin. The view from the windows splendid over the lake and mountains. It is an excellent house, well furnished and the various rooms cheerful and large. We have rooms besides kitchen and servants' rooms and 12 beds. The cost is £12 British a month. We anticipate a profitable winter as there are a great many good people within our reach and we already know and like some of them.

Unlike other locations earlier in the family's continental tour, their stay near Vevey was virtually entirely among Swiss people – the only Englishman with whom they made acquaintance was one who was married to a Swiss woman.

Hamilton wrote that he believed 'it has hardly ever been the case that an English family has been so entirely in Swiss society than we are. We have more invitations than we can accept. . . .'

The family lived quietly in their house overlooking Lake Geneva and the Chateau de Chillon to the French Alps on the far side. John heard from Donegal that the crops at home were thriving and that 'the terror of famine diminished'. While, from England came news of rioting by the Chartists, a movement which was organising monster meetings and petitions to obtain political reform. Word also came from Ireland that John's sister, Katherine, had recovered from her serious illness, and John was also able to record that Bella was 'rather better', that Helen was 'quite recovered – her sore healed', while James was much stronger after his fever. He, himself was 'tolerably supple' after an attack of lumbago.

John Hamilton continued to observe and discuss aspects of religion, 'the real state' of which, in Switzerland, he found different from Germany. It was not long before he organised a local weekly Scripture-reading meeting which drew an attendance of around 35, mostly poor people including 'notorious frequenters of the drinking houses'. Later, he started another meeting at the far end of the town 'where there is also a miserable population sadly neglected'. Hamilton took the view that the Christian people there were 'sadly lazy about the welfare of their poor ignorant neighbours'.

> My meetings with the poor go on and those who attend every Sunday are very attentive but in visiting them I find the cares of this life so absorbing in their minds that it is hard to lead them to higher things. Not only is it hard for me to do so but impossible, yet the Lord by his word in my hands can absorb their hearts and attention still more, but my faith is so little; Lord increase my strength.

DEATH OF A DAUGHTER

Early in the New Year of 1840, a journal entry noted that young James 'is at an age which causes much anxiety and his faults come more and more to light. Want of thought in the principle – a common want at 15–16, but not the less to be fought against – principally, however, with the weapon of prayer'. James had recovered from his Scarlet Fever (and none of the girls had caught the infection) but Helen was again suffering from 'a sore', while the father continued to endure lumbago. More seriously, Isabella continued to be an invalid and her health soon took a turn for the worse:

> We are much disturbed about our dear Bell who, besides making no progress in the disease which has so long harassed her, has for the last

> three weeks been attacked by a most obstinate complaint in the bowels which defies all remedies . . . . She is still kept always patient and I trust happy in the Lord.

Isabella's health soon became the cause of even more concern, and after two further weeks her father wrote: 'My dear Bell continues very unwell so that our purpose of moving homewards this Spring is almost quite laid aside'. As the weeks went by, Isabella's condition deteriorated steadily and in April, John wrote about the family's ' week of trial':

> Having ordered mustard poultices to her feet and legs, I ran for the doctor and in half an hour had the Mayors, father and son, but the poultices had begun to act and having been applied so early in the attack their effect was rapid and a decided turn for the better had begun, but the thing was evidently an intense and painful business and she could not express what she wanted to say.

In a further journal entry John recorded that:

> On Good Friday, our dear Bell wrote herself the last writing which she was to write with her dear hand; it was a little composition of her own.
>
> *He died, the Lord our Saviour died,*
> *And what a cruel death.*
> *Behold they pierce his holy side*
> *As God's own pure words saith.*
> *And t'was for us the Saviour died*
> *To save us from our sin,*
> *T'was for us he was crucified*
> *That we might be made clean.*

As might be imagined, most of the journal entries at this time centered on Isabella's illness which, though described in its various manifestations which included her lameness, bowel problems and what were called 'suffusions' of the brain, continued to be something of a mystery at the time and remain so to this day. John's descriptions are vague and it is impossible to state with any certainty what exactly was wrong with Isabella. Some of the Hamilton descendants think that she may have suffered form tuberculosis, but there are various other possibilities, including some congenital problem, or something which had its origins in her early childhood but which did not manifest itself until her teenage years. The reference to suffusions of the brain may even point to a form of Spina Bifida, or Hydrocephalus – water on the brain.

Whatever the problem, it is plain that she was very seriously ill, and father, mother and Miss Bagot, the girls' governess, took it in turns to sit with Bella at night and, as far as possible, the other children were kept away from her – even though John commented on one occasion that she would talk quietly with her sisters whenever this was permitted. Significantly, there was not one single entry in the journal during the entire month of May but on 2 June, John Hamilton recorded that: 'on the Sunday night (3rd May) after I wrote last, our dear child, Isabella, was taken to rest with our Saviour'. It continued:

> Her different opposing sicknesses required different treatment; what was good for one was aggravating to the others, and on Sunday May 3 she was evidently quite worn out. On Saturday she was attacked by violent inflammation of the foot and leg. On Thursday she had been threatened by inflammation of the bowels, and the lowering treatment required for these reduced her strength so that when the inflammation gave way it gave place to mortification . . .

Even a few days before her death, Isabella had been able to recite passages from the Bible including, as noted in the journal, Romans 8: 28, parts of Psalms 27, 61 and 118, and Proverbs 22. John commented: 'She herself, as well as me, was astonished at the readiness with which she recalled to mind the passages which were her comfort and joy'. A few evenings before she died, after he kissed her, she put an arm around his neck saying: 'O father, I should like to live to nurse you if you are sick'. The same entry went on to describe her final evening:

> Towards Sunday night she sank fast, hands and feet and face became cold – and colder; severe suffering ceased . . . . At half past eleven she seemed just departing, her poor eyes seemed to see no more. I asked her 'My Bell, do you know me?' She said 'O yes, dear Papa'. 'Do you know that I am always with you holding your hand, and dear Mama too?' 'I know, I know' These were her last words.

She died with her father and mother each holding one of her hands, sitting on either side of the bed. Next day, her body was placed 'in a leaden coffin', after which the family travelled more than three-hundred miles to Karlsruhe. Describing the family's melancholy journey to there from the shores of Lake Geneva, John Hamilton wrote that they may have met many disagreeable happenings during the journey, bringing Bella's coffin with them, but these he dismissed as of little consequence. He had tried to see the Baden Minister in Bern (Germany was still composed of separate kingdoms and grand duchies, including Baden and Prussia) so that the party would not have to undergo 'a disagreeable and distressing search' when crossing the Swiss border. The Minister whom John sought was away so he called on the Prussian Ambassador in his private house. The Baden diplomat's absence was, at the very least, a piece of extraordinary good luck in that Hamilton was thus led to call on a man who was not only a very distinguished and influential diplomat but an extremely religious man as well. This Baron Christian Karl Josias von Bunsen, who was appointed Ambassador to Britain the following year, was Christian by name and Christian by conviction, a biblical scholar and interested in theological research, and had published a book of more than 900 hymns and a number of other religious works in German, French and English. Strangely, there is no mention of any of this in the journal but it is plain from what John wrote at the time that they got on very well together and, as a result, Bunsen agreed to 'do the Baden business'. So, when the family reached the Swiss frontier, they 'met no hindrance, vexation or delay' and Hamilton had no doubt that this was a mark of God's kindness to him because, as he wrote, 'the law allows the clergyman and other officers who are concerned in funerals, to claim, in every parish through which a dead body passes, all the fees as if it was buried there', adding that he had been 'unaware of this toll until we were safe in Carlsruhe'.

Two days before they reached the latter city, John Hamilton left the family at Offenburg and drove ahead to make arrangements to rent a house. Arriving in Karlsruhe, he went to a coffee shop and was recognised by the landlord who remembered him from the time of the family's outward journey nearly four years earlier. On hearing that John was looking for accommodation, he told him he knew of a house which would exactly suit him. Owned by Herr Himmelhaber, it was situated in a pleasant street 'only three minutes from a cool forest' which surrounded the town. Having secured it, and after visiting a few former friends, he returned in the direction of Offenburg to Rastatt where the family was re-united that evening. They proceeded to their new quarters the next day and 'in the evening we all assembled in the chapel in the burying ground, our good friend Mr. Frommel officiated at our dear child's burial and her body was laid beside Rebecca's'. It will be remembered that Rebecca McClearn, had been buried at Karlsruhe during the second year of the European tour, and it seems likely that the existence of Rebecca's grave there had prompted John's decision to bring Isabella's coffin all the way there from Switzerland.

Later, he was to write that Isabella had a vision, in April of the previous year, that God had come to her in a dream and told her that she would die in May. She had confided this to her sisters who were so horrified and confused when they heard this that they did not mention it to their parents until after her death. At that time, twelve months before Isabella died, the family had just arrived in Geneva where, on 3 May she suddenly felt both unwell and very cold and thought she was about to die, thereby fulfilling the prediction (as she thought), until she realised that the 'prophesy' was not to be fulfilled until May of the *following* year. It certainly seems quite remarkable that she died on that exact date one year later. Her father also noted that, during March and April, when the family was gravely concerned about her condition, Isabella had told her sister, Helen, there was no immediate need for concern because she would 'linger on until May and then die'.

KARLSRUHE TO BADEN

John found himself again afflicted with Lumbago, so the family turned back to the spa town of Baden-Baden, where John had been ordered to take the waters 'to restore me after the illness I had at Carlsruhe'. With the delayed funeral finally over, the change of scene at Baden was greatly appreciated by family, where they enjoyed:

> many delightful excursions among the hills and magnificent woods of the Back Forest skirts. Mr. F. and James were generally mounted on asses, sometimes we have spent many hours in the thick woods . . . . Such air as we found on the tops of the hills, clothed with immense silver firs, I never tasted – for really it tastes so fresh, like soda water, and so aromatic from the young growth of the fir trees that it gives quite an unearthly feel when one breathes it and must, I think, tend much to health . . . .

Baden-Baden dates back to Roman times when the original baths (still to be seen) were established, and during the nineteenth century it became 'the summer capital of Europe', noted for its fine buildings and an especially beautiful promenade planted with exotic trees – all in an attractive setting between the Black Forest and the Baden vineyards. The Kurhaus with its elegant portico and columns – the scene of glittering balls – had been built almost 20 years before John Hamilton arrived there, and the city boasted a fine Casino, so it may say something about the man when he described the town as having 'in itself nothing beautiful or remarkable', But if the town held little attraction for him, he obviously liked the surrounding countryside:

> Its situation was delightful. It lies in a valley opening into the great and fruitful plain through which flows the river Rhine – it is surrounded and sheltered by high hills, almost worthy to be called mountains, which are covered to their very tops with magnificent woods, some of oak and beech, but mostly of silver firs. These woods form a part of an immense forest several days' journey long, called the Black Forest, from its awful and dark shade caused by the enormous silver firs. The hot springs of Baden rise out of a rock pretty high up on a hill, and yield great abundance of water. I found both its taste and effects more disagreeable than those of the waters of Aix-la-Chapelle and of Wiesbaden, and was obliged to soon cease drinking it, but afterwards continued again, and, by God's

blessing, before we took our departure from Baden I was able to walk a journey with my son (each of us carrying a knapsack on our back) of more than a hundred miles through the Black Forest.

The people of the Black Forest seemed to me a handsomer and more intelligent race than the people of the richer lands of Baden or Würtenburg, and their dress and houses are much more comfortable, notwithstanding their worse soil and climate. These people are obliged to work hard to get enough to live, and then, having industrious habits, they go on diligently, add comforts to their necessaries and are much better off than their neighbours whose land yields four times as much with less labour. Perhaps you will think that the people who have the least land are kept poor by a higher rent. Not at all, for in these countries the farm almost always belongs to the farmer, and the great object of every peasant is to save up as much money as will buy a few acres for himself if he does not inherit some land from his father.

The houses are in general built entirely of wood and are often very pretty. If it please God that I return home in safety, I shall have much pleasure in showing you some pictures of these houses. The walls are made of whole logs, such as you see landed from America or Norway. These logs are well united together, and often curiously carved and ornamented. The roof comes far over the walls and keeps them quite dry, often sticking out ten feet beyond the house. The rooms in these wooden dwellings are very warm and comfortable, and are heated by stoves such as I have described in a previous letter. The women wear very broad straw hats, full a foot broad in the brim, and in some districts they wear short blue woollen petticoats, a tight black body [bodice], white wide short sleeves, and red stockings. A number of women thus dressed and busy on a fine day in a hay-field look very pretty and curious. Both men and women are very well mannered and intelligent.

The Hamiltons were, during this time, accompanied by the Rev. Vicarus Frommel who had officiated at Isabella's funeral, and with whom the family had got on so well that Mary Hamilton suggested to her husband that he be asked to act as tutor to young James, and this arrangement was then agreed. After a month at Baden, the family moved north to Neuwied am Rhine, back to where they had stayed for almost a year at the beginning of their continental tour, and where 'a good many English resided'. En route, they stopped overnight at Karlsruhe where 'much of our short time was spent at that loved spot where we laid the bodies of two [persons] dear to us in the Lord, and where now two stones with inscriptions surrounded by iron railings mark the spot where their remains rest'. The Reverend Frommel, who accompanied them as far as Heidelberg, decided at that point to go no further. Among the 'English' families with whom the Hamilton's became very friendly at Neuwied were the

John Hamilton's drawing of the entrance to the Kuhloch cave near Bamberg, north-east Bavaria, in an area known as 'Franconian Switzerland' which reminded him of Derbyshire.

McCarthy's who were, not unexpectedly, Irish. John's attachment to Mr. McCarthy was heightened because 'he had begun a meeting for searching the scriptures every week in his house'.

John Hamilton made no reference in his journal to the house where the family stayed in at Neuwied, but his daughter's second journal explained that they stayed with two sisters at the *Brudergemeinde* Inn run by the Moravian *Hernhut* community there. From there, the Hamiltons travelled eastwards into Franconia in north-east Bavaria, an area known in Germany as the *Fichtelgebirge* -literally, the Spruce Mountains – which he described as 'lying in a triangle whose angles are Bamberg, Bayreuth and Würzburg'. In fact, these three places, when looked at on a map, are almost in a straight line and he must have meant Nürnberg rather than Würzburg, and this would seem to be confirmed by the fact that the tiny village where they stayed, Muggendorf, lies almost in the centre of the latter triangle. This district is known as Franconian Switzerland, which he described as:

> very curious, much like part of Derbyshire, with deeply cut valleys in high undulating country. These valleys are full of the most fantastic shaped rocks from 10 to 200 feet high, with some pretty streams, but a fall near the castle of Babeneck [Bad Berneck?] prevented me from being able to explore as much as we should have liked. We had, however, gone into two curious caves, the Kuh Loch or the Cow's Hole, and another which was some thousand feet into the rock and is full of remarkable stalactites, and in which are some interesting animal remains, stags' horns, bears' skulls and the bones of some gigantic animal, all more or less embedded in the calcareous deposits on the ground of the cavern.

The family also went south-west to Würtzburg; its connection with the Irish monk St. Killian seems to have escaped him though he was, not surprisingly, astonished by the almost arrogant grandeur of the Episcopal citadel of Marienburg, overlooking the city, one of the biggest Baroque castles in Germany. Describing this bishop's palace, he thought that 'the number and style of the reception rooms was like the palace of a great king', which in turn prompted the remark that 'certainly those bishops were more princely than apostolic in their habits'.

It seems curious and it is very disappointing that although the next entry is headed 'Prague, Aug 25, 1840', and although it runs to fourteen pages, there is only a tantalisingly brief description in the journal of this diversion into Bohemia. Instead he wrote at great length about his own private thoughts on life and religion. The entry opens with the sentence: 'Again in a strange land . . . . I am this day forty years old' but he did not mention the route taken to reach the Bohemian capital, let alone describe it. Later, he was to write retrospectively that:

> Prague far exceeded my expectations as a fine and beautiful city, the effects of its spires and towers is most pleasing and imposing. I did not know what view of the town to prefer – from the bridge [by which he must have meant the statue-lined Charles Bridge], from the Hradschin [the medieval castle district overlooking the city],or from the [nearby hilltop] Niclausberg – all were fascinating.

After leaving Prague, the family travelled through northern Bohemia to the small town of Teplitz (now Teplice). Hamilton gave no explanation for this diversion, bur the reason becomes clear when it is realised that it was an old spa town and Hamilton, with his aches and pains, had become greatly attracted to these places. Teplitz was especially favoured at the time by musicians, including Beethoven, Chopin, Liszt, Paganini and Wagner, but it later became overshadowed by the more fashionable spas of western Bohemia. The Hamiltons then crossed the Prussian border into Saxony, staying at Bad Schandau where, in one of his sketch books, John drew a number of views of the River Elbe near this pretty little resort, as well as several sketches of the nearby 'Saxon Switzerland' with its spectacular sandstone pillars high above the Elbe. From there it was only a short distance to Dresden, where his next journal entry was written. Incredibly, John Hamilton was unimpressed by this city – the *Elbeflorenz,* 'the Florence on the Elbe' – as the capital of the Kingdom of Saxony came to be known. He virtually dismissed this city of palaces, churches and museums in a few brief sentences: 'Dresden disappointed me, I had formed too high expectations and looked for a brilliant effect on arriving'.

Given John Hamilton's continuing interest in the Moravian Brotherhood, it seems strange that he does not appear to have taken the opportunity to visit Herrnhut, only a short distance east of Dresden. It was to there that the remnants of this old religion fled from persecution, finding shelter and protection on the estate of the Lutheran Count Zinzendorf, after which the Brethren embarked on their extraordinary, but now almost unknown missionary work. The influence and outreach of this small church, with its strong missionary zeal, was quite remarkable – it seems almost unbelievable, for example, that they had established a mission on Greenland by 1733.

The Hamiltons stayed in Dresden for a few days at least, for the oldest surviving Hamilton family photograph was taken in that city by Teich Hansstaengl, a professional photographer who had begun working there. Considering that Fox Talbot and Daguerre, independently credited with the birth of photography, both published details of their respective experiments to produce from negatives, positive pictures on paper only a year earlier, this picture must have been a great novelty at the time and may now rank among some of the oldest surviving photographs. From Dresden, the family then travelled by Leipzig and Weimar back to Neuweid in preparation for the homeward journey.

RETURNING HOME

Towards the end of their stay at Neuwied, there were 'rumours of war between France and England, taking in, of course, the other continental powers, [which] made us determine, after much prayer and deliberation, to travel homewards. . . '. Forced to leave in a hurry, they sold the furniture they had bought for their rented house 'at considerable loss'. On the way 'in the steamer'[presumably on the River Rhine, but this is not stated] they met Arthur Pakenham who was on a tour 'for health'. Notwithstanding his hasty decision to depart for home because of the threat of war, John then mentioned in his journal that they then spent a week with friends at Wiesbaden from where he and his son made a quick tour of Homburg, Frankfurt and Nassau!

When the family eventually set-out for home, John was delighted and flattered to find in Cologne a local who, hearing Hamilton speaking in German thought that he *was* a German! The family continued through Aix, Liege, and Ostend by train (the first mention in the journals of this form of transport) and, after sailing overnight to London, continued via Liverpool to Kingstown, where they stayed for a week. When, at last, they got back to Donegal, the family resided for three weeks at Brownhall 'because at St Ernan's all is still very unsettled and unfurnished but where we were all well'. They eventually moved back into St. Ernans in mid November, four years and three months after their departure to Europe.

An early nineteenth century engraving of a scene on the River Rhein - possibly at Neuwied – which 'Moll' Hamilton used to illustrate her own travel journal.

EIGHT

Back in Donegal

While much of his writings during the family's sojourn on the conti nent centred around his religious experiences, and rather less on descriptions of the places visited, it would have been disappointing – given his interest in improving his own estate and the conditions for his tenants – if he had failed to record something of what he saw of foreign agricultural practices. Fortunately he wrote some of his observations in letters to his tenants, of which the following are some extracts:

> As soon as any one from our country arrives in France, or in most of the countries I have seen, he begins to wonder where the cattle can be, and is astonished to see no hedges or fences.
>
> Not a cow is to be seen upon the land, and the whole country for miles is in one great field, not an inch in a thousand acres is taken up with fences. But there must be cattle for there is no scarcity of butter, milk and meat. The truth is the cattle are all fed in the house, except in places where the land is quite mountainous and unfit for cultivation. The gain by this plan is wonderful, as you may see if you calculate the loss of ground in fences, the loss of money, time, and labour in making and repairing them, the loss of crops by loose cattle straying into fields, the loss of cattle themselves, hurt by breaking over fences or hunted out of the crop they have been damaging, and, what is no small thing in the account, the loss of good neighbourhood through disputes about cattle breaking out and breaking in. Besides all this gain, those who feed the cattle in the house can keep twice as many on the same land, and raise a vast deal more and finer crops also, because they make such a great quantity of manure.
>
> Even along the roadside there are no fences at all, but generally rows of apple, pear, and cherry trees. When cattle are driven to market, or for any other purpose along the roads, the drivers are very careful to prevent them from doing the smallest injury to the crops on either side. The people all live in villages or towns, so a farmer never has his house upon his farm, which makes the country look very bare and deserted. I think it is also a great loss to the people, for they must drive all their manure so far out and their crops so far home, and lose so much time whenever

> they want to do anything upon their land. But they find some advantages too in their plan. The children can be sent to school more readily, and the people go more easily to church, for nearly every village has a school and a church, at least in Germany, but not so generally in France, and they think it dreadfully lonely to live in a house separated even by one field from others. But I think all the advantages are far more than balanced by the evils of having all the people in villages and towns
>
> It makes these much larger as well as more numerous, and there is always more temptation to vice in towns than in the country; the children learn bad habits much more in the streets than in the fields, and the men are much more likely to go to the public-house when it is in the same street, than when it is a mile or two distant from their houses; still we may learn much from their plan, for with all its disadvantages they keep more cattle and raise more crops upon equally good land than we do.
>
> I should like to see each farm well fenced round for shelter as well as for protection, each house upon its own farm, and no cross-fences unless the farm is very large, but a nice garden, well enclosed, and some good trees planted by the tenant and registered so as to be his own property round the house and garden and along the outside fence. There would be much gain in this if the cattle were fed in the house, as every one of the hundreds of thousands are in the rich parts of France and Germany. But the place where I saw the best farming and the finest crops was in Belgium. A great part of Belgium is very rich and quite flat. The people do not neglect it and leave it to itself, because it is so rich that even then it would give good crops, but they are very careful and industrious farmers. In a day's journey you do not find as much weeds as would fill a hat. They pull them out as soon as they begin to appear and never let them seed, and as they are careful in other respects also; their crops are rich and plentiful as they are clean, and their fields, their cattle, their horses, all are so well kept that it is a pleasure to see them.

Shortly after he had settled as proprietor of his newly-inherited Donegal estate, John Hamilton had remarked on the absence of carts locally, so it is not surprising that he was intrigued by the oxen carts which were at that time a feature of many parts of Europe. He commented that :

> cows, even while they are giving milk, all do a little work. They are always harnessed by the horns, and by the carts in this part of Germany would surprise you, especially those drawn by oxen and cows . . . A cushion is laid on their head and a bar lies across upon this, and is fastened with two straps round the roots of the horns. When one ox draws a cart there is a hole in each end of the bar upon the beast's head, and the

> points of the shafts are fixed in these holes – when two work together there is a hanging link in the middle of the bar which rests on both their heads, and the pole is fixed to this. The beasts push with their heads and draw steadily and seem to be very much at their ease. The people treat them kindly and they are generally fat and sleek. The women in particular are careful to get a good meal for the cattle – they let nothing go to waste, but gather leaves, roots of grass, and weeds in the ploughed fields; wash, clean and boil them, and give them to the cows, with a little coarse bread sometimes cut into it when it is cool. Indeed the Germans are very careful to let nothing go to waste, whether of their own or what is entrusted to them. Thus they avoid a great sin, which among us is, I am sorry to say, is very common – for wasting food or fuel or any other thing that God gives to us to use, is a sin against the Giver whose kindness we thus make light of.

COMPARING CLIMATES AND EDUCATION

John Hamilton observed some of the advantages and disadvantages of the continental climate compared to that in Ireland:

> One of the causes why a person who has been unwell in Ireland often recovers in these lands, is the difference of the climate, chiefly the dryness of the air. Our country being an island surrounded on all sides by the sea is not only subject to much more rain than fails here, but even in fine weather there is not that dryness which I have observed in these countries, nor is the power of the sun in fine weather nearly so great. This heat and dryness makes corn and fruit grow and ripen very fast indeed, and in general these are better and finer than with us. But I do not think that on the whole they have any advantage over us, for if the dry climate is good for diseases brought on in a damp one, I find this climate too dry to live in for a continuance, and its very dryness causes many complaints to be more frequent than with us, as well as more violent. People are on the whole certainly neither stronger, healthier, nor longer lived here – and if the sun has more power and the finer kinds of grain and fruits ripen better here, the same power of the sun often dries up the springs of water and parches up the ground, and is much more terrible than a rainy season with us. It is also very oppressive to both man and beast to labour in such heat, and the more common and useful crops, as potatoes, oats, barley, cabbages, and all garden vegetables, and grass, grow as well, if not better, in our climate – as well as apples and pears and other common small fruits.

Given that John Hamilton had established seven schools in his part of south Donegal, it is hardly surprising that he took an interest in schooling while he was abroad. He wrote at some length on the subject of education in the Kingdom of Prussia – which may seem surprising given that most people's perception of Prussia is that it lay in the far north-east of Germany, an area which he did not visit while abroad. However, during the period when the Hamilton family was in Europe, Prussia extended westwards as far as the Rhein and beyond it, and Neuwied, where they stayed for almost a year, was at the time in the province of Rhenish Prussia. While there, John commented that the King of Prussia, Frederich Wilhelm IV, had 'given much attention to this part of his duty as the father of his people':

Mary ('Moll') Hamilton (1827-1877), John's second daughter, photographed at Dresden in 1840. This was only one year after the technique of transferring photographic negative images onto paper had been discovered, so that this picture must be among the oldest surviving early photographs.

> In every village there is a school, and in every town, according to its size, several, where the children both boys and girls are well taught by masters placed and paid by the Government out of the taxes paid by the people. Every child must be sent to one of these schools, and must attend regularly, unless the parents can show that the child's health is quite too bad to allow of its going to school, or unless they satisfy the persons appointed over these matters that they provide a good education for the child at home or at a private school. Of course a great many rich people have teachers for their children at home, or send them to schools where many more things are taught than are needed for the children of those who are poorer; but these public schools are so good, the children so

well taught and well kept in order, that many rich parents send their children to them, and I have known the child of a wealthy gentleman to be in the class with the child of the poorest labourer.

The children are all obliged to be clean and tidy, and to behave properly. One of these schools was held next door but one of the house in which I lived for twelve months in Neuwied, and the children, of whom there were above a hundred, passed under my view every day going to school and returning home, besides being allowed twice a day to play for a quarter of an hour in the street opposite to my windows, for it was a quiet retired part of the town. So excellent was the order in which the school was kept, that in all that time I never saw a blow given, nor heard any angry words among all those children, but they behaved well and decently while they ran and jumped and sang and laughed as merrily as any troop of little ones could do. How much happier is this, while they continue children, than to be allowed to have their own way which always leads to so much roughness in word and deed among children, and how much better for them afterwards, when they are men and women, to be accustomed early to restrain their evil passions and to behave themselves like reasonable and civilised beings.

Nowhere, perhaps, is the effect of this careful education of the whole of the children more remarkable than in the fairs. These are held much more rarely than with us, so that there is a great collection of all sorts of people when a fair takes place, and booths are set up in long rows and furnished like good shops. I have often walked through such fairs with ladies accompanying me, and never met with or saw anything unpleasant or uncivil among all the crowds of men and women, no crushing and pushing, no drunkenness or fighting, every one taking care to annoy others as little as possible. How different is this from some fairs that I could mention! I often asked myself, is there any reason why Irish men and women should not behave as well as Germans do?

Now, my dear neighbours, I know you pretty well, I am acquainted with most of your faults, and I am certain that God has not created you one step behind these well-behaved Germans in any point whatever, yet, certain it is, you are behind them – far away, in these things. I ask you why? I beg of you think of this question and each of you strive for yourself and for your children that there may be no room to ask so humbling a question for the future.

After the family had settled back in Donegal, one of the first entries in John Hamilton's journal reflected how deeply affected he continued to be over the death of Isabella:

Yesterday was the birthday of my dear child, now a blessed spirit with

> God. How little did we expect a year ago, when we all brought our little presents of texts of Scripture in token of our love, that our next union on her birthday would be no more in the body but only in the spirit. My wife and I passed the morning fasting and with prayer, and we met all the dear children in prayer and remembrance of our dear Isabella in the evening.

In the New Year, John Hamilton added some further thoughts on Isabella:

> This year began again in my earthly home, safe brought back with all from Neuwied. . . . But of our party of girls who left thus, two are no more among us. A wild dream it sometimes seems that we have been above four years abroad, and that I have seen my child die, and laid her body in a foreign land, and shall see her no more on earth, that the reality of those scenes at Lausanne, the sinking life, the parting breath, the cold lifeless clay – the coffin, and at Carlsruhe, the grave, the stone tomb. . . .

Many years later, after the Famine, John Hamilton with his wife and three remaining daughters, returned to Karlsruhe in order to visit Isabella's grave, that 'pilgimage', as he was to call it.

During 1837, while the family had been abroad, two sisters who were daughters of the Bishop of Derry, when touring the area had called to Brownhall where John's brother was still residing. Frances and Emily Ponsonby recorded the occasion: 'We passed through Donegal and drove to Brownhall, a most beautiful place on our road, belonging to Mr. Hamilton. We had a great deal to see there, as there is a very curious subterranean river running through the place, which is well worth going a great distance to see. . . .' [Known *The Pullins*, this is described in chapter two].

Back in St. Ernan's, John Hamilton was full of ideas as a result of his observations during his visit to the continent and he now renewed his determination to improve his estate and the conditions for his tenantry. He was well aware that he had been needlessly profligate with his inheritance, becoming wiser in this respect almost too late. He found his Sunday schools and adult Bible reading classes continuing much as he had left them, and he continued to avail of any opportunity, as he put it, to 'address congregations' and at the same time sought ways and means to achieve his own personal spiritual fulfilment. In March 1841, more than four months after coming home, John Hamilton was finding it difficult to settle down to the routine of running his estate:

> I have been doing very little since my return except setting my house in order. James, I have with us, reading with a tutor, he is deficient in energy, but the medical brain in Germany told me to expect this for a couple of years and not to fight against it too much. . . . In everything else his mind is well enough. . . .

> I trust God has wound me up, and made me see more strongly the state of those so under my care as servants and tenants. I have considered their case with much care and am persuaded that a radical reform is called for, and I will, with God's blessing, begin before I am compelled. My object is to raise them, both in the scale of society as well as to be the means of (if God will use so unworthy an instrument) furthering their religious improvement. I shall have to face every prejudice, many in myself, many more in my friends, agent, tenants, servants, but if God be with me I shall succeed. I have hitherto given too inconsiderately to my tenants, and they have learned to lean upon me in a way that is disreputable and degrading. It is my fault and I must change my way – but prudently. I have helped my poorest tenantry to live on in poverty, while the same or less expenditure judiciously and firmly administered would have helped them out of poverty into comparative affluence.

VISIT TO OXFORD

Having made up his mind to find yet another tutor for his son, John Hamilton brought James to Oxford in the Spring of 1841. Typically, his description of the journey was more concerned with his spiritual discussions on the way rather than with the scenery. After travelling to Ballyshannon, father and son continued by coach to Enniskillen, and John soon discovered that one of the other passengers, an army captain, was as he expressed it 'a bold soldier of the Lord, who seemed truly desirous, whatever he did, to do all to the glory of God'. Missing the connecting coach to Dublin, the three shared a *chaise* and reached Lisnaskea before nightfall, where they stayed at the inn, and John Hamilton with typical forthrightness in these matters invited 'the landlady and her house to worship'.

> There was some objection made on account of some being Roman Catholics but, on being invited they, contrary to the landlady's expectation, came willingly and seemed much gratified at least. God grant it may prove more. The landlady told us, thanking us warmly, that during the many years she had kept an inn, notwithstanding hundreds of clergymen had frequented her house, it was the second time she had had such a thing proposed.

On the next stage of the journey, Hamilton found a new travelling companion, a divinity student:

> with whom I had much conversation and partly about the Roman Catholics. I was happy to meet one who spoke so kindly of them without

> being indulgent to the errors of Popery. On his getting outside for a stage, a middle-aged lady and I entered into conversation. She said it was a great privilege to hear such conversation instead of the kind too common in coaches, and seemed really happy to speak of heavenly things. I afterwards asked the young gentleman who she was, and he told me she was a Roman Catholic lady. How thankful should I be that God led and enabled me to bear a good witness for Him before this person, it may be the means of letting her see that a Bible Christian is not a furious Papist-hating creature.

En route to Dublin, their coach had been stopped by snowdrifts near Navan (this was in March) and John took the opportunity to stay for four days with his uncle and aunt who lived nearby at Ardbraccan Glebe, 'until the frost broke up'. When he reached Oxford, he settled his son with a Dr. Greenhill in a room overlooking the High Street opposite All Soul's College, and John took the opportunity to attend several church services at Oxford to hear for himself some of the views of celebrated members of the Oxford Movement and its adherents.

This 1841 visit to Oxford came at a very interesting time for both Protestantism and Catholicism in England. John Newman had been appointed vicar of St Mary's in the town 13 years earlier and had become noted for his sermons. Originally a supporter of the Evangelical, and Low Church wings of the Church of England, he had already changed his views when John Hamilton heard him preach, becoming a High Churchman and Anglo Catholic, and one of the foremost members of what came to be known as 'the Oxford Movement'. Newman, along with his fellow members, published many religious tracts (hence 'Tractarians') propounding a kind of middle way between Catholicism and Protestantism. Critically, one of Newman's tracts interpreted the doctrinal *formularies* of the Church of England as in basic agreement with the doctrines of the Council of Trent, as drawn up three centuries earlier. This brought an outcry from a broad spectrum of Newman's fellow churchmen who took the view that some of the decisions made by the Catholic Church at Trent were frankly anti-Protestant. Indeed there was a feeling that certain religious practices at that time had been condemned by the council simply because they were in use among Protestants, notably the translation of both the Bible and the liturgy into the vernacular. Newman was greatly disturbed at this hostile reaction and, despite his deep regret at leaving what he termed his 'beloved Anglicanism', he became a Roman Catholic in 1845. He subsequently played a significant part in establishing the new Catholic University at Dublin, of which he was Rector from 1854-58, and was created a cardinal in 1879.

It is, therefore, of no little interest that at one of the services attended by Hamilton, the Anglican preacher was John Henry Newman, whom he described as one of the foremost of the Tractarians:

> The tone of his sermon on baptism was good, the matter bad, that is, built on traditions, not on Scripture, and not only so, but according to the system of this set he preached up tradition as equal to Scripture and the word of the Church, that is, in his acceptation the clergy as equal to the Word of God. He and Pusey [who, along with John Keble, were the main leaders of the Oxford Movement] I take for sincere and well-meaning men, devout, and superstitiously inclined who, seeing the neglect of all discipline and the loose manner of life of so-called Christians, have gone into another extreme. . . . I had much opportunity of conversation with some of the warmest adherents of the doctrines of Newman, etc., and certainly they do carry beyond all that I had an idea of, their doctrine of blind submission to the priesthood, which of course, they extend and confine to the clergy.

AGENT DISMISSED

The years between his return from Europe and the on-set of the Great Famine were, for Hamilton, ones of consolidation and progress. Although he was aware that his finances were stretched, his impatience continued to cause him to spend large sums of money that could have been reduced or even saved had he been satisfied with a slower rate of progress.

He had extended and partly re-built his house at St Ernan's but a decade later it seems surprising that it was still in an unfinished state. John Hamilton's hint that he was not entirely satisfied with it perhaps partly reflected his still unsettled state after the long trip abroad:

> Much of this past season has been taken up in the fitting and preparing of this house which, though built a dozen years, was never finished, papered or painted. Yet it is not in my heart. I am conscious that however much I am interested in it, I should not be grieved to leave it, not from disgust or dissatisfaction, God knoweth, for few – very few – have such reason to rejoice and be glad in their house and family. . . .

However, there was another reason for the unfinished state of his house – he had been building houses for his tenants, over a hundred in the previous year. He mentioned this in a letter he sent to his tenants which, while couched in typically friendly language, was critical of those whom he had assisted earlier but who, due to laziness, had failed to take advantage of the help given, in contrast with those others who by their own efforts, had since been doing well:

> MY DEAR TENANTS, – In taking the agency of my estate into my own hands, I wish to make myself clearly understood by you all upon a

few matters of consequence to us both. But, first, I must say a word about our excellent friends Mr. Andrew, Mr. Abraham, and Mr. Alexander Hamilton of Coxtown, who since the death of their father have all so faithfully and in so friendly a manner acted as agents between you and me. I do not now take my agency into my own hands from any misunderstanding or anything unpleasant between me and any of them – on the contrary, every year of the many during which I have known them has made me esteem them more and more.

But I am desirous of coming myself near to my tenants, knowing them better, and thus being better able, as I hope, to be of use to them. But here comes the difficulty, my friends; how shall I be of use to you?

I have been above twenty years your landlord, I have lived very constantly among you, and have spent nearly double the amount of my yearly rent here, and that not in costly living, but mostly in paying labourers and tradesmen, and building or assisting to build tenants' houses. My own house, though eleven years built, is not yet painted or in any sense finished, and as I had last year above a hundred tenants' houses to renew, and a considerable number every year for some time before, it is no wonder if I could not afford to finish my own sooner. While I was absent from this country, I did not in the four years that I was away draw £50 a year from Ireland, but continued to spend at home, what belonged to my home.

I have not only spent my money at home and among you, but I have also considerably reduced my rents, although they were not before any higher than those around us – so that in ten years I have received less by above £2000 than I should have done if I had not reduced my rents . . . . Consider what I have lost and what you ought to have gained by this. A very heavy arrear which I found upon the estate twenty years ago, was in part forgiven and the rest taken in labour. And since, when it pleased the Lord to send us a season that almost caused a famine [1831], I gave up the whole year's income either in remitting part of the rent or in providing provisions from a distance. There is a multitude of lesser matters in which I have tried to benefit my tenants, not to increase my own riches, for my rental shows above £200 a year less now than it did a dozen years ago, although several valuable old leases have fallen in during that time.

What do I, then, look for in return for all I spend and have spent among you? I look for an improvement in you. I expect to see an improvement in respectability and independence in yourselves, your houses, and your families.

Now, I ask you is it too much to seek this? There is but one side from which I have reason to expect anything to prevent the improvement which I look for, and that is from your own selves.

> I complain of you as being your own enemies, while I am happy to say you have, with few exceptions, shown yourselves as far as you could my friends. You have honestly done more to pay my rent than you have done to make yourselves comfortable and respectable. And, worse than this, by dividing small farms you have reduced yourselves in numerous cases to many more difficulties than you would otherwise have had to fight against.
>
> JOHN HAMILTON

He indicated in his journal that he was giving more thought to his future plans, hoping thus to avoid impulsive decisions which had resulted in expensive mistakes in the past..

> I have nearly completed the time I allowed myself for looking around me, making myself more perfectly acquainted with estate matters and forming my opinions before entering on the regular plan of improvement of my Estate. . . .

Most landlords ran their estates without any training in the business whatever. Some young landlords, if they were lucky, may have benefited by watching

Coxtown was for a time the home of another, unrelated, Hamilton family. Alexander Hamilton of Coxtown was an innovating land agent who acted for John Hamilton as well as for a number of other proprietors in the Ballintra – Ballyshannon area.

how their fathers coped, but the majority were far away from the family estate – perhaps in the Indian Army – when news came that they had just inherited the property. John's son was more fortunate than most having been at home for much of his young life and he would have seen his father's innovations as well as his serious misjudgements. His father, conscious of his own costly errors, had just decided to send young James away to learn the business of running the very large family estate, an opportunity afforded to very few young heirs at that time.

> My dear son is in Dublin working at Messrs. J. R. Stewart's office at estate agency business. [John Robert Stewart through his mother, the Hon. Elizabeth Pakenham, was John's cousin, and his business continued in the family for two more generations]. I am anxious he should get what I find the want of sorely – early knowledge of, and habits of this kind of business . . . '

A small diary kept by Mary (Moll), one of John's younger sisters, at this time consists mostly of very brief entries about very ordinary day-to-day events. From it, it is clear that her brother, James, was spending a considerable amount of his time at the Fintown estate (and she recorded several times that he had walked home from there). It would seem that this was another means of introducing the young heir into the business of running the Brownhall estate. One entry from Moll's diary gives a flavour of its contents:

> All Saint's Day. Morning fine. Went to Laghy, heard the Vicar's farewell sermon to a crowded congregation – two baptisms. Shook hands at the gate. Very stormy coming home and the sea dashing over the mound [causeway]. Would not go to the meeting in pit [perhaps a reference to the makeshift chapel at Greggstown]. Jimmy at Fintown.

FATHER MATHEW IN DONEGAL

Father Mathew's temperance campaign between 1838 and 1842, which resulted in an estimated five million persons taking a pledge of total abstinence, must rank as one of the most under-rated personal achievements in Irish history. After he had visited Donegal town in June 1841, John Hamilton recorded that he had heard that the 'temperance priest' had cured a local man who was a cripple:

> A very remarkable thing has just occurred here. Last Sunday as I was going into Donegal I heard that Father Mathew, who has been the means of turning thousands of our poor people from whisky, had been in the

town on Friday, induced many to take the total abstinence pledge, and had healed a cripple. On the pump in the midst of the market-place I saw his crutches exhibited.

After church I asked a merchant in the town who the cripple was, as I wished to trace the matter and expose any imposture that might mislead the people. He told me the name, and accompanied me to the house. I was surprised to find that he was a poor man whom I knew well, having visited him several times, he being very ill, hopelessly so, in my opinion, and on the previous Wednesday I had seen him very ill, but able to go on crutches. He was also well known to the Independent minister and to the Methodist preacher, both of whom had ministered to his necessities, for he had been ill about three years. He had been sent to the county hospital, but dismissed because epilepsy was joined with other ailments. He had almost no power of digestion, and when moved by medicine suffered dreadful tortures, was swollen in stomach and bowels, and as if palsied in his limbs.

His wife was in the house when my companion and I arrived. To our question 'How is your husband to-day?' she answered, 'Quite well, your honour'. 'Where is he?' 'He is gone to the chapel to return thanks to God'. 'How did he go?' 'Walking on his two legs, God be praised'. 'Well', said I, 'let us go towards the chapel', which was a mile distant, 'and we shall see how the matter really is'. As we drew near the chapel we saw a party of men in advance of the crowd returning to the town, and amongst the foremost I recognised at a distance a white hat, once my own, which I had given to McGrorty, and whoever wore it now was certainly no cripple. On coming nearer, we saw it *was* McGrorty, walking as stoutly as any man in the parish. When I came up to him, I said, 'McGrorty, I am astonished'. 'No wonder, your honour, so am I all in wonderment too' and, opening his waistcoat he showed me his skin hanging like a loose bag about his body. 'Look', said he', I am quite swamp, and yesterday morning I was like a blown bladder'. The next day, I went to see him, and sat half an hour with him and his wife. They seemed both simple and decent people, full of thankfulness to God for the mercy, shown him; he was well in health, but not a man of strong frame, low in muscle from long wasting, his digestion well and all swelling gone. I drew him into conversation on many subjects, but could find no feeling to be in him but, thankfulness to his Lord. W. Foster afterwards accompanied me to see him, and examined him closely. He declared that he had prayed long that God would restore him so far that he might be able to 'travel', that is to walk, even though he should be only able to go and beg with his wife and children, that he had believed God could and would cure him by means of Father Mathew, but that he did not believe – nor had been taught – that Father Mathew had power to heal,

> but that if any one had faith in the Lord and believed he was able and willing, then Father Mathew's prayer would be heard, and a cure given through his means. 'How do you say you were healed?' 'Through faith in the Lord, and by the Lord's mercy'. 'Whom do you mean by the Lord?' (Taking off his hat): 'The Redeemer of the world'.
>
> My brother Edward and his wife came to us in the evening, and when I told them the story they seemed, especially Edward, very sceptical, and no wonder, as one not knowing the man can hardly think that others have not been deceived as to his state before. However, it occurred to me that some time ago McGrorty's wife had mentioned with gratitude, that she had one day met Edward and received two shillings to buy a flannel roller. I told Edward this, and he said, 'Why, that was McGrorty's wife of Trummon'. 'Yes, that is the man'. 'Why, I know the man well; he formerly worked much for me, and I think him an honest, simple man, quite unlikely to be made a tool of for any deception, and I know how hopelessly ill he has been for a long time'.
>
> Thus so many of the very best witnesses seem to have been prepared most wonderfully to testify that this man was a really miserable object in his bodily state up to the very time of his cure. What shall we say to these things? Lord, incline us to judge fairly and enable us to judge right. The Protestants in general are furious and blindly outrageous in denying the matter; one denying the cure, though the man is there walking and praising God; another denying the previous miserable state, though so clearly authenticated; another saying it is a work of the devil, though done in Jesus' name and the glory given to Him.

Hamilton added in a margin note that McGrorty became very ill in May 1842; he partly recovered two months later and then, was unfortunate enough to be involved in a freak accident in the Catholic church in Donegal town when the floor collapsed under the weight of the congregation. McGrorty was present at the time but, though he was not physically hurt:

> the fright brought back the fits, and they continued severe for some time. I went to him and told him I would cure him, and by the use of quite simple means, not at all calculated to cure him, he was restored, he attributing it more to the continuance of the former cure than to what he then took and he is now, after nine years, a strong healthy man. The last time I saw him he was carrying eight stones of potatoes home in a basket on his back, a distance of three miles at least, without the least difficulty.

Hamilton returned to this story some time later to add the following additional detail concerning McGrorty's plea to Father Mathew for help in June 1841:

> He [McGrorty] told me that he had heard that Father Mathew could cure ailing people, and when he knew of his coming he felt sure he would heal him. Accordingly, as soon as he [Father Mathew] arrived on Friday he went to him on his crutches and applied to him. Father Mathew told him he had no more power than any other man. 'But', said McGrory, 'you have healed many a one'. 'No, I only prayed God to do so, and often those for whom I prayed remained cripples or sick'. 'Well, can't you pray to God for me?' 'Surely, my, brother, I do and will pray for you'. 'But, Father, your Reverence, if you would pray over me before all the people I am sure God would hear you and cure me in a minute. Won't you grant me my request, and do what you can?' 'Yes, my poor man, I will; but mark me well, don't expect I can do anything for you, I can do no more for you than you for me'. 'Well, God bless your Reverence then; for I thought indeed till now that your Reverence could do it; but I see it all plainly now, it's God's power and goodness all entirely, and I'll come to-morrow and take the pledge and a medal, and then you will pray and I'll be cured in a minute, I will'. So he went, and having with difficulty dragged his feeble limbs and swelled panting body to the market-place on his crutches, he walked stoutly away after the transaction, carrying his crutches to the pump, and tied them there and went home cured.

The accident in Donegal Catholic church was to have another interesting outcome. Fr Eugene McCafferty, the Parish Priest, wrote as follows to John Hamilton:

> DEAR SIR, – On the part of religion, I beg leave to tender you my most grateful and sincere thanks for your very charitable and liberal donation of five pounds towards the repair of our new chapel. I am now fully convinced, by awful experience, of the necessity of having the flooring firmly and permanently supported. Your suggestions on this point are most excellent, and as you have kindly offered me the means of taking the necessary precautions against any further accidents, I will be particular in seeing them carried into immediate effect. Praying that the Lord may grant you happy and lengthened days here among a people to whom you are and always have been so useful, and reward you with a crown of never-ending glory hereafter, I have the honour to subscribe myself, most faithfully and sincerely yours,
>
> EUGENE MCCAFFERTY, P.P., Donegal.

In May 1842, on the second anniversary of his daughter's death in Germany, John Hamiton recalled that even yet it seemed 'like a dream to me and I have allowed myself to live this year in a sad, dreary state, doing less than I ever did in a year'. He added that his wife, 'with whom I have conversed on the subject feels exactly as I do'.

In December, 1844, Hamilton reviewed his three years since he had taken back complete control of his estate, during this period he had taken the opportunity to bring into his possession some 300 acres on the mainland adjacent to his house which had previously been let to tenants, writing that the means by which he had completed this were 'such as are honourable'. As he laid his plans, he was, he hoped, now giving his estate his personal attention:

> I know the best plan will have its faults . . . and I know a faultless plan would not be easily worked when such stuff is to be handled as an Irish tenantry; and I know that friends looking-on, who perhaps would not or could not mend my plan on the whole will be ready to point at its defects and prophesy failures; but a plan I must make and follow without any great digressions from its original sketch, or else I shall attain to nothing; therefore I propose, if God leave me as my stewardship here, to complete my plan and begin it with the year 1845. . . .

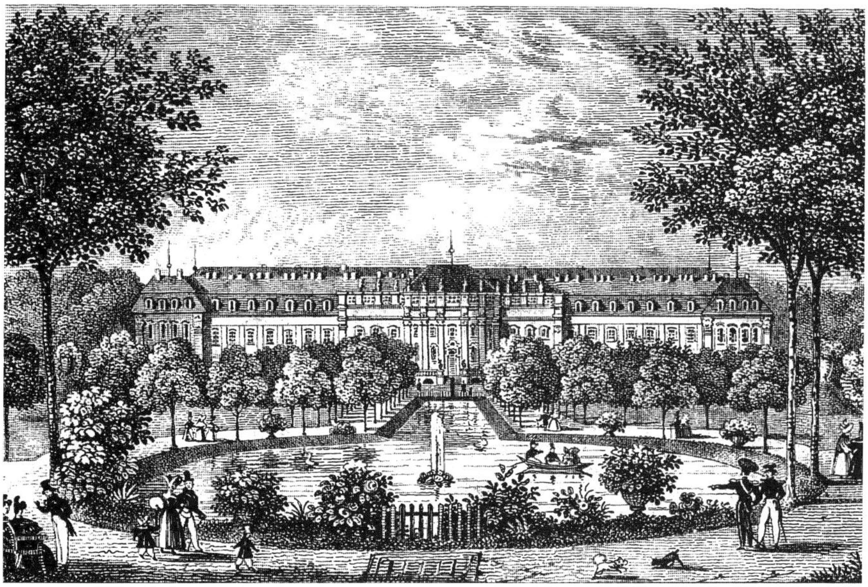

The Royal Palace at Heilbronn, near Stuttgart, one of a number of pictures which the then twelve year old 'Moll' Hamilton used to illustrate her own travel journal.

NINE

The 1845 Famine

By the summer of 1845, John Hamilton's efforts at improvement had met with substantial success. The area of arable land on the estate had been almost doubled, and the sanitary arrangements for the tenants had been improved under his direction with the result that fever had all but disappeared locally. Between 1830 and 1845 he had reorganised much of his estate, having 'squared' most of his tenant's irregular-shaped holdings, ensuring that they lay alongside roads where possible. The tenants drew lots for the re-arranged holdings, and rents were fixed by arbitrators. As part of all this, Hamilton had also built new houses for most of the tenants sited (as far as possible) in the centre of each holding, and mentioned in his journal that he had built or re-built one hundred tenants' houses in a single year. Sadly, there is very little detail available about all that he did during this hectic period, but one unsubstantiated reference claimed that he built over two thousand homes for his tenants during his first fifteen years at Brownhall. Under his guidance, 'industry and comfort were advancing rapidly', and he was able to stand back and view the cheering signs of success all around him. But not for long. Just when, at last, nearly everything seemed to be going well, a hitherto unknown disease struck the vital potato crop upon which the majority of the people depended for food, rendering it a stenching, decaying mass. His first reference to this began with the words:

> The year 1845 was ordered under providence to be one of a series of sore trials for Ireland. The potato crop upon which the mass of the people depended for food was smitten, and a season of fearful want followed.

TOUR OF THE MIDLANDS AND WEST

Donegal, Sligo and Mayo – the north west generally – was the last region in Ireland to be affected during the first year of the blight, and when John Hamilton set-out to travel on a short tour of parts of the midlands and the west of Ireland in the autumn of 1845, he had not yet seen any sign of potato disease. He recorded what he observed in a small pocket notebook which has only recently been discovered, along with Moll's travel journal, at Brownhall. As an 'improving' landlord, owning a very large proportion of extremely poor land, it would seem that the main purpose of his trip was to see for himself the methods being employed by other landlords coping with similar conditions, and his account is additionally interesting because of his several references to 'potato rot' at a time when the awful consequences of the newly arrived potato blight were not yet foreseen.

'Thursday, October 19th 1845: Left Ballinasloe, and passing through the fortifications of Shannon Bridge, arrived at the pretty little town of Birr in the evening. One of the prettiest and nicest I have seen in Ireland'. He continued next day through 'the picturesque town of Roscrea in the county of Tip. with its castle and round tower' to Mountrath, situated in what he described as well wooded and fertile country'. Saturday morning started 'intolerably wet', but in the afternoon he drove 'to Cardtown (W. S. Trenche)' but not finding him in, he went on to his farm at Buneigh, which he described as containing 'about 1800 acres of which about three hundred are at present reclaimed', and he detailed the method being used there to convert a 'moory' upland into productive land capable of producing about 2 ½ cwt potatoes to the acre. Having so much bog and mountain land on his own estate it is not surprising that a description of the reclamation work occupied three pages, with details about lime and Peruvian guano, taking note of Trenche's practice of draining *along* the contours. After growing potatoes on the reclaimed land for two years, the subsequent grazing land 'now will carry nearly seven sheep to the acre', and on the farm 'there are from 80 to 100 labourers in constant employment, and from 8 to 13 horses'.

John Hamilton then went to Esker, near Ballinasloe, where he visited the convent 'where Dr. Smithe is establishing a very large agricultural school, the model farm is to be on very poor, boggy and swampy ground – the friars very good, humorous lads'. At Ballinakill, near Loughrea, he visited another estate where reclamation work had begun in earnest and where the manager, Mr. Charles Lermont, explained his methods to Hamilton: 'He sticks entirely to the up and down drains', and recommended 'running clay by means of a wooden railway down upon the bog; this railway may be very portable'. Lermont also recommended diverting streams into newly made drains and so, by what would, to-day, be regarded as environmentally unfriendly means, 'one man cutting sods and letting the stream carry them away, can do more than six without the aid of the water'. Thinking of his own wild, and largely unproductive Fintown estate, he added: 'This would be very applicable below the roads towards the Finn'.

After several wet days, John Hamilton arrived in Galway where on Sunday he 'went to the church, an old cathedral, it is a fine old building with windows not matching'. In fact, because the Church of Ireland cathedral is in Tuam, the journal reference must have been to St. Nicholas Collegiate Church. John thought the houses in the town were very curious with 'old cut stone arched doors and windows, and arms over the doors, quite Spanish in all its features'. On Monday, he drove to Oughterard, staying in Flynn's Half Way House, and walked 15 miles 'to Kilkerrin' [Kilkieran] next day by bridle path, 'most of it no path at all'. Here he visited Mr Hazell the manager of the estate, which John described as:

> A very wild property to work on, more than half the surface being rock, every little field is fenced with great stone walls from 5 to 10 feet high to bury the stones – the ground between these granite rocks gives fine oats in many places. There is here a curious husk-less oat called Poor Man's oats, pretty commonly cultivated as it grows upon land where other oats will not do, and having no husk can be easily ground and makes a very good meal tho' not marketable.
>
> This property has the great advantage of the sea coming round the whole part that is cultivated, about five miles of coast, so they boat all their oats to Galway. There are no roads to it, but next Xmas, one will be open from Roundstone'.

Hazell told Hamilton that he could get lime delivered to his quay; and he used seaweed 'about 12 rowboats per Irish acre', and mentioned that 'there is a great supply of coral along the coast which is very fine manure'.

John arrived at Clifden after 'driving along the twelve pins, a pretty, wild drive, part of the way along a lake – the descent into Clifden is rather pretty, and if planted would be beautiful'. On Friday he went a further six miles to see the marble quarries run by Mr. Martin, who told him that he sent a good deal of the stone to Liverpool. Next day, Hamilton drove to another estate, which had been 'lately bought for £13,000, and now it brings the owner near nine hundred a year'.

> Graham does not farm at all himself but lets land to enterprising farmers in lots of from one to four hundred acres at long or perpetual leases. His small farmers are all five to six acre holders and paying about five pounds (well paid). There is a great deal of sea rack (seaweed) which causes some poor land to let very high; land I should not value at ten shillings he lets at a pound'.
>
> On Sunday we walked across to Renville [Renvyle], Mr. Blake's, a very bleak spot on the very shore. Trees take a long time getting to any size here, the house is built very low but contains a great number of rooms, and is all-weather slated on the outside and panelled inside, so that it is quite comfortable tho' so exposed. He is an exceedingly nice gentlemanly man and very hospitable.

He then visited Ballinahinch Castle, 'a very comfortable but very ugly house'.

The owner, Mr. Martin was, like so many landlords at this time, busy improving his property: 'draining deep bog, pretty extensive, all with four foot deep shore drains. . . '. In his first reference to the potato blight, during this tour, John added that:

> There seems to be a very great deal of rot thro' the potatoes in all this country, both in the ridge and in the pits; the only tolerable preventative in the pit seems to be dry mould.

Hamilton drove back through Clifden to Kylemore Lake and went by

> a very beautiful pass through the mountains of Connemara, about six miles long to Killeries [Killary Harbour], a long narrow bay about ten miles long and one broad, with high steepish mountains on each side coming right down into the water, along the foot of which the road runs, winding round the various projections into the bay. Altogether a more beautiful day's drive I can hardly imagine.

At Westport, he noted Lord Sligo's demesne close to town – 'but tho' a nice walk for the citizens, is no great thing in the way of beauty'. Here he wrote that 'the potato rot, as far as I could find out, is not in any great extent in this neighbourhood, and the people seem not inclined to give credence to the generality of the disease'. He continued in the direction of Castlebar, and thought that his back-ward glance towards Westport gave it:

> the idea of a foreign town in situations; in the background you have the fine mountain of Croagh Patrick rising to a very great height like a Sugarloaf. I think it decidedly the finest shaped mountain I ever saw. It is a great station for pilgrims who come here from all parts, like to Lough Derg [Lough Derg lay just outside the eastern limits of his Donegal estate].

Between Castlebar and Ballina, he thought Pontoon Bridge very beautiful with Nephin mountain reflected in Loch Conn, and he considered Ballina's shops 'capital'. John stayed there for a week-end, visiting Mr Jackson's estate 'three miles out of the town, a flat place with no features at all', where he inspected the newly-made drains and noted the method being used there of fertilising with guano, after which Jackson introduced a large stock of cattle on the land, which provided it with a very good quantity of manure:

> We saw here a great failure in the potatoes; when picked the heap of bad was as large as the good. Mr. H. feeds his cattle on the bad ones raw and steamed, but principally raw. On Thursday I went over Mr Jackson's

potatoes and found on the whole one fourth rotten. The experiment ran thus:

Potatoes	**Sound**	**Unsound**	**Doubtful.**
Cork reds	5	—	—
Old Apples	3	4	—
Red	4	—	—
Cups	9	2	1
Lumpers	6	—	2
Pink eyes	3	4	—
Total	30	10	3

He had hoped to do a further examination on a larger scale but he found this to be impossible because of 'the several days of tremendous rain from Wednesday till 7 a.m. on Friday I ever witnessed'.

Hamilton drove from there towards Tubbercurry through wild and desolate scenery to Glenesk Lodge, at Lough Talt, where he spoke to Mr Learmont, the steward there, 'who is an intelligent man, an old Scotch man from near Calrosie'.

> The estate of Glenesk contains about 3,500 acres for which £560 is paid, a high rent for high lying ground from 500 ft. upwards. So much so that seven years at work it does not pay the rent yet'.

He mentioned that 'the society both take land at too high a price and lay out too little capital improving it, or it might be better'. The 'society' referred to was, in fact, the Waste Land Improvement Company, which had purchased the property following the death of the previous owner, Mr Taaffe. Hamilton speculated that the land was 'very improvable' and thought that the new owners 'might make it work well'.

His description of this tour suddenly ends here, presumably because he then drove back to Donegal.

THE POTATO BLIGHT

With the approach of winter, it became increasingly clear that what Hamilton called the 'potato rot' was turning out to be very serious – much worse than anything experienced before. He had coped well with the 1831 famine and he now began to apply some of the lessons learned at that time. As it turned out, the situation during the first winter was not as bad as originally feared, mainly because the blight arrived comparatively late in the season so that much of the early crop was saved, but what was to follow over the next three or four years was, of course, to prove a great deal worse.

Hamilton concluded that for the people to depend upon the workhouse or on alms meant demoralisation, and his principle object, after the bare necessities were met by the soup kitchens and similar measures of temporary relief, was to employ people on land improvement works, by which they could earn wages benefit themselves and permanently benefit the district, It would appear to be almost impossible to exaggerate what John Hamilton did for more than two thousand desperately poor and vulnerable people around him. He had to curtail any plans for further estate improvements – apart from those likely to improve the lot of the tenants who, as the situation got worse, found it increasingly difficult to pay their rents. Little of what he wrote covered this aspect of his work, whether because he felt no need to record the details in his personal journals or because he was too busy in other matters. Almost all of what has survived of his writings at this time consists of lengthy correspondence with officialdom, including letters to the Lord Lieutenant and the Chief Secretary, arguing the case for altering the means by which the government was endeavouring to relieve the worst of the suffering. The impression thus given might be that most of his exertions at the time were confined to writing extremely long letters to extremely important people who were – in the main – extremely

John Hamilton's son James (1824-1915), who inherited the Brownhall property in 1884 when it was in a very perilous state. He married Dorothea Stewart of Horn Head, one of three marriages between the Hamiltons and the Stewarts which were closely connected with John Hamilton.

unimpressed by his arguments, but his practical good works were more important locally. When the 1845 Famine was over, Hamilton was to claim that virtually none of his tenants had become inmates of the local workhouse and only one had died from starvation. Starvation itself was the cause of relatively few famine deaths, less than 250 in the case of County Donegal. Most of the deaths resulted from famine-induced fevers and diseases – notably typhus and dysentery – but even so one can only speculate what might have been the situation nationally if officialdom had listened to him more carefully, and if all other landlords had acted as humanely.

The advent of the Famine meant that most of the landlords' income vanished, and as the magnitude of the potato failure became evident, and as its duration lengthened, it became obvious that even if willing, the landlords alone would be unable to meet the situation. When relief areas were initially set up, Drumholm was united with Rossnowlagh and the active local committee opened a relief fund to which Archdeacon Fenwick and Colonel Conolly contributed £400, and Hamilton £200 Much rested on the government and while the Prime Minister, Sir Robert Peel, acted at the outset with commendable alacrity, the sheer scale of the disaster was probably more than any government could have adequately dealt with at that time. It is easy to see that many of the decisions made were plainly wrong, or totally inadequate, or grossly bungled. It is even easier to make these points confidently with the benefit of hindsight, but the views of people who commented at the time seem more relevant, and few appear to have had as much to say as John Hamilton of St Ernan's:

> The Government took hurried means the next year to meet the famine, the potato disease rather increasing in virulence and nearly the whole crop lost. Immense sums were raised by a kind of road sessions for the employment of the people on roads, after soup and stirabout kitchens had been tried and had demoralised the population more than relieved the poor. For present means the Government advanced the money, charging it on districts – not on Estates – so that the landlord who employed or relieved all his population had to bear as much taxation as those who threw all their poor upon relief. . . .

He was to repeat the latter charge over and over again, but in the meantime, the terrible effects of the Famine all around him stirred John Hamilton into action and seemed to leave him with little time to sit down to record his actions at the time He never mentioned Indian corn in his journals, which seems strange in view of the fact that he had, near Coxtown, one of the two mills in the whole of the county capable of grinding it. A quarter of a century later, at the age 71, he wrote about these events from a more distant perspective:

> Terrible as the word 'famine' is, and treble-terrible to any one who has

> witnessed the progress and ghastly consequences of famine, still the famine of 1846 and following years did not fail to bring out some traits of character worthy of being remembered.
>
> This district is on the western coast – the side of Ireland which suffered most; but our people, nevertheless, did not suffer as much as those in some other parts. Still, it was terrible in Donegal. The Government was taken aback, and seemed not to know what to do. Apathy and spasmodic action alternated, and the result was that those landlords who did least came off best pecuniarily. A person having property in two parishes found fellow-landlords in one of them who united to meet the Government proposal that its contribution for the relief of the sufferers should be met by an equal sum. Several hundred pounds were raised and augmented by as much from the Government; so far, good.
>
> In the other parishes the proprietors refused to join him, and the destitution was altogether met by the Government alone. This, however, was only the first temporary measure of relief, and did not involve large outlay, merely stopping absolute starvation till plans could be formed to meet the emergency. Then road-making was resorted to, and loans which were not at the choice of the borrowers to take or decline. The roads were laid out by officials who paid little regard to the mischief they did by running the roads through the fields, or to the probable usefulness of the roads if finished, or to the prospect of their ever being completed, which very many never have been to this day. An instance is before me. An estate had lately been re-let to tenants, the farms laid out square and fenced. The omnipotent officials laid out a road diagonally through the lands, cutting both farms and fields into triangles and leaving the landlord no redress to his expostulations, no alternative but such as would deprive the destitute in that neighbourhood of the prospect of earning a living. The road begins in a field and ends in a field; there is no access to it at either end. By cuttings and fillings it makes a permanent hindrance to tillage, and abides to this day one of the many monuments to red tape in the Irish famine.

Hamilton embarked on his own relief works with the aid of money from the Board of Public Works, preferring what he called 'the straightforward road' not letting any of his own people to be a charge on public charity. He employed not only his own poor but those others from other nearby properties and argued that rather than expend huge sums on soup kitchens and roads, it would be far better to enable the starving people to grow more food for the next year. He criticised the authorities for sending officers 'to secure that there should be nothing done with [any money advanced] which would tend to increase the produce of the soil by any means'.

When the scope of the Land Drainage Act was extended to encourage landlords to give further employment, Hamilton applied for the sum of £1,800 which was to be repaid in instalments, but when a government inspector arrived, he recommended an outlay of £46,000. This was a staggering amount, but as the Act gave a reasonable time for repayment, allowing for the improvements to become remunerative, he agreed to go as far as £34,000 'with the understanding that I might stop at any lesser sum, and that I was to work for three years without any demand for repayment'. Matters were, however, to become greatly complicated as he was soon to find out.

BORROWING GOVERNMENT MONEY

When the Famine was over, John Hamilton wrote 14 pages of notes, hand-stitched into a home-made booklet, in which he explained why, by then, he was in a very serious financial situation. This had come about partly because he had borrowed government money under terms which were later altered, forcing him to borrow further elsewhere and also to sell stock and other goods at a time of great economic depression. Entitled, *My transactions in the Famine, '46, etc.,* he began by describing the government's initial reactions to the famine crisis, including the expedient of employing people 'on the roads'. Holding the view that it would have been better to help the poor to prepare their own land for the following year's food supply, Hamilton sent petitions to the Lord Lieutenant, to the government and to parliament, 'but in vain', and he described how he had to watch useless roads being built at great expense, much of it being spent on administrative costs.

> This was called a charity to the Irish from England, though the funds came out of the Imperial treasury, and though the repayment of instalments is now exacting . . . from the impoverished people whose last calf or pig is often seized and sold by the collector to repay the charity, the repayment being demanded while the distress still continues . . . . The Government did, however, listen to the application for advances of money to enable landed proprietors to employ their tenantry profitably . . . but delay and sufficiency of obtaining these advances was great.
>
> I early urged this plan on the government and took the earliest advantage of the privilege when made available. In October, 1846 I made application for a loan under the existing Acts for drainage and asked for 1800£ to be repaid in instalments according to the plan laid down in the existing Acts. In December I arranged for the loan, having had my Estates viewed by Mr E. Murphy, sent by the Board of Works, who recommended a loan of about £44,000, forty four thousand pounds, and gave it as his opinion that the outlay would repay 8 per cent at least, but on going to Dublin and consulting with the Commissioners, the loan

> was fixed at about £35,000, to be in three loans on three districts for drainage and restoration of land. Under the Act, I was to lay out a sum, say 100 or 200£ and then on the inspection and approval of an officer, the Board of Works was to pay me the sum laid out . . . . An Act of Parliament allowed advances from the Treasury for this purpose. I received official notice that the Lords of the Treasury approved of a fresh advance of 4,000£ on account of my works, and I began immediately.
>
> In order to be in a position to lay out a large sum with advantage, I saw it as necessary to get a considerable extent of land into my own hands. At the same time there was a great tendency in many of my best tenants to emigrate in a panic. I therefore desired to enable a number of the poorer tenants to emigrate – who could not occupy their land to any advantage and could hardly expect to support their families, much less to pay rent if they remained. To enable me to do this I raised about £4,000 to £5,000 – as well as a further sum to enable me to erect buildings, make [a] mill course, and cultivate the lands which I was to improve under the Board of Works.

John Hamilton saw an important advantage in that the first repayment on the loan was not due until October 1850 after which, over a period of 20 years or so, the principal and interest was to be paid off in instalments. Even so, the interval did not give a lot of time for the improvement works to make a return on their outlay, especially on items such as 'the many miles of stone fences, roads etc.', nor did it allow for any unexpected set-backs including (as it happened) the disastrous repetition of the potato failure for three more years. Nevertheless, he undertook all this work, as he expressed it, 'with energy' but soon found the need to borrow further. Before this could happen, the Board of Works had to be satisfied with the work already undertaken with the aid of government money:

> I therefore applied to have [the work] inspected . . . and approved from the Commissioners, but no further money was sent. I went on, and asked for another inspection of more finished work, again it was approved but no money sent.

Despite the fact that he was having great difficulty in getting the money from the Board of Works, he continued to embark on additional schemes which gave considerable employment while improving the land for himself and his tenants. This forced him to borrow elsewhere and:

> I was obliged to sell my milk cows, my farm produce – everything I could make money of at any price to go on with my works, for I was too deeply involved to be able to stop without much loss (though it would

have been well for me if I had done so).

Sometime later, he was informed by the Lords of the Treasury (to whom he had complained) that he would only get about one third of the sum he actually needed and that if he required any more than this from the Board of Works he would have to borrow 'under the new law'. This meant that instead of the £36,000 which he had requested, he would have to settle for £12,000 and, under a newly introduced new Act, the repayments on the sum would commence, not in 1850 but in 1848.

> I remonstrated but in vain. I had many engagements entered into, and could not stop. I contemplated the sale of part of my estate rather than submit to such decided injustice and loss, but I was unable to effect this, in a satisfactory manner.

He travelled to London to remonstrate with the Treasury, where he was told that he could, if he wished, take an action at law, stop all the works and (though this was not stated) let the people starve. He failed in his intention to persuade the officers there that he had a special case for increasing the amount of the original borrowings. The point he had made about being unable to sell part of the estate 'in a satisfactory manner' was a reference to the devalued state of land at this time and he had, additionally, incurred considerable expense in his efforts to 'extract my right from the government' which, to date, had involved seven journeys to Dublin and one to London, besides which he had also lost the sum of £500 on a cargo of provisions which he had imported for the local people. Over and above the financial implications, Hamilton was concerned about the lengthy absences from his home and family and, perhaps more importantly, from his estate – at a time when he had up to 1,000 men 'working on the schemes ... while my affairs were left to servants who were not always faithful nor always equal to the task without my supervision'.

He continued to correspond with the Commissioners of the Board of Works complaining about the difficulties he was experiencing in obtaining the money already due to him for work completed which made it difficult for him to 'continue in the same manner'. When at last, he received a reply stating that 'the Commissioners will pay monthly', he felt himself 'safe' and he immediately embarked on further improvement work, only to find that the delays continued as before.

> During all this, there never was once room for complaint against me – either that I asked for money before my work was inspected and approved, or that there was error on my part. There never was any such excuse attempted by the Board of Works, nor indeed any other excuse for the ruinous delays to which I was subjected.

John Hamilton may have overstated his case for being entirely blameless for his own difficulties. For example, a letter was sent to him by the Office of Public Works in July 1847 explaining that the reason for his application for an advance of £36,000 being reduced to £12,000 was because the Land Drainage Act specified that the latter sum was the maximum available 'unless under special instructions from the Treasury'. The same letter went on to make the point that in Hamilton's application for the advance, it appeared 'there are items included which are contrary to the arrangements made with the Drainage Office'. This was a reference to a claim 'for draining bog', and the letter reminded Hamilton that he had been 'informed in the Draining Office that the sum was sanctioned to the improvement of arable land, and not to include any deep bog'. The letter continued: 'There is also a certificate in Aghadory ... [for reclaiming about 16 acres] at £3.16.8 = £63.5.8. Now there is no such rate as £3.16.8 per acre as contained in Mr Murphy's [the inspector's] report'. The letter concluded: 'As soon as the above difficulties are removed, payment will be made'. Other correspondence at this time indicates that some delays were caused by Inspectors filing incorrect returns or sending them to the wrong addresses, and there were several instances where returns sent to Dublin could not be traced at the Office of Public Works. He estimated his losses sustained by the delays alone at £3,000 – this was over and above losses incurred around the same time for other reasons, included the 'forced sales' and additional borrowings. He commented:

> While my works have been most successful and the actual outlay on land very remunerating, the whole transaction has been ruinous – solely the result of the unjust dealings of the government, first in not keeping faith as to their payments to me, and secondly in compelling me by a *post facto* law to pay three years before the time I had engaged to pay, and then attempting the poor subterfuge that I had *voluntarily* come under the new law when I had no option but to do so, or give up all I had undertaken . . .
>
> I did not certainly expect myself to make a profit by these works, but I did expect that without serious diminution of my own income, I should by my exertion save many times, improve the condition of the tenantry, and have my heir double the income (or near it) which I enjoyed – and if I have failed in a material fashion of this expectation, it is because I put my trust too much in government and in the promises and engagements they made. And now looking back, I can not see that I acted wrong, though the result is most injurious to me and my family. I could not have suspected what I have experienced.

Thus ended John Hamilton's notes on some of his Famine experiences, written in 1850. There is a hint, in that last paragraph, that he may have written the details with a certain sense of guilt – perhaps desirous of putting on record for his descendants, especially for his son (then aged 26), his personal explanation of why Brownhall Estate emerged from the Famine years in a such a serious financial state. Part of the estate had been mortgaged in 1847, and further mortgages were necessary in 1850, in order to pay off debts, resulting in him, eventually, having to sell some of the land. His desire to explain matters seems to be confirmed by a footnote added in slightly shaky writing, in his old age:

> I find, many year later, that the loss to my son James is far greater than I had anticipated. The sum I raised to enable me to do many things for which the government loan was not available, such as [assisted] emigration, buildings, etc., were borrowed from various sources . . . . These I have been paying off as I found it possible, but they have, by interest yearly on all debt, kept me down and disabled me from clearing the debts which James involved himself with me, and this is what weighs heaviest upon my mind – for he never failed me in the days of famine nor hesitated to give up his security for the higher weal.

It does seem that this post-script confirms the likelihood that John Hamilton wanted to put on record his view that it was government policy or bungling, rather than fault on his own part, that had put Brownhall in jeopardy. It is a matter of some regret that his son James does not appear to have left any written comments of his own to indicate whether or not he shared his father's view, though John's grandson, as mentioned later, was openly candid in his criticisms of his grandfather.

CORRESPONDENCE WITH THE LORD LIEUTENANT

John Hamilton's frustration over the government loans caused him to write detailed letters of complaint to anyone whose influence might be brought to bear favourably upon his plight. He wrote at least three letters to Lord Clarendon, the Lord Lieutenant. His first was written in September, 1847, covering a number of topics including the sale of encumbered estates. The famine had already ruined some of the landlords and many more were to follow during the next few years, but what should be done with the collapsed estates continued to be a vexed problem. It is quite possible that Hamilton's detailed letter at this time, followed by an even longer one a year later, may have played a part in the enactment of the Encumbered Estates Act in 1849, the purpose of which was to side-step the many legal complications which unduly delayed the sale of bankrupt properties

His letter ranged over many of the problems facing landlords, especially those proprietors who were making some effort to help their people, and he conveyed his strong views on the system of levying Poor Rates which, he argued, simply discouraged landlords who were trying to improve both their estates and the conditions for their tenants. He took the opportunity, not for the last time, to re-state his view that the notion of lumping good and bad landlords together in 'unions' or 'divisions' was grossly unfair to the former.

With his letter, he enclosed a copy of a resolution passed by the Donegal Board of Guardians and cited the very different state of Arran (as compared with his own property) as proof of his argument that each estate should be dealt with separately:

> I state the fact that in the wretched Union of Glenties (Co. Donegal) is the island of Arran, now perhaps the most wretched portion of that Union. A capitalist has been negotiating about the purchase, believing that, wretched as it is, he could un-pauperise it, but he makes it a *sine qua non* that it shall be made free from the supporting of the destitution of other properties, thus marking the conviction of the capitalist that the separation of even a most diseased member of the body is the first step towards its recovery and, where the whole body is more or less thus diseased, the power to isolate any member from the neighbouring portion and giving a property its share of poverty to deal with, is necessary in order to its cure; and being rendered attainable, its cure is possible, and will be undertaken.
>
> In the same Union there is an electoral division, Fintown, belonging to one proprietor, [Hamilton himself] the valuation £425 a year, the population 1,123, the Poor Rate merely nominal because the proprietor exerts himself, while in other divisions it is overwhelming. The same proprietor has property in the Donegal Union, where he makes much greater exertion and employs many more people in proportion. Now the Donegal Union has considerably less population than the Glenties, and its valuation is about double that of Glenties. But this proprietor's land in Donegal Union in one instance has paid, since harvest last, a rate of 5s. in the pound, and is now subject to another of 3s. which will not bring it on to harvest 1848, because he is by law joined to other proprietors whose poor are utterly neglected.
>
> Further, his property being improved, is liable to be rated upon the improved value. Thus in a year (1847) in which he has not received half his rents, and in which he has expended several years' income (borrowed) in employing the poor on his own and the surrounding properties, he is obliged to pay fully 10s. in the pound valuation or 20s. in the pound received, to support the destitution caused by the neglect of others.
>
> The foregoing is my own case and, if there are few quite as striking, it is because few have worked against the tide as I have done. But were it not for the discouraging circumstances which I have laid before you,

> many would at once enter upon a system of improvement. Where the proprietor has a whole electoral division, even with the unfair and impolitic arrangement which allows or rather incites the throwing of paupers on the Union at large, he can with advantage to himself stem the torrent. But where he is joined with those who will not co-operate, he cannot attempt it but with fearful loss. No one has tried it more fairly than I have, and success could not be more complete both with regard to improvement of land and rescue of people – many besides my own – from destitution; but this one tyrant-hand seizes us all, proprietor and tenantry, and for the sin of energy and perseverance in doing good, hurls us into the abyss from which we sought to rescue ourselves and others. Is this to go on?

Stating that he was sure a recommendation from the Lord Lieutenant would have the maximum effect in changing the system, he asked him to believe that his submission came from one:

> who does not cry till he is hurt, and who does not make a noise till he has tried what can be done quietly, and who sees the immense advantage of attaining any desirable object rather by an appeal to the Government rather than to the people. And I may assert that never did a Government more easily attain the object of pleasing a large portion of the people by an act that can wrong no one . . . [than] by enabling improving proprietors to separate their properties as I have proposed.
>
> The effect upon national prosperity would be marked and rapid, and great would be the blessing upon the Government which opened such a door of improvement. Pardon my long letter, and believe me always, faithfully yours,
>
> JOHN HAMILTON

A second letter written a month later, in October, 1847, began: 'As Viceroy only, and not in any claim of acquaintance, I beg your attention'. This was an allusion to the fact that he and Arthur Villiers, now Lord Clarendon, had been fellow students at Cambridge. This approach was an appeal for support in his 'battle' with the Board of Works, and he enclosed a copy of a letter which he had just sent to the Board complaining that he had 'lost fully one thousand pounds directly and indirectly, by delays in payments' and that nothing could induce him 'to bear up against the disappointments from repeated breaches of agreement but the fact that, depending upon the money to be advanced, I have too deeply involved myself in land improvement to retract'. After quoting from his letter to the Board of Works, Hamilton added that : 'It may seem no such very materialistic thing to cause the loss of 1,000£ or delay of 1,500£ to a landed proprietor, but in these times *it is most serious*. I am working to the utmost of my steam, and the stoppages are quite intolerable '.

During 1848, John Hamilton published a 50-page pamphlet entitled '*Ireland's Recovery and Ireland's Health*', much of it covering (in even greater detail) the already stated points which he had been making over and over again in his letters to anyone whom he thought might be in a position to influence some change in the situation. He sent a copy of the pamphlet along with his next letter to Lord Clarendon who, in his reply, made it clear that he did not altogether agree with the views expressed in it, gently adding that he was not alone of that view:

> VICEREGAL LODGE, 9th May, 1848.
>
> DEAR HAMILTON, – I have read your book [*Ireland's Recovery*..] with the greatest interest, and I wish I could entirely concur in your views; but my fear is they might neither do the extent of good you anticipate to the landowners or the poor, as the latter might find themselves minus all means of subsistence on the absentee estates until the bankrupt owner was able to part with his property, or was compelled by law to make provision for the poor; and that the duty-fulfilling residents might find themselves called upon for a rate in aid, which would be all the more onerous because wholly unexpected. I wish you would send me two or three copies of your book, in order that I may collect opinions upon your views; and if you stay three or four days in Dublin I should beg of you to see Mr. Power, the Poor Law Commissioner, and Captain Larcom, after they have read the work. Do you know them? A very experienced man in the Poor Law administration called on me this morning, and I lent him my copy of the book, with a request to hear his opinion about it. I enclose his answer, as I am sure you will care more to know what is thought by those who differ from you than those who take your view of the subject. – Very truly yours,
>
> CLARENDON

In one of a series of letters circulated to his tenants during the famine, Hamilton began by stating that at such a serious time, it was only natural that they would look to him for advice. He suggested that they would need to be more watchful than ever, and advised that all the exertions of the government would be of no avail unless everyone helped themselves, and the advice of landlords would do no good if the tenants were not themselves industrious:

> Sometimes I am told as an excuse for doing nothing, that a man does mot know what to do, and cannot see what crops he is to prepare for in place of potatoes. Now my friends, this is an idle excuse. . . . There is plenty of

work wanting on your farms that will tell well for *whatever crop* is to go into the land – drain some of it. Dig some [land] up, and leave it in the best form to get the benefit of frost and weather. Mend your fences, that your winter crops, if you hereafter have any, may be safe. Level old useless fences, and above all, collect a great heap of manure – whatever crops you grow, this will be wanting . . .

I advise you, even if potatoes would grow as well as ever, never trust to one crop for food, as you did to them. Sow *turnips, parsnips, carrots, cabbages of different kinds, peas and beans* – all these are good to feed people, as well as pigs and cattle.

Wherever I see a real endeavour to prepare for a crop, I will, as far as I can, help any tenant who is really unable to buy seeds, so that his labour may be followed by its reward in a profitable crop – and I will, with God's help, be as I always have desired to be, your sincere friend,

JOHN HAMILTON

THE POSITION OF THE LANDLORDS

On 28 August 1847, the London *Morning Chronicle* posed the question: 'What is the use of the Irish landlords?' which prompted John Hamilton to write down his own thoughts on the subject. He wrote (typically, at very considerable length) giving his own view as an Irish landlord – a point of view perhaps only slightly better appreciated to-day than when the London journalist posed the question. Hamilton's considered response – even though his outlook was not shared by the majority of landlords at the time – may surprise those who continue to take the view either that all landlords, without exception, treated their tenants ruthlessly, or that the government acted in collusion with landlords against tenants. What follows here is his very detailed response, abbreviated here and there, to the London newspaper:

There exists a confusion in many minds as to the nature of a landlord's position in the community. . . . It would be of incalculable advantage to the class of landlords if they would look upon themselves, and cause the public to look upon them, as lords of acres only, and not lords of their fellow creatures. . . . The signal failure of some well-meaning landlords, who in Ireland have sought to benefit their tenantry, is enough to prove that something very radical prevents their success. . . .

All landowners, ship-owners, mill-owners, fund-owners, shop-owners, etc., all whose ownership is profitable to them through the custom of the mass of the people, and whose ownership is defended for them by the laws of the land, are bound to use their position for the general weal, and are liable to be called upon, in extraordinary emergencies, to contribute extraordinary means for the public good.

There is a very prevalent feeling, it does not merit the name of an opinion, that land is not rightly the subject of individual proprietorship, and the property in land is not as defensible in principle as property in corn, in cattle, in ships, in merchandise. Persons who from this feeling become enemies of the landlord class do not consider that land in itself is utterly without value, and that it only is in respect to its productions that land is worth anything. . . . Some venture an argument against the principle of property in land, apparently founded upon the very fact that land is only valuable on account of the possibility of obtaining valuable produce from it. The argument is that land owes its value to the produce, and the produce is obtained by the labour of the occupier; therefore he who occupies an acre causes it, by his bodily exertion to be of value, is the rightful owner of that acre. This argument is plainly that of a prejudiced opponent of a particular class; or else, the same argument would be applied to the ship, which is only valuable by the labour of the crew it produces a return. The shop, mill, log of timber, hide of leather, bale of cotton may be argued about in the same fashion. . . . Should the journeyman-tanner and the shoemaker be made owners of the hide of leather because by their work the value was produced from an otherwise valueless skin?

But to the question, 'what is the use of Irish landlords?' Why not ask what is the use of Irish merchants, Irish tanners? Why make Irish part of the question at all? What is the use of *any property owner*? The use of the owner as an owner, is the means for increasing for the general benefit the utility of the article of which the law permits his being the owner. The use then, of the landlord (landowner) is to be the means to increase the utility of the land for the benefit of the country. . . . The writer is no mere theorist as to the capacity of the Irish soil . . . to yield immense increase in return for increased outlay and labour. As a landlord on the west coast of Ireland he is a sufferer under the present calamities of the people. . . . Left without funds in consequence of the general insolvency of the tenantry under the present visitation, while the clergyman's tithe, the Poor Rates, the public burdens, the interest of money are demanded full payments. . . .

The result is a large quantity of land producing now such increased quantity of crop that there is no doubt of the success of the undertaking – a larger quantity of land prepared under superior advantages for next year's crop, and the population of my estate saved from the pauperism and degradation that surrounds them. None of them have been in the poor house and none of them need have been on the public works or soup kitchens, though a few of them did prefer the drone's fare and the

> lazy work upon the public roads; but these are exceptions and by no means numerous. The population of this property are now much improved in their moral position, they only desire to be enabled to live by their industry. . . .
>
> Land improvement to be efficiently executed and to pay well must as a rule be done on a large scale. The profits of a small undertaking are apt to be eaten up by the staff and machinery, which are relatively more expensive than in a large one. Good wages are both directly and indirectly among great means of facilitating land improvement . . . and in Ireland the effect ought to be most advantageous in gradually inducing the wretched holders of very small farms to become the comfortable earners of good wages...
>
> We have been taught, and it is to be hoped learned, very important lessons in this past year of misery and of attempts to relieve that misery. Among these lessons one of the chief is, that doing for people what they ought to be doing for themselves is mistaken benevolence. . . . Some well-intentioned persons cry: 'Make the landlords take care of their people'. The people do not belong to the landlords, God forbid they should. . . . *The real remedy is to alter and improve their social condition*. . . . It is by no means meant . . . still less conceded that Irish landowners are alone answerable for, or guilty of, the present state of the Irish people. . . . Irish landlords are not guiltless of the misery of the poorer Irish; but an ample share of the blame and of the shame is due to that class [the government] from whence has flown a stream of vicious legislation under which Ireland has deteriorated, while every other European country has been advancing.

Following a meeting of the Donegal Union Guardians in May, 1848, Hamilton wrote a letter to the editor of the *Saunders' News-Letter* in Dublin. In it, he repeated the point that those landowners who were willing to provide employment for their tenants were being discouraged from doing so when they realised that they had, additionally, to pay a full share of the rate for supporting paupers living on adjacent properties neglected by their owners. Also, if the employment so provided resulted in the landlord's property being improved – say to double its value – that landlord was then additionally 'punished' by being obliged to pay double rate for, as he put it, 'keeping paupers from other properties'. Referring to the recent meeting of the local Guardians, the letter pointed out that among the members, there were some who:

> possessing small properties in the same electoral divisions with large but neglected properties, declared that they would at once expend considerable sums in improving their land, were it not for the dread of the injustice and discouragement mentioned in the above resolution. They also de-

clared their willingness to support the full share of population, according to the plan in my *Ireland's Recovery* . . .

When the public mind is led to see the horrible evils which must follow the present unfair and impolitic system of laying the heaviest burdens on the most zealous improvers of the condition of the people, and applying this tax to perpetuate and increase a pauper caste, and when the obvious possibility, not to say, facility, of altering the law is generally seen, this will be changed; and the public mind is opening to the truth.

Your obedient servant,

JOHN HAMILTON

Four months later, in September, John Hamilton wrote to the Chairman and Guardians of the Donegal Union informing them that he was no longer prepared to bear the unfair financial burden being placed upon him by misguided official policies and red tape. After informing the Union that he was being forced to cease the operations 'which have employed so many of the poor of the Donegal, Lough Eske, Clagher, and Laghey divisions', he stated that he felt he was being forced to consider becoming an absentee proprietor:

I do not mean to insinuate that I alone have employed all the poor in these electoral divisions. Lord Arran and Mr. Brooke have also employed many, and are in a degree sufferers with me, though I hope not so severely. I merely call your attention to the effect which the cessation of my works will have.

I will not say how much it grieves me to be driven to this determination. I have the funds prepared, and plans laid down for doing as much the next season as in the last; but I have been so severely punished by the Poor Law and its executive while I have employed so many poor, that this last stroke finishes me. I cannot swim with such a burden as is imposed upon me, as an improving resident landlord. But if I am to be driven into absenteeism and to take refuge in England on what property I possess there, it shall only be to watch the opportunity of returning to my place and works as soon as the Legislature and the administrators of the law take off the fetters, which I am persuaded they will at length do; for, fatal as is the Effect, the Purpose cannot be to ruin those who exert themselves most for the country.

Long afterwards, Hamilton wrote a note across this page of his journal: 'The result of all this was that some hundreds of men were thrown our of work, and much misery and many deaths; but red tape prevailed'.

Hamilton also instanced one of the results of what he termed 'government red tape-ism':

All the destitute within a certain distance of a road, which was being made under Government officials, were appointed to work at it. The Ordnance map had not the mountain elevations then marked, which, I suppose, is the excuse for the clerk at his desk, who included in the list of persons, women as well as men, who were to work at this road, the inhabitants of valleys separated from it by mountain ranges. However, these poor people did put in an appearance at the required place, and those who lived nearer came and worked at it. At the end of the week they expected to be paid. But no pay-master appeared.

It was Saturday evening, and I happened to be in the little town of Donegal. I saw a crowd of hungry-looking mortals ankle-deep in the snow, surrounding the Government official, a young artillery officer, who was endeavouring to pacify them. They were the workers at this road, which was five or six miles off, and had come to him as the ostensible manager of the concern. He was in great trouble, deeply moved with pity. 'But', said he, 'What can I do? I must send up the accounts of all the roads to the office in Dublin. I have to make them up after I receive them from the various overseers, which will take time; and I shall receive orders to draw the money and pay the people probably by this day week'. A groan rose from the crowd. 'This day week ! We were destitute a week ago, we have struggled through the week working on starvation (and their faces showed it) and now we are to wait another week!' 'Oh! Oh! Good God, sir', said the officer, 'what can I do? It is really terrible'. After a moment's thought I said: 'I see a way through it. I will pay the men, and when the money comes you can just hand it to me'. 'God bless you, sir', replied he; and I verily think he was as thankful as any of the poor hungry souls before us. I managed to borrow from the shopkeepers in the town about forty pounds, and sent the poor fellows away contented, though many had ten weary miles through the snow to their homes. Three days after, I went to the officer who met me with a doleful face. 'I don't know', said he, 'how to look you in the face. I have got into a sad scrape myself, but I chiefly regret having drawn you into it too. I have orders not to pay you your advance, but to pay each labourer; and my application to have the pay sent down each week is refused, and I am reprimanded for the irregularity of our proceedings on Saturday. So you see the poor fellows can't – if they would desire me to – give it to you, nor can they hand it to you when they get it, for I shall not have it for them til Saturday and then another week is due'. Remonstration was in vain. The Government *never* repaid me. But I was repaid with that interest which is invaluable, of one who loves and respects his neighbours. They could not, as was plain, repay me at once; but these poor fellows appointed one of themselves who, each pay day, took an appointed proportion from each and handed it to me, so that all those who

> lived through the work repaid me in full. Some failed having died very soon after the occurrence related above, and a few fell off from the work and only paid part, but fully seven-eighths of the sum advanced was repaid me with every expression of gratitude.

Hamilton had some other interesting comments to make about the famine, including his assertion that deaths from starvation were uncommon. From his experiences in County Donegal, he thought that most of the fatalities were the result of 'long privation', and he instanced the following as an example:

> It was the effect of long privation in breaking down the constitution that was so fatal. One of the saddest cases of death direct from famine, was in the family of a small tenant not far from St. Ernan's. He had several children. They and his wife seemed to support the privation tolerably; but the father was failing fast, a hale middle-aged man, and one who would make every effort, submit to every hardship, rather than go upon the rates. He died. The doctor said nothing apparently ailed him that he should die, and it was known that his little store of potatoes was not quite exhausted. He and his family were seen making a scanty meal of them daily. The doctor made a post-mortem examination to discover his malady, and found that he was full of indigestible potato skins, of which he had been in the habit of making his meals, giving the insides to his children.

ARDNAMONA EXPLOSION

A few years before all this, at the end of 1846, Hamilton wrote a letter concerning one of his neighbours, George Wray, who lived at Ardnamona, beside Lough Eske. The nearby townland of Tawnawilly (spelt in a variety of ways, all derived from the Irish *Tamhnach a' Mhullaigh*), bordered the two men's properties, and Hamilton regarded many of the people living there as troublemakers, rent-defaulters, poteen makers and probably Ribbonmen to boot, and the fact that many of their number turned-up to help in the building of the causeway several decades earlier was the cause of some surprise to Hamilton at that time.

Situated near Barnsmore, much of the area consisted of poor, mountain land, and almost all of the people there were tenants of the Royal School, Raphoe, established in 1626 by Charles I with a grant of nearly 7,000 acres at Tawnawilly to provide the school with an income. In fact, the school was almost perpetually chronically short of money, especially after Waterloo when prices of agricultural produce plummeted and tenants – especially the poorest – were unable to pay rents which generally remained at pre-Napoleonic levels. Unable to pay its teachers, the school rents were further increased but, because most of the Tawnawilly holdings yielded little more than subsistence levels for the tenants, most of the rents simply fell further into arrears. The agent, James Anderson, had the unenviable job of trying to collect the rents which, not forthcoming, resulted first in the seizing of livestock, followed by harrowing scenes of evictions.

George Wray of Ardnamona had been a well-to-do landowner, but when he found his fortunes in decline he took-on the agency of the Raphoe School which Anderson had given-up in despair. Some accounts credit Wray with being a decent, mild-mannered person, kind to both his own tenants and workmen, a view shared by Hamilton, but if this was really the case it seems all the more surprising that he appeared to act so cruelly against the tenants, many of them by then ten or more years in arrears, who could not (or would not, as he and some others saw it) pay their rents. On Christmas Eve 1846. he tactlessly impounded cattle or served eviction notices on the defaulters.

Two nights later, on St. Stephen's Day, a home-made bomb which had been placed on a window-sill directly below Wray's bedroom exploded, resulting in some damage to the house but fortunately causing neither fatalities or injuries to any of the household. Inevitably, this led to the district being proscribed under the Coercion Act, and notices offering a reward for information about the perpetrators were posted around Tawnawilly. A number of men were arrested but, poor as the people were, nobody came forward to give the evidence which would have secured the reward. John Hamilton comes into this story because he was chairman at a meeting of the local magistrates held on New Year's Day, 1849, when a resolution was passed regretting 'the vile attempt' made to blow-up Ardnamona House. The meeting raised 'the sum of £300 to be added to the sum offered by the government for the conviction of the offenders'. £800 was additionally collected, of which £100 was contributed by Hamilton, presumably to assist Wray. Hamilton felt sufficiently strongly about the matter to write a letter to the Secretary of the Board of Education, expressing his concern for his neighbour:

> I possess property adjoining . . . and . . . have had opportunity of constantly observing Mr. Wray's conduct, and way of dealing with the tenantry. It has been judicious, considerate, kind and firm. I do not think so fit a person could have been appointed to rescue them and the property from the state into which they had been allowed to fall, and made that estate a plague-spot in the county.

The letter went on to state that Wray had given considerable employment in the area, and most of the tenants regarded him as a friend but:

> a few rascals who would rather idle about and make whiskey, according to the old habits of the place, have kept up a feeling against Mr. Wray and . . . his resolute determination to do his duty has exasperated some of

> these to that deed of horrible wickedness which, but for a kind providence, would have de- stroyed both him and his wife on Tuesday night.

Expressing the hope that the 'ruffians' would be detected, as otherwise 'all the good that Wray had done for Townawilly will be thrown away and it will become more unprofitable, more lawless than before', Hamilton signed the letter 'as the oldest resident proprietor in these parts'.

ABSENTEEISM

John Hamilton printed and distributed an open letter in 1847, setting out his views about the relationships between landlords and their tenants in some detail:

A letter from an Irish land owner,
by John Hamilton, A.M., Cantab., (St. Ernan's),
Deputy Lieutenant of County Donegal, 1847.

On the Extreme urgency of the present crisis, joined with the manifest opportunity afforded by the present transition state of the country, especially of the poorer classes, is the moving cause – and may be the excuse for – the writing and sending of this letter.

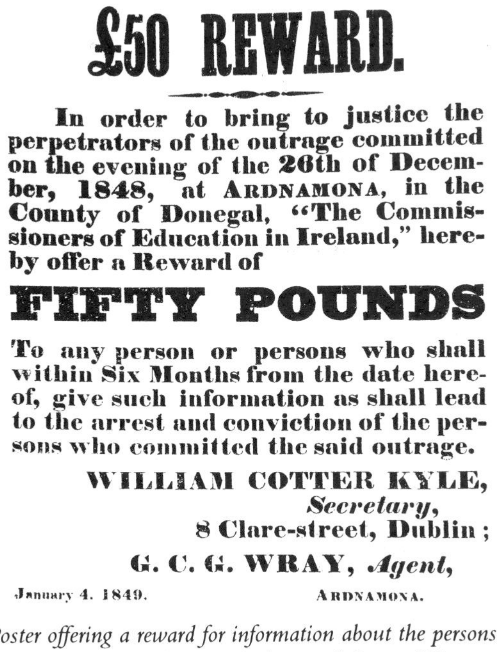

£50 REWARD.

In order to bring to justice the perpetrators of the outrage committed on the evening of the 26th of December, 1848, at ARDNAMONA, in the County of Donegal, "The Commissioners of Education in Ireland," hereby offer a Reward of

FIFTY POUNDS

To any person or persons who shall within Six Months from the date hereof, give such information as shall lead to the arrest and conviction of the persons who committed the said outrage.

WILLIAM COTTER KYLE,
Secretary,
8 Clare-street, Dublin ;
G. C. G. WRAY, *Agent,*

January 4. 1849. ARDNAMONA.

Poster offering a reward for information about the persons who attempted to blow up the house of George Wray, a neighbour of John Hamilton, at Lough Eske.

The letter opened with a statement of his view that 'the welfare of the stability of the Empire' was dependent on the state of the poor, pointing out that 'when the poor are irritated and hardened by extreme and habitual suffering and degraded and demoralised by the efforts of class pauperism that they, in mad ignorance, become opposers of government. The condition of the poor must depend to a great degree upon the rich'. Hamilton explained to his tenants his view that, if a landlord who took care of his tenants was to be forced to have those poor from the neighbouring neglected properties, especially the properties of absentee landlords, as he put it 'cast, upon him', this would be 'a direct punishment of the good and a direct premium to the bad'. The letter went on to emphasise this point at considerable length, adding that 'the only class who will benefit in the end by the unfair plan of taxing the larger districts all over equally, will be the absentee landlord . . . ' But he was careful to make the point that not *all* absentee landlords had failed to do their duty to their tenants, and some of the local *resident* landowners had 'totally neglected it' – a reminder that the actions, or in-actions of the landed proprietors at that time demonstrate that the landlord/tenant situation was a great deal more complex than is usually supposed today. In this respect it is worth noting that the majority of absentee landlords were, in fact, resident elsewhere in Ireland. Arthur Young, who toured Ireland in 1780, listed 195 absentee landlords even at that time long before the Famine, though he made the point that some absentees spent large sums on their Irish estates. While defending the reputation of those absentee proprietors who saw to it that everything reasonable be done for their tenants, Hamilton was in no doubt that the majority of them cared little about their tenants' welfare:

> One of the most crying evils, most evident and acknowledged causes of Ireland's diseased condition, is absenteeism, or the leaving of landed properties without a resident proprietor, or agent of the stamp fitted to fill a proprietor's place. This, while it is not removed, is a self-increasing evil for, those proprietors who are resident are often worn out in the anxious but very vain endeavour to do the work which should be borne by many.

The worst effects of the Famine were over by 1850 although one of the consequences, large-scale emigration, continued. No one knows for certain how many died and how many left the country but the best estimates seem to be, in round figures, one million dead, while up to a million and a half emigrated. These figures in total represented over one quarter of the population and, in proportionate terms if not in actual numbers, may well have been the single greatest human disaster suffered anywhere in the world during the nineteenth century. One can only speculate how different the position might have been if all landlords had acted like Hamilton and taken steps to provide advice and encouragement to their tenants. The Viceroy, Lord Clarendon, perhaps influenced by Hamilton's correspondence, suggested that the government should employ instructors for this purpose, but the idea was dismissed out of hand by the Chancellor of the Exchequer.

FAMINE RECOLLECTIONS

Hamilton wrote some interesting reflections on the those years, feeling that the awful event had drawn together 'all the educated and wealthier part of the people, parson, priest, landlord, merchant', adding that 'the individual knowledge of the priests among the poorer portion made their hearty aid doubly valuable'. On Christmas Day, 1850, he wrote the following letter of encouragement to his tenants:

> There are, I suppose, none of us so foolish as to expect to get through hard times without some trouble, a good deal of hard work and of pinching. I have lived among you and you all can judge if I have shrunk from trouble, hard work or pinching myself – had I done so I could not have given the employment or the assistance or carried out the works I have done; and I tell you that if you shrink, and do not work beyond what is usual, and bear up against loss and trouble, you will not do. And any help I could give would be of no use to a man who is not determined to help himself by God's blessing on his honest endeavours.
>
> I must say in your praise that there have been much industry and great exertions among you, I wish I could say it of every one of you, and very little complaining – indeed the greatest complainers are in general those who are the slowest workers. I have, as far as I could, set you an example, and employed many of you in improving land. You see many acres producing from five to ten pounds worth of corn or of hay which used not to produce much more than as many shillings worth. Some of you have tried such works yourselves and found the benefit.
>
> If any tenant, whether he has a lease or not, finds that with all due attention and industry his land does not produce enough to afford the rent now laid on it, let him come to me and say: 'Look over my farm, see the order I have it in, and how I take the most out of it, and judge if it is able to pay the present rent, for I find it too heavy'. I will not be so unreasonable as not to attend to him, but will give his case my best attention, and if I find he has done his best, I will do *my* best. But if I find that his farm cannot pay its rent because it is not worked as it should be, shall I be ready to lose my rent that he may occupy my land without industry?
>
> No, that would indeed be unreasonable. Let us understand one another, we each want the other – you want the use of my land, and I want you to pay me what is fair for it. Now it would be unreasonable on my part if I were to require of a tenant that he should pay me more rent than the land he holds could fairly afford when it is well worked and the most is made of it, and it would be unreasonable of me if I were to take advantage of an industrious tenant to exact the last penny his industry

> could enable him to pay for the land he holds. But it would be unreasonable of any *tenant* to expect me to bear all the burden of bad times, and to make him as well off as if we had good times, as we shall have, I trust in God, before long.

Hamilton recalled an incident which, he wrote, showed something of the character of what he called his poorer fellow-countrymen:

> After the famine was over, though we were still smarting from the wound, the Government sent some gentlemen round the country (I do not exactly remember what designation) to inquire into the state of the people. One of these officers came to me, and saying that my name had been mentioned in the report of the Board of Works, begged of me to allow him to make use of me in his investigation. Among other things he asked me, if among the many labourers he saw I still had at work, I could show him one, not living on my land, who had worked with me steadily through the three bad years 1846-47-48, and begged of me to let him speak to the man without my interfering at all.
>
> We went to my farm, and I pointed out such a man to him. He accosted him. The man rested on his spade, and returned his salute. 'How long have you been working here?' 'Pretty regular these three years, sir'. 'How much are your wages' 'Why, sir, you see we work by measure. Ten pence the day used to be the pay'. 'And is that what you can make now?' 'Oh no, sir, if we work as much as the leading squad, whose work sets the price of whatever is doing, we get eighteen pence. But I have a bit of land, and it suits me and the rest of us to work by measure, for we can come and go, as it is convenient, and need not leave our little industry at home behind. But I and my son work here pretty regular, and generally have twelve or fourteen shillings a week to take home with us'. 'Did you ever get any of the relief meal?' 'Is it the charity meal that they gave to them that were starving? No, sir, I thank God I never did'. 'Did any of your neighbours get any of that meal' 'Well, I suppose they did'. 'Why did they prefer that to coming to work?' 'I'm sure I don't know. It's nothing to me. They might have come if they had liked, for the work was open to all. May be they got more by the way they took'. 'How many of a family have you?' 'Nine of us all together'. 'Could you think of any neighbour who got the charity meal and who had about as many?' 'Just as many. I do know of such a one'. 'Now, do you know how much worth of meal his allowance was weekly for nine people?' 'To be sure I don't. What's it to me?' 'Well, I will tell you'. And taking out his pencil and pocket-book he calculated the quantity and price. 'Just one or two shillings worth more than you got by working. So which do you think was better off, you and yours or he and his?'

My man looked very indignant, and was silent for a minute, and then said: 'Aye, poor fellow, he might have more meal in his belly, but can he have the soul of a man left in him?' And he turned abruptly away to his work. The inquirer said to me: 'I would have gladly come all the way from London to hear that fine fellow's words. He has a sense of what he is saved from by the opportunity of earning his support, and by the manliness to choose the earned bread rather than the gratuitous. I dare say there are many others who would give nearly the same answers'. I assured him that that was my belief. Then I followed my man to speak to him. He accosted me gruffly. 'I wonder, sir, what made you bring that Englishman here to insult us, the way he talked about us taking the charity meal'. But when I explained the matter to him he said: 'Well, then, I'll forgive him; but he need not think too hardly of them that took it. There is many a one besides a poor labouring man that would be tempted, if he'd be offered more for idling than working. Only I thank God I did earn all I got, and with his blessing will do so'.

This is one of the very many instances in which the poor peasantry show a character that commands respect much more than it excites compassion. Unfortunately, the violent, hot-headed, misled, or broken-spirited pauperised beggarly portion of the population, being naturally in the position to attract most attention, have been taken as samples of the Irish peasantry. This has occasioned scant respect to be felt or shown towards the mass of the people; and it must be confessed that the want of respect shown even by benefactors who exhibit pity and benevolence enough, has tended to lower the respectability of the people.

If these reminiscences should lead some of their readers to believe in the existence of a high, noble, virtuous spirit in my poorer fellow-countrymen, and to respect them accordingly, I shall be thankful to have been able thus to discharge a little of the debt of obligation to those among whom I have lived so long, and whose kindly and neighbourly intercourse and behaviour not merely make me their friend but also make me proud to call them mine.

TEN

Post-Famine Years

With the Famine years now behind them, most of those who were left gradually improved their position, though many others continued to seek a better life in far distant lands. The population of Ireland in 1841 had reached over eight million and projections forecast that the figure would rise to above nine million by the next (1851) census. The Famine not only prevented this figure from being achieved but resulted in the actual figure shrinking initially to around six -and-a half million, with further declines following. So much has been written about the Great Famine in recent years that these details, and much else, must now be almost common knowledge. Perhaps the least-known aspect of the famine years relates to how the landlords themselves were affected, and without understanding the dilemmas facing *them,* it is impossible to comprehend why so many acted as they did. Most landlords were persuaded by agents that they had no option but to resort to evictions, and some did so with great reluctance. Large numbers of landlords – perhaps one quarter of the total number – went bankrupt, and when their estates were sold, the new proprietors, many of them Irish, were often more ruthless than their predecessors.

RETURN VISIT TO GERMANY

At the end of 1851, with conditions returning to something like normality, John Hamilton took his wife and their three surviving daughters to spend eight months in Germany, leaving John behind to look after the estate. Only a few sketchy details of this trip appear in the journals, but it is clear that the main purpose of the journey was to visit the grave where Isabella had been buried 15 years earlier. But apart from a brief description of their visit to the grave, some references to visiting two persons in London en route, and to a business transaction in Paris on the return journey, no other incident during this tour seems to have been recorded:

> *Carlsruhe, 20th May, 1852.* – My wife and I, with our three daughters, Mary, Arabella and Helen, are here on our pilgrimage to our dear Isabella's grave.

> I feel deeply the loss I have personally had in that dear child. I do not repine, but I feel it. There was a peculiar agreement and consent of our hearts and minds, we understood each other and felt together. And do we not so now? Oh that my mind and heart were more above with hers.
>
> God our Father, make our communion brighter. I have much blessing in my three remaining daughters, and if I cultivate it I may find as much agreement and fellowship. Lord, help me to do so.
>
> Our dear child's grave, where her body lies at the corner of the middle walks of the cemetery along with our faithful servant and dear sister in the Lord, Rebecca McClearn, is quite overgrown with weeds, among which a few flowers peep out. It was for several years nicely kept; but the graves of our kind friends Madame de Struve and Elise her daughter, who showed this token of love, are in the cemetery, and these, too, are overgrown and neglected.

The family had Isabella's grave put in order on the following day, planting it with evergreen periwinkle. They also tidied the grave of Madame de Struve, with whom they had become friendly during their earlier continental tour, but were unable to tend the grave of her daughter because it was 'so in the crowd that we could only have its grassy mound green as it is'. It was, he added, 'a sad pleasure, but a pleasure to do this'. Inevitably, many of the people whom John Hamilton had remembered from his previous visit were no longer to be found, adding to the general poignancy of the occasion. 'We have gone about our old haunts here, but it is very sad to do so, the old faces are nearly all gone. A Mr. Hase, who used to attend our Sunday Meetings, recognised and spoke to me, and expressed his thankful remembrance of former times'.

On the outward trip to Germany he briefly visited an old friend, the Rev. Frederick Denison Maurice, in London:

> When passing through London I visited Frederick Maurice in Queen's Square, going in the evening to make sure of find him, and met Fredericka Bremer at tea there, a nice little elderly lady just returned from a tour in America. Though I only saw her for an hour, it will give additional pleasure to the reading of any of her works.

In Paris, on his way home, Hamilton recorded without explanation that he had 'a painful business to do there, how it may succeed I know not'. Whatever it was about, it took only an hour to complete, leaving him some time to see something of the city's sights. He penned his thoughts on the attitude of the people there rather than on the city itself, which he virtually dismissed in a single sentence:

> A strange, fine city it is, with wondrous mixture of grand and mean, of

> elegance and indelicacy. A strange capital of a strange people. They seem to want an emperor already, after so much blood shed for freedom from despotism. Here and in Germany the mass of the people seem, at least, to have learned that in the putting down of the rule of kings and aristocracy there is not certainly more freedom attained, and still less, certainly, by the setting up of the rule of the lower class. What keeps down the revolutionary spirit on the continent is dread of the rise of the extreme democrats to power, and the consequent anarchy.
>
> The people are not yet fit to rule because they are not yet capable of willing obedience to any rule for the general benefit. Till they are so they cannot rule, and it is better till then that they be ruled even by despotism; and they feel it so, but do not see the remedy. I am in principle a more utter democrat than any I ever met with, but before the people can govern, they must be able to govern, the test of which is willingness to be governed for the general good; for the people who govern must govern something, and in this case that something is themselves. In England, reform, continually open and continually advancing, though with very imperfect principles or practice, still seems to prevent revolution by a much higher and better principle than that of mere fear of the evils of the democracy of a barbarous people.

Back in St. Ernan's, Hamilton found 'all thriving' on his estate:

> At home again. God give us a blessing here and make us a blessing. Have much to do to bring things into a trim condition. My wife is busy arranging house and household; my daughter Mary planning the getting up of her school of girls and little boys under the maligned National Board of Education. The alteration of the condition and spirits of the people is great since last year, all is now thriving, no one grumbling, but almost all saying they are doing well, and tenants ready to pay their rents

DUKE OF WELLINGTON'S FUNERAL

Little over a month after his return from the continent, John Hamilton had to interrupt his affairs in Donegal to attend the funeral, in St Paul's Cathedral, London, of his uncle, the Duke of Wellington, 'having been bidden as a relative'. Arthur Wellesley, the Irish-born Duke of Wellington (1769-1852), had a distinguished military career starting as a young ensign when he was made aide-de-camp at Dublin Castle. He became a major-general before he was 35 and in 1807 he was appointed Secretary of State for Ireland. His army career culminated at the Battle of Waterloo after which he turned to politics and was appointed Premier in 1847. Though he at first opposed Catholic Emancipation, he is credited with subsequently persuading both the Tories and King George IV to accept it. He had criticised several defects which he noted in the state of Ireland – the substitution by landlords of land for cash payments in exchange for labour; the malign effects of absenteeism; and the repeated sub-division of land which resulted in holdings becoming uneconomic.

Funeral of the late

Field Marshall The Duke of Wellington, K.G.

Admit John Hamilton, Esq.

to the Procession

Norfolk.

Earl Marshall.

Funeral of the late Duke of Wellington

CARRIAGE No. 67.

To be admitted to St. James's Park at the Horse Guards, and turn to the right towards the Admiralty. The Carriages will be formed in numerical order according to the number on the Card.

Those to precede and those to follow the funeral car will be formed in separate lines.

NORFOLK,
Earl Marshal.

Invitation and admission card to the funeral of the Duke of Wellington sent to John Hamilton. Wellington's wife and Hamilton's mother were Pakenham sisters.

Hamilton described the pomp and ceremony of the 'Iron Duke's' funeral in some detail:

> In company with William Foster [married to John's sister, Catherine] and Thomas Stewart [his first cousin], I made a prosperous voyage and journey, and we three went yesterday in a brougham to the Horse Guards to take our place in the funeral procession. It took us two hours to reach the rendezvous, and we were half an hour late, so great was the throng at that early hour. We arrived at 8.30 a.m., the head of the procession had started, but many greater 'guns' were also necessarily late. Our turn to start in the mourning coaches did not come till near 10 o'clock.
>
> I was in the sixty-seventh and last coach, having made up my mind late to come, and written to my cousin, the present duke, who kindly applied to the earl-marshal who put on another coach, sixty-six being the number and these all filled.
>
> We went in Court dress mourning, which not possessing we hired at Nathan's in Tichborne Street. This, however, was not our case alone, for I saw honourable names in abundance, Wellesleys and Pakenhams, in Nathan's order book. The weather had been fearfully wet for a week past, and at six o'clock yesterday morning it was still pouring rain in torrents, but, thank God, it cleared and was a fine day, though at night it poured again. I saw most of the procession set out, and at length the funeral car with its bronze wheels and the coffin high exalted on the top, drawn by twelve enormous black horses – then the forty last mourning coaches, in the last of which I was. We went through the Park to Apsley House [presented to Wellington by a grateful British people], the road lined with crowds. I observed that multitudes suddenly showed great emotion, and many persons burst into tears as we came up, though the car and coffin were a quarter of a mile in advance of us. At first I could not guess the reason, but looking behind I saw that next after our carriage came the duke's charger, led by his old groom, with the empty saddle and boots reversed. This sight made those feel who had resisted the sight of the car and coffin. All through the streets to St. Paul's the crowd was enormous, yet not one loud noise, not one unreasonable advance or push called for the interference of the police, all was orderly, still, solemn. The clubs and other buildings had ascending rows and benches prepared, and hung with black.
>
> When we passed large openings, as Cockspur Street, Trafalgar Square, etc., the sea of faces was wondrous, yet no jostling or pushing. From Temple Bar the streets were lined with troops, the duke's old regiment, the thirty-third, next to the cathedral.
>
> The arrangements inside St. Paul's were excellent. I feared the black hangings would hide the architecture, but all was admirably managed.

> There were 16,000 or 17,000 persons [?] in the cathedral. The service was not very impressively performed, and the music and singing paltry in so great a temple, still the committing the body to earth and the spirit to God of our 'dear brother' was very striking, the coffin sinking slowly into the dark pit while a 'dead march' toned through the lofty cupola, had all the effect of the highest scenic art and all the reality of fact, such greatness and glory at an end.
>
> The behaviour of all in the cathedral was excellent. Prince Albert stood close to where I was placed, and seemed in real earnest. The whole was over by about four o'clock, and the rain recommenced in the night. I met many friends and acquaintances at the funeral, and was kindly received by the present duke, whom I visited next day, as I am to leave town to-morrow.

Returning from London, Hamilton called to see his cousin, Mrs. Ruxton at Redhouse, near Ardee. Frazer's *Travellers' Handbook*, published seven years after this visit, includes the slightly curious entry: 'Ardee House, the seat of Mr. Ruxton, and Red House, the seat of Mrs. Ruxton, adjoins the town'. Presumably the references were to son and mother, respectively.

> On my way home am staying with my good friend and cousin, Mrs Ruxton, here. She is a wonderful old lady, eighty years of age, and active in body and mind. Harriet Fortescue lives with her, and is progressing good, seeing God in the plenitude of His loving kindness, and exerting herself for the spiritual and bodily weal of her fellow-creatures. She has by much exertion, and fighting through many difficulties and discouragements, established a shirt-making industry among the females around Ardee, by which many earn from two to five shillings a week, a great thing in poor families where the females were either useless consumers or obliged to do men's work in the fields, but chiefly the former.

Hamilton went on to state that Mrs Ruxton's factory had been supplying a hundred dozen shirts per week to an outlet in London but she had sold the business to that firm with certain conditions regarding the welfare of the workers, adding that this was 'a witness that she has succeeded in doing something for poor Ireland'. Also on his way home to Donegal, he called to Lord Clermont who lived at Ravensdale Park, half way between Dundalk and Newry. Hamilton was planning to establish a library in Castle Street, Donegal, the following year for the benefit of the people of the town, with over 500 volumes, and the purpose of this diversion was to collect from Clermont:

> a number of duplicate books and others for our intended library in Donegal in connection with our Literary Institute. This I succeeded in getting

> formed lately by subscription, beginning with a reading room for newspapers and periodicals. We have nearly twenty newspapers between daily, bi-weekly and weekly, and several magazines. The Donegal folk seem to appreciate it, and to feel themselves a step up the ladder of civilisation. I suppose it is the smallest town in the United Kingdom that supports such an establishment. I am proud of my neighbours, and proud of having stirred them up to it.

LOW AND MISERABLE LIFE

Hamilton was back in London at the end of the following year, when he took the opportunity to call again on the Rev. Frederick Denison Maurice whom he had first met in Germany on the family's first continental tour. Hamilton enjoyed discussing matters concerning theology with Maurice, and even though they often found themselves in disagreement, feeling that 'an hour with Frederick Maurice is always pleasant and profitable to me'. While he had mentioned his friend several times before, Hamilton left it until this occasion to explain the origin of their friendship:

> I became acquainted with Maurice in Germany many years ago (1840). His sister Priscilla was left by him and a party of friends at Neuwied on the Rhine, where I was residing, and my wife heard that a young lady was taken seriously ill at the house of one of the Moravians, of whom there is a congregation there. She found Priscilla Maurice dangerously ill, and ministered to her as a sister. When Maurice returned to Neuwied, Priscilla was much better, but not fit to travel: He could not prolong his stay, so she remained and returned to England with us, and afterwards visited us for a summer at St. Ernan's. Maurice's house in Queen's Square, and afterwards in Bedford Square, was my hotel when I frequently visited London alone, and many a night we sat with our feet on the fender after the house was at rest, enjoying a communion of mind and of spirit which was to me so pleasant and profitable. Then he was so easy to understand, which in his preaching and writing was not always the case. Priscilla continued our intimate friend till her death at St. Leonard's, where we happened to be at the time, and were much with her then. Maurice's sons were often with us in various places, notably once at Clifton, where I taught them to swim in the tepid bath.

It was during this visit to London that John Hamilton was, as he expressed it, 'led into some acquaintance with low and miserable life' in the metropolis. His description, expressed with a Victorian restraint, reads like one of the many morality tales popular in magazines and other publications at the time:

I questioned two decent-looking girls as to their way of life, their loitering manner leading me to suspect them, while their dress was not that of persons of improper life. The elder, about eighteen years old, told me they were sisters, their father and mother living in Westminster; the father getting good wages, but eating and drinking most of it, and furiously ill-treating his family, beating his wife, whom the daughter represented as a hard-working, broken-hearted woman. They used to have two rooms, there being six children, but by the forming of the new street, 'Victoria Street', through Westminster, lodgings had become so dear they now had but one room. Her father had, a few nights before, attacked her with a knife and hunted her out of the house, and she was afraid to return.

The occasion was: Her brother is employed in a colour factory, – he is fifteen – and he made and painted some little piece of furniture, his master having given him the paints. The father on coming home inquired about it, and accused his son of stealing the paint from his master, and on his denying it, beat him. His sister Anne told him next day to get a certificate from his master that he had given him the paint; this he did, and Anne laid it under the father's plate at supper. When he lifted up the plate and saw it he said: 'Ah, Miss Nanny, this is your saucy doing, but I'll do you now in earnest'. He got up, took a stick and came to her, but she sat still and said: 'No, father, you are not going to, I have done right, and you know it, and I won't be beaten'. He seemed cowed and sat down, but soon after having drunk a good deal, he snatched up a knife and rushed at her with an exclamation, and she ran out of the house, he chasing her along the street and swearing he would stick her.

She acknowledged that when driven out then, and before, she had taken to wicked courses, but seemed to desire really to escape from them, and assured me she prayed to God every day to make some way of escape for her.

She was employed in shirt-front making, which was a profitable business when work was plentiful; she then sometimes made three in a day at ten pence or a shilling each, but not often, and sometimes work was so slack she got only two in a week to do. I asked her how she came to be so plainly and poorly dressed, thinly and insufficiently. She said she had pawned some things to pay beforehand money for a lodging, as otherwise she would have to go into a house with regular prostitutes, which, she said, fallen as she was, she could not bear. I asked what she had pawned and she told me, but they were only such things as a shirt-maker would wear, and not such as a girl who wished to attract attention would have. I asked her, therefore, how she came not to have better-looking clothes as she confessed having received a good deal of money. 'Ah, sir, it is because I had to get good clothes for my sister'. 'Why so?' 'She is a pretty girl and bigger than me, for I am the eldest and was kept down in

> my growth to work and help mother with the little ones, and I lost my education too, for all the rest went to school, but I can't read; and you know, sir, if my sister saw me nice and smart and herself poorly clad, she might long to be fine, and might go and be as bad as I am, and it is bad enough to have one of us lost; so you see I had to give her things and not to get for myself, and she is now, thank God, out of father's way, for a kind woman that takes washing from a large hotel, and has a family of her own, employed her sometimes, and when she found how it was with us at home, she made her come and live with her daughters entirely and never go home'.
>
> I asked her how much she had pawned her things for, and she reckoned it up. I gave her enough to release them, and, on thinking how I might possibly put the poor girl in a position to leave her wretched way of life, it occurred to me to ask her if she knew of any clergyman who visited the poor in her district. She said: 'Oh, yes, Mr. X.; he goes a good deal and has schools'.

Due to leave London the next day, Hamilton went to the clergyman the young woman had named and he seemed glad to co-operate in order to 'rescue this poor girl;' but when told that Hamilton had given her some money, the Rev. Mr. X expressed surprise at Hamilton's misplaced trust, saying that she would already 'have drunk it with her fellows that associate with her', adding that he had '20,000 in my district and there are not 200 decent livers among the lot'.

Apparently somewhat hurt at the clergyman's reaction, Hamilton tried unsuccessfully to contact the young woman's parents and that evening he confided his experience with a friend who told him: 'God has not left His poor there quite without a helper, there is a Mr. Nash who has set up a kind of refuge for culprits, and endeavours, in a really Christian spirit and way, to save as many in that wretched neighbourhood as he can':

> I determined from what I heard to stay another day in town and seek him out, and, if possible, commit my poor acquaintance to his care. The next morning after breakfast I met Anne again in the street near where I had first seen her. I asked her if she had got the clothes from the pawnbroker. She said: 'Oh, sir, there is a mistake about that, you know we calculated how much it wanted, and we did not reckon it right'. 'What', said I, 'you did not get enough money?' 'Yes, sir, I got the clothes all out but I got just twice as much money as it took; indeed, sir, I did it by mistake and I hope you will forgive me, and here is the rest, and thank you, sir, I will never forget your kindness'. I took the money and gave it again to her, saying it would keep her from want and its temptation for a few days, till something might be done for her. She said she was just going to be paid for some work and would not be in want; however, I

Helen Hamilton (1830-1909), John's youngest child by his first marriage, photographed in Jersey in 1861. She married the Rev. Gustavus de Veer and corresponded regularly with her father from Paris during his latter years.

gave her the money, and went on to seek Mr. Nash, to whose care I committed her, and then went to see her mother at the wash-house. I found her a civil-spoken, broken-hearted creature. She corroborated all her daughter's story, and told me her daughter had come home at dinner-time and given her some money (the very same I had given her that morning) to get things necessary for herself and children, but she said: 'Sir, I wish the money may be well come by; she declared it is or I would not take it, but, sir, I am afraid, for it is hard for a poor girl to be right, driven as she is'. Hamilton concluded the story with the words:

In Mr. Nash's care I left her, and to her God and his God and my God I commend her and him, and also poor Mr. X. who has so strange an idea of God's glory.

MESMERISM AND HYPNOTISM

As far back as 1849, John Hamilton had been interested in mesmeric experiences and had come to the conclusion that 'in regard to the nervous system, and the medical effects of medicines, imagination, change of air and scene, and now of mesmerism, being all of the same nature, viz., that all are by the excitement of currents or vibrations in the nervous system . . . thus checking disease or actually producing healthy action'. Friedrick Anton Mesmer (1733-1815), a Swiss-born physician, had discovered that a powerful influence could be exerted by one person over another, a power which he called 'animal magnetism' but which is better-known today as hypnotism. Mesmer went on to claim that he could 'magnetise' various objects which in turn could produce, at a later time, the same effect. After discovering the technique for himself, and suffering from various complaints, Hamilton had not only been practising mesmerism – or hypnotism – on himself but discovered that he too could 'magnetise' objects:

> I have always been subject to inflammatory and relaxed sore throat, frequently recurring on every exposure to sharp wind, especially if followed by exposure to much warmth; also to inflammation of the nose and lips from like causes. I have within the last year had at least twenty such attacks, and in every case have succeeded in banishing the evil in a few hours by mesmerising, by passes, with the will and expectation to do so. The habit of my constitution almost always was to suffer for several days whenever these attacks had any beginning. Incipient cough I have in the same way stopped. I have allayed the pain of hurts from violence, and never failed to mitigate and soon remove attacks of rheumatism in wrists and ankles, the former of which I had often been plagued with. I am subject to lumbago or some similar pain in lower regions of back, extending to hips. Whenever I can succeed in fixing my will and resolve upon it I banish this pain. Last week I was much affected with it, and it was increased by a false step on rough ground. I was particularly annoyed at it and felt that I could concentrate my power to conquer it. I succeeded perfectly in half an hour; from much pain I was perfectly easy, had no return for several days, though I drove eighteen miles in a gig one day, and have kept it under – though it has threatened again, and I drove thirty-six miles in my gig yesterday.
>
> About eight weeks ago I was called to see the daughter of one of my tenants who was, they said, in dreadful suffering. I found her with wrists, ankles, and knees swollen from rheumatic fever, and screeching with agony, so that several friends left the house in tears unable to bear her cries; her face was highly flushed, tongue loaded, pulse 120, and she had had no sleep for more than ten minutes together for five days, and when she did sleep for a few minutes, her sister told me it was a very troubled sleep, and she always wakened crying out loudly. She was panting and sweating with agony, and alternately moaning and shrieking when I went to see her. I had never mesmerised any one regularly except myself, but I made up my mind at once. Neither she nor any of her people knew what I was doing. I said only: 'I will try what gently rubbing down her limbs will do'.
>
> She had also sore throat, pain in shoulders, oppression of heart, and was cutting a back tooth which caused great pain and inflammation in the jaw and swelled her face. She is a healthy girl of twenty-two years of age, used to all the work of a farmer's daughter. She continued to groan, writhe, and cry out for twenty minutes, then after a great cry she said: 'Ease is good', and in a moment she slept quite quietly. I made passes

> from her head to her feet, and she lost her flushed colour, her pulse sank and skin cooled. She wakened in ten minutes in some pain, but I put one hand on her head and the other over her knees, as she lay quite covered in bed, and though she groaned and cried I persevered, and in ten minutes she was again asleep and slept like a child on its mother's breast for an hour. I do not think her sleep rendered her insensible to feeling, though it was so deep that a clock striking loudly or conversation did not wake her. Her sleep was so natural looking that I left her sleeping, desiring that she should not be disturbed, and that if she wakened they should coax her to sleep again. This was about six o'clock p.m. She soon wakened when I was gone, but not in severe pain, and passed a tolerable night. I visited her, repeating the mesmerism every day at about the same hour for a fortnight, always putting her to sleep and always in the same quiet natural-looking sleep from which she wakened always quietly, and generally within half an hour of my going away, but usually dozed off again. The pains continued to recur, sometimes rather violently, but only once anything like the first time I saw her. She got up too soon, and threw herself back in the cure; til after a fortnight I left her able to sit up and fairly recovering, and on my return in ten days' time, though she had in the interval taken cold, she was going about the house complaining only of some stiffness and occasional twinges in the joints that had suffered most. She is now well and nearly strong again. Some months after she was married, and has continued well.

On one of his visits to Edinburgh, John Hamilton made the acquaintance of a Mrs Gregory, wife of a professor at the university there who studied and wrote about mesmerism and had translated some of Reichenbach's works on the forces and phenomena connected with vitality and will over matter and organisation. It perplexed him that while he had often relieved himself of pain by mesmerising, he was puzzled why he was sometimes successful and sometimes failed. During the following Summer he had several opportunities to apply his strange skill on other people. Hamilton travelled with his brother Edward who had been invalided, to Aix-la-Chapelle, staying there and in the nearby Belgian town of Spa, to 'take the cure'. During their two month stay, John wrote further on the subject of mesmerism:

> The first case concerned a Mr. Davison of Tulloch, who was the husband of his wife's half sister, whose health was 'quite broken down with sickness, hardly able to walk leaning on a friend; he was so Herculean a man when we saw him here in 1852'.

Hamilton travelled from Aix to Spa and found that the doctors there had been unable to diagnose his relation's illness except that it appeared to have been caused by, or was a consequence of 'a general ulceration of the bowels and stomach'. Whatever the cause, the result was that the unfortunate man suffered from terrible spasms and pain which had been for so long treated with opiates that they had almost ceased to have any effect, and the only thing which now gave him any ease was chloroform. John Hamilton decided to see if he could apply mesmerism with any beneficial effect:

> He, poor fellow, jumped at the idea and I tried it at once. In fifteen minutes he slept quietly, his face assumed a happy look in place of the haggard, anxious expression it had before, his hands, which were like those of a corpse, got colour, and when in about an hour he awoke, he said he felt as he had not felt for months, but remarked: 'I am quite frightened, it is so pleasant, too pleasant to be so free from pain and tremor'. The doctor came and he told him what had occurred. The doctor laughed at him, but Davidson held his hand toward the candle and said: 'You know how that hand shook during the weeks you have seen me, see how steady it is now'. Still it was 'stiff', and being invited to stay and see me mesmerise him tonight at ten o'clock, he said: 'If I saw it a hundred times I would not believe it, for it is impossible'. However at ten I mesmerised him. He had told me that his bowels always required medicine, and that the bladder and kidneys were all astray, as gravel and thickness of the discharge proved, besides great pain and uneasiness accompanying it. He now sleeps calm and quiet while I watch by him; God give His blessing to the means I am led to use, and make me useful to him.
>
> *Aix, 12th July.* – Davidson wakened about one o'clock, and in a half-asleep state got up and relieved himself by copious discharges. This occurred twice, the second time he wakened fully, told me he felt so well and comfortable, and free from all pain, but very sleepy. He fell asleep immediately, at half-past two, and I left him at three o'clock. At eight I returned to his room, and found that at half-past six he had called for his breakfast from a feeling of hunger, and eaten a good breakfast and an egg. He had had no appetite for months. He got up about nine o'clock. and soon after ordered a carriage in which he drove himself about all day, every one observing how totally he was changed. He promised to let me know how he gets on.
>
> *Aix, 24th July.* – I have been at Spa again, went on Wednesday, found Davidson much better, though very imprudent, dining sometimes at *table d'hote*, etc. He has had no return of uneasiness or illness, the functions are regular, and his whole state much improved, but he had been attacked on Tuesday with a painful swelling of the knee, like gout. The

doctor said he thought it was so, and bandaged it up tight, which threw him into a fever of torture as the knee went on swelling and tightening the bandage. I removed the bandage, and at night in the presence of his wife and mother-in-law mesmerised him. He was in great pain and could not move without some one to handle and turn his leg, and though done with the greatest care, it made him roar out. However in fifteen minutes he slept. His wife said he was not asleep for he did not snore, but I find, in general, those whom I mesmerise do not snore, though they sleep a natural sleep. He slept all night, turning himself without wakening, though he often groaned when he did so. I sat by him till about two o'clock, and got up whenever I heard him and mesmerised him, which always made him quiet again. In the morning his pulse was down and the pain so much better that he got up and drove me all about. Mrs. Davidson told me that his disease came on with paroxysms, and that now, three weeks after the last bad attack, was the time to expect it. He told me it came on with anxiety, pain in the stomach, loathing, and violent green vomiting, followed by such spasms for several days that he often wished for death to release him, and each attack left him weaker than before. I therefore determined to stay a couple of days. On Thursday evening Davidson looked anxious and nervous, and told me afterwards he felt all the premonitory sensations of his attack. On Thursday night he slept well under mesmerising, and on Friday was rather low and drove out but little. On Friday night I mesmerised both for sleep and for relief of the internal ailment, and in the night all the peccant [source of the trouble] matter, as the doctors call it, was discharged, and he wakened every way relieved, knee easier, appetite good, anxiety of feeling and of face gone, and he drove me four leagues to Verviers. I had a good deal of opportunity of conversation with him as I lay in bed resting in the mornings, and he was eating his breakfast. I hope and trust these conversations will be of use to us both.

Aix, 30th July, 1854. – I have had peculiarly great joy in recollections of home and thoughts of those I am separated from, since I came here At all events, it is a bright spot in one's life to be able to be of comfort to a brother and sister like Edward and his wife as I am enabled to be here, for I do not think they would do at all alone, there would be no chance of benefit to Edward from the waters of Aix, for he wants some one to cheer and encourage him, and sometimes to force him a little. Besides, God has given me the great blessing of using me for Davidson's good and even more.

John Hamilton returned to the health resort of Spa from Aix three weeks later to visit Davidson, who, though greatly recovered, continued to be unwell:

> *Spa, 22nd August*: He wrote lately to me, he who a month ago could not write a word without great exertion, and then hardly legibly, wrote three sheets of note-paper full, in as steady a hand as I ever read. He had told me of his still being not altogether as he should be in his bowels and circulation, his feet often swelling. I had sent him a mesmerised sheet of paper which he placed on his breast going to bed, and slept delightfully, although suffering from a severe attack of bowel complaint, with great uneasiness which quite destroyed his rest the night before, and threatened to do the same again. To test the mesmerism, he tried in the forenoon the effect of the paper after a good night's rest. It put him to sleep immediately and for some time. The next night also, and he slept some hours longer than he had been accustomed to do since I had first mesmerised him. The other distressing symptoms also ceased Davidson said he would come to Aix on Saturday, but as he did not do so, I came this way to see him, fearing he might be ill. I find he has gone to Tavigny, his chateau in the Ardennes, and intends to return here to-morrow, and on Friday last had batted at a cricket match, dined with the cricket party and gone to a ball ! Well as he is, for a man whose life a short time ago was not worth four days' purchase, this was indeed overdoing it; however, he does not seem to have suffered.

Soon after Hamilton's earlier visit to Aix, a Countess Bernstorff who was staying in the neighbourhood with her daughter and grand-daughter, heard about his mesmerising and asked him to call upon her. She told him that some years earlier one of her daughters has been cured of 'a long and hopeless illness' by mesmerism, and begged Hamilton to try this method on her thirty-eight year old companion who was very ill and whom the doctors has failed to cure:

> I found her with fearful headache, pains in back and limbs, cold feet, and unable to take even liquids without throwing up, though she was parched with thirst, pulse hard 120 to 130 degrees.
>
> In half an hour she slept quietly and wakened soon with warm feet and still aching head, but a second operation sent her to sleep, and she wakened quite free from pain and, in general comparative ease. This was on Tuesday last at five; at five o'clock on Wednesday, Thursday, Friday and Saturday I visited her; she has had no headache or pains since, warm feet, desire for food, and generally a stomach to take it, sleeps well every night.
>
> She always slept well under my mesmerising, except yesterday, I have not seen her since, but I think she was affected by the mesmerising though she did not sleep. In this family I have made pleasant acquaintances, and though they go away soon, I have already enjoyed some pleasant hours with them, and I look upon them as friends sent by God to open to me

> a door of some usefulness to a fellow creature. The Countess Bernstorff goes to Paris, where her daughter is, then for the winter, generally, to Nice, the others go home to Hanover.
>
> Aix. 5th August. I have received a letter from Mrs Bruce at Spa, Davidson's cousin, saying they only fear what of his over-exerting his rapidly returning strength. My other patient is gone to Paris with her mistress, still better than when I left her. How much have I to thank God for in thus using me to relieve others!

Many years afterwards, John Hamilton's grandson, living at Brownhall, related that when he was about five or six, his mother's jaw was so badly swollen that she was 'practically lockjaw'. The doctor was sent for and leeches were applied but all to no avail. She got so bad that her husband decided as a last resort to try John Hamilton's hypnotic powers and a land steward was sent on horseback to St. Ernan's with some wrapped up handkerchiefs without being told what was in the parcel:

> He gave it to my grandfather who put the handkerchiefs in his pocket or somewhere about him, carried them for about an hour or so, packed them up and David (the steward) brought them home. That night my mother could not think why my father and uncle were so very particular about the putting on of her poultices, but that night she . . . woke up my father and said: 'Oh, Jimmy, Jimmy, I can get my finger in my mouth'. She was so much better next day she was able to come down and sit in the drawing room. My mother soon got well, but I think it was some time before she was told the story.

John Hamilton's house at St Ernan's, enlarged several times during his lifetime, is now a hotel, surrounded by many of the trees which he planted.

ELEVEN

Journal Closes

At the end of November 1855, back once more at St. Ernan's, Mary Hamilton became ill. In a journal entry dated 19th December. John Hamilton wrote:

For my future reminding, and for the advantage of my dear children if I am taken away from them, I make these few memoranda about my dear Mary, their blessed mother.

On the 11th of this month (Monday) my dear wife was removed from the sight of our eyes. She had been unwell for three weeks; at one time so suffering as to cause me much anxiety. I wrote fully to Dr. Cusack who knew her case, and he did not anticipate any danger, or recommend any active treatment, in which I am sure he was right. No man could have foreseen her danger, or, if foreseen, could it have been prevented. An old confirmed disease of the veins, chiefly of the legs, had extended itself towards the heart, and at half-past seven on Monday morning the power of that heart to act ceased.

Sunday the 10th we had passed together. I had a cough and stayed with her while our daughters went to church. We walked in the garden and had sweet communion together. I carried her up the hills and upstairs, but she said: 'To-morrow you will not have to do this, I feel so much better'.

We read the [scripture] lessons for the day; she read (as I had a cough) with our maid, Catherine, who stayed at home, and we felt happy fellowship with our fellow-worshippers elsewhere. Her appetite and spirits were all day very good. In the evening, as our custom was, we came together at the Lord's Supper, and with our dear daughters ate of that bread and drank of that cup in remembrance of Him who loved us and gave Himself for us. Our prayer at this time was especially for increase of that communion with Him, and with each other, which neither separation nor bodily death can mar. The Sunday – the last we were to see together in the body – was altogether a blessed day. I hardly can allow myself to say how blessed. But not that day only, the last few months had been most peculiarly blessed.

I had felt as if I now only had begun to love her, so much was my love beyond what it ever had been, not indeed greater attachment, but far greater oneness, far greater mutual endeavour to bear and forbear and, I am sure, from her side . . . I anticipated an old age together of far more love than the warm sweet love of our youth. But there is no old age for us, she has left the body which could grow old, – but we have waited on Thee, O Lord, shall we not renew our strength? Shall not our youth be renewed?

Yes, the night is far spent. I have passed my fifty-fourth birthday, and the time since, when in my twenty-third year I wooed and won her, seems to me but a few days for the love I had to her.

Mary Simson (1825-1906), who married John Hamilton three years after the death of his first wife, bearing him two further children, John Pakenham Hamilton and Katherine.

Mary Hamilton, who left £3,614 to be divided between her three surviving daughters, does not appear to have enjoyed robust good health throughout most of her life, and apart from her final illness, she was seriously unwell for a very considerable period after the birth of their last child. The journal mentions her being ill at various other times, beginning almost as soon as the young couple first moved into Brownhall. Her death must have been a considerable set back to him, causing him, after 27 years, to cease keeping his journal which ended with a very long reflection upon his 34 year marriage, of which the following is just one paragraph:

A month ago, one little month, my Mary was here in the body, convalescent, gay, busy. About this hour I knelt beside her in her bed, and we prayed together our last prayer of united voice. She desired to be called before sunrise, for she had much to do. As the maid came to the door to call her, I was springing out of bed alarmed at her manner of breathing. A light was brought in which showed me her dying features, dying the body was, but in God's kind mercy without a pang. How every hour of our long married life passed like a vision before me as I held her in my arms and she breathed her last. And that vision remains living before me with all its blessing and all its reproach. May it never fade. May every blessing be seen in its full brightness, and every cause of reproach be seen in its full blackness, that God may be thanked, and I may be ashamed, humbled, but not in despair.

Over the previous year or two, the entries in John Hamilton's journals had become less detailed and more infrequent. Their brevity was often matched by their frustrating vagueness and lack of explanation, as the following example demonstrates:

> Came to London to try to forward my business in putting the funded money kept on our land. . . . Found I was much needed at the solicitors. Every day at Tothams, law terribly slow. In all this legal delay I am much tried. . . .

While it is a matter of regret for posterity that John ceased writing in his journals at this point, he did at least continue to write elsewhere, often at great length, on topics close to his own heart – especially concerning matters which related to his position as a landlord. He wrote numerous letters and a number of pamphlets on such topics as the Poor Laws, Tenant Right, the various Land Acts, and about agrarian movements such as the Fenians, and he wrote regular open letters about these and other matters to his tenants. He also continued to express his views on religious topics, some of which found outlets through various tracts which he published, and he expressed his opinions on wider religious issues such as Catholic Emancipation, and Disestablishment. From these sources, and from surviving letters to his family, it is possible to paint a picture of the remaining decades of his long life, albeit in less detail.

SECOND MARRIAGE

Within three years of the death of his wife, John Hamilton had married again. Coincidentally, both women came from the east coast of Scotland, and both were called Mary. During the period after Hamilton succeeded to the Brownhall estate, many of the old native cattle breeds were being ousted by imported pedigree animals, and John became interested in Shorthorns, then widely regarded as the premier breed, for which he won many awards from the 1840s onwards. It is quite possible that this interest led him to visit George Simson to purchase stock from the prize Simson Shorthorn herd in Fifeshire, established around 1790. Whatever way it happened, John Hamilton met Col. George and Mrs Mary Ann Simson's eldest daughter, Mary, at their home, Pitcorthie House, not far from St Andrews. They were married on 29 April, 1858 in the local parish church a few miles away at Carnbee, and it may be presumed that Mary's younger sister, Frances, was a bridesmaid. Mary was 30 at the time, so it seems that there was an age-gap of about 27 years between the newly married couple.

When John took Mary back to St. Ernan's, she brought with her a ready-made family of four orphaned Simson children who had been in her care: a nephew, Frank, and three nieces Marjorie, Mary, and 'Tiny'. Three years later, a son, John Pakenham Hamilton was born, followed by a daughter, Katherine, four years after that, and all six were reared together under a governess who, it is still recalled, was very good with the children, encouraging them to make the most of their various talents. As already noted, John Hamilton was quite an accomplished artist, a talent which was also evident in the Simson family, and two of the children of this extended second family became competent artists. Firstly, the daughter, known in the family as Kitty, who went to the Slade College of Art where she met Augustus John, the eminent British painter and Royal Academician, and the two remained lifelong friends, and secondly, the nephew in Mary's care, Frank, became a good painter too, later becoming a member of the Scottish Royal Academy.

Having given-up keeping his journal, very little information about John Hamilton's family life seems to have survived. During the next ten years he published a number of books, the first of which appeared in 1865 – a novel about three Fenian brothers. In 1867 he completed a three volume novel, *Philo – a Romance of Life in the First Century,* which described a man's search for goodness, which led him to be attracted by some aspects of Christianity and to repudiate others. This work, as well as one that followed, reflected some of Hamilton's personal views on religion. Two year's after that, he wrote *Arthur's Seat, or a Church of the Banned*, in which he told the story of an Anglican, a Roman Catholic and a Presbyterian passing through 'unrest in mind' before finding 'in a broader church the place that they had in vain sought in other ways'.

Carnbee Church, about 10 miles south-west of St. Andrews, was the parish church of the Simson family, where John Hamilton married Mary Simson in 1858.

His estate, his writing and his new adopted family and, in due course, the arrival of two babies, must have kept him busy, though it appears that his first written reference to the estate following his re-marriage did not come until the Spring of 1871:

> I have got my farming operations into good train so that I think that all will go on well under [Samuel] Fyffe's direction [he had appointed an agent once more]. My joint stock plan failed. If I had begun it thirty years ago it would probably have answered, but it would require some years of great personal and constant activity to bring me to see and feel the benefits. I am

> too old [he was then 70]to attempt it, and am more and more led to the opinion that good of this sort *arises* from the lower class requiring it, rather than from the upper *graciously* granting it My sheep and cattle have thriven well, my crops have been good.

THE FENIANS

As the after effects of the famine continued to recede, agrarian unrest began to take shape once more and the newly emerging Fenian Brotherhood prompted John Hamilton to print and circulate an open letter to his tenants and the people of the neighbourhood. He was concerned that Fenian agitation would culminate in an armed rebellion and his message was an exhortation to the tenants and others in the area to remain 'loyal, well disposed and honest', and warned that participation in Fenian activities would probably bring those involved loss rather than gain.

The Fenian movement in America gave considerable backing to its offshoot in Ireland but the latter was be-devilled by informers. James Stephens, its leader, was betrayed and put in jail, from which he made a remarkable escape. Urged to launch open rebellion he decided to postpone action while he went to America where he was deposed as leader. Plans to stage an uprising in February 1870 had to be cancelled after another informer struck, and a month after that the details of the re-arranged uprising were again betrayed. Sporadic attacks were launched, mainly on police stations, but while the Fenian rising was to prove a disaster in the short term, arguably the long-term effects were something else.

All this prompted Hamilton to write his novel based on the activities of the Fenians, the story of which which centred on three Donegal brothers, sons of a well-to-do farmer who joined the Fenian Brotherhood. In the tale, one of the brothers had fought for the Federal cause in America from which he emerged alive but maimed. When first approached by Fenian agents in Washington, he rejected their overtures: Told by them that Ireland was to be made as free as America, and separate from Britain, he replied: 'Ay! Like as the South boys were wanting to be free and separate from the United States, and see what they got. That's what you call freedom here, I suppose?' The recruiting agents persisted and eventually he agreed to join the Brotherhood as an officer on full pay and allowances, returning to Ireland as a captain.

The story then followed the fortunes of the three brothers and ended with two of them evading capture by escaping abroad, while the third, the captain, was captured and sentenced to five years penal servitude. The preface to the novel is interesting, conveying as it does something of Hamilton's political outlook at this period of land agitation:

To my Fellow countrymen of the United Kingdom

While I hope to afford some amusement to those who read for amusement, I hope also in these pages to suggest some ideas which may be of use in cultivating a good and growing feeling between English and different parties in Ireland.

It is too often forgotten or overlooked that a people who have been oppressed will learn certain vices which cannot be unlearned as soon as the oppression ceases, and will feel a certain acrimony against their oppressors which, also, will continue for a considerable time after the causes are removed, especially in the minds of the most ignorant.

These faults can only be eradicated by strict and impartial justice, united with that social intercourse which will take a healthy complexion from a true view and right feeling of the case, especially and primarily by the more educated and ruling class. As long as these assume the demeanour and tone of domination, it is not to be expected that the less educated, less thinking class will cease from the vices in thought and action which make them dangerous to others, and present the great obstacle to their own advancement. The near neighbourhood of Great Britain, which has gone through phases somewhat similar to those through which Ireland is now struggling, is in some respects a disadvantage to Ireland, of course, and the question is often asked: 'Why cannot the Irish do as the English do?' As if the half-grown boy could do what the man ten years his senior can do, or the people who are a century younger than their neighbours be as forward in political freedom or wisdom.

Ireland has to attain an adult state, which was certainly retarded in bygone years by misgovernment and oppression. A great deal of what is attributed to the character of race is really due to national youth, and time – with national advancement – will with the blessing of God, show it.

TENANT RIGHT

Even though the Fenian movement collapsed in 1867, agrarian agitation continued and gradually developed into the Land League, when the disturbances centred largely around 'Tenant Right', a system which allowed an outgoing tenant to sell his interest or goodwill in the farm to an incoming tenant. Tenant Right was already widely practised by landlords in many parts of Ulster, usually subject to the landlord's approval of the incoming tenant. Some proprietors in the other provinces also sanctioned the principle, notably Lord Portsmouth in Co. Wexford, Lord Portarlington and Lord Devon, but the system did not come under Act of Parliament statute till 1870. Long before this, in 1849 and again in 1852, John Hamilton had written to his tenants on the subject, a system which he personally endorsed and practised, stating that 'no tenant was ever dispossessed of his land on my estate without being allowed to sell his holding . . . and where good houses or other improvements had been made, they were always paid for besides'.

Post-famine conditions had continued to improve, and at the beginning of 1853 Hamilton wrote to his tenants a wide-ranging letter covering many different aspects of life at the time, encouraging them towards self-improvement and better education, and advising them to decide for themselves – rather than being influenced by others – when voting at elections. The land question continued to be one of the most important political problems facing the country, and tenant societies had sprung-up to represent the aspirations of the larger farmers rather than the land-less labourers in what was, in effect, the beginnings of the Land War. This movement succeeded in extracting concessions, piecemeal, through a series of Land Acts culminating in the Wyndham Act of 1903 but at this stage Hamilton was concerned about his tenants being led, pointlessly in his view, into violence, especially because, far from putting an end to evictions, it only provided landlords with further reason for more of them:

> MY DEAR FRIENDS,– I thank God that by His blessing our country is in so different a state as to outward prosperity from what it was the last time I thus addressed you. It has pleased God to bless our land in many ways, and by means of some things which were by many persons thought likely to be injurious to us. I pray God we may show more thankfulness under His mercies than we did repentance under His chastenings.
>
> It now lies in a great degree in our own hands to become a prosperous people, more than we ever were before. We have learned some severe lessons of late years, let us now profit by them. Necessity has driven us to more exertion, and we have learned that our old methods of cultivating our land and of managing our crop and cattle could be much improved. We have still a great deal to learn. We have been taught, too, not to despair in the worst circumstances, but to trust in God and do our best. When the fruits of the earth in a great degree failed, when the spade and the plough brought little return for the hard labour of our men, it was so ordered that the needles of our women and girls should bring what was wanting, and a door of relief was opened which saved us from sinking when all seemed nearly hopeless.
>
> I have observed with much satisfaction a spirit of manly independence increased among you. There is, however, still much room for further increase in this respect. It must be a vain attempt to make laws which will put tenants in a good position, until tenants learn to act like men and like honest men, honest to themselves as well as to those whose land they take for rent. While tenants are afraid of landlords, or while they think to make landlords afraid of them, there is want of manly honesty. While

tenants let themselves be deceived or over-reached by their landlords, or while they try to deceive or over-reach them, there is again want of manly honesty.

Thank God there is an improvement in these things, and I trust there will be more, until it shall be felt and seen that both the owner of land and the occupier understand and feel that the true interest of each is in fair, open dealings, in an honestly made bargain, honestly kept on both sides. . . .

There have been, I am sorry to say, some attempts hereabouts as well as in other parts, to stir up a bad feeling between landlords and tenants. I think, however, that most of you have good sense enough to see through them, and good feeling enough to resist them. The last election of members of Parliament gave occasion for much agitation on this subject, and plenty of bad feeling was excited by parties who care not one straw what evil consequences may come to the people, if they only gain their own ends. These people raise a cry of Tenant Right, or whatever tune they think they can make the ignorant people dance to.

Now, I should be acting strangely if I were to oppose the real rights of tenants, but I oppose the iniquity of deceiving people with false pretences, and taking advantage of a word like Tenant Right to carry the political plans of any person into effect. I do not seek to compel any man to vote at elections contrary to his own real opinion. And I think and affirm that any man who does seek to compel a voter, acts wrongly as a man, and unconstitutionally as a subject of our Queen and member of our commonwealth. Whether he be landlord or clergy, if he holds out the terrors of his power to force any one to vote, his conduct is utterly unjustifiable, and if he were my landlord or my clergyman I would not submit to it.

The law of our country appoints certain persons to be the voters or electors, and if the opinion of any person be that some of these voters are not competent to choose whom they should vote for, that person has no right to go against the law and deprive the voter of his choice by threats or by any form of coercion. It is indeed my duty to my country and to my neighbour to advise him, and to show the reason why one candidate is more or less worthy than another, and why in some cases it may be better for a voter to take my advice, as an old friend, than to listen to the tale of a stranger or the threats of either clergy or landlords . . .

There is no man more decidedly for civil, commercial, and especially for religious freedom than I am. But I know that these are mere empty sounds used for electioneering and other selfish ends . . . Ignorance robs men of their freedom and makes them slaves to some one thing or another. It makes men bad subjects and bad rulers, bad children and bad parents, bad congregations and bad clergy, bad in every way, for it robs

> them of their real freedom as citizens of their country, as traders or farmers, and especially as religious beings with immortal souls.
>
> And, my dear friends, all this concerns us in our present matter of communication; for, ignorance also makes bad landlords and bad tenants, and while it does so, all the Acts of Parliament that can be thought of will never mend the matter.
>
> JOHN HAMILTON

During February, 1870, John Hamilton wrote another long letter to his tenants, in which he referred to Tenant Right, but also provided a good idea of his general thinking as he approached his seventieth birthday:

> My position gives me an advantage in seeing what is going on in the land, and I see that, because there are in some places instances of cruel and unjust conduct of landlords towards tenants, some persons use this as a means of stirring up discontent among tenants as if all their woes were caused by such landlords and would be removed by a law against unjust and cruel conduct by landlords.

Hamilton again argued that landlords were little different from other businessmen, adding that most landowners would consider themselves well paid if they got 'anything near one shilling yearly for each pound the land cost or would bring . . . . Would any merchant keep people clothed or fed at the same rate?' he asked. As to his tenants, his advice was to get a lease before they expended money or labour in improving the value of their holding, adding that he had 'no confidence in any law that interferes in business between man and man in the way some people expect a new *Tenant Right* law to do. Even if the law could make all landlords do right it would be little use unless it could make all *tenants* wise, prudent, industrious and good'.

> I would, however, gladly see a law that if a landlord turned out a tenant without allowing him to sell his Tenant Right, the landlord should be liable for the whole cost of that tenant and his family if they should become charged upon the poor rates – and further, that all tenants should, if at all possible, be secured from being unreasonably or cruelly turned out without being allowed to sell, or without a just compensation for the improved value of the holding through their expenditure of money or labour.
>
> I confess I do not foresee how a law is to be framed that will even seem to do this; but I do foresee that if anything beyond this is attempted by a law, that law will not only fail to do good, but it will be the means of putting the sinking, poor tenant more into the grasp of a bad landlord

and his attorney, while it will put a great hindrance in the way of a good landlord who wishes to help forward the prosperity of his tenants . . .

As to my tenants, no landlord who has as many was ever better satisfied with them. Since the sad days of famine, 1845-49, when they were sorely pinched, I can say they have paid honestly, and I will add that I do not think that in the last twenty years I have had one unreasonable request or application from any of them . . .

Thus, my neighbours, I give you my mind on the subject that just now agitates many minds, and remain now, as ever, your sincere friend,

JOHN HAMILTON

In fact, by 1874, Hamilton had 'voluntarily' paid out some £4,000 in compensation to tenants during his programme of consolidation – most of the settlements ranging between the equivalent of five to fifteen year's' rent of the holdings concerned. The Tenant Right Act did not become law until nearly six years later, just before Hamilton's eightieth birthday, when he wrote once again on the 'Ulster Custom'. His comments are especially interesting coming from the perspective of one who, while favouring the Union, saw merit in some form of limited Home Rule.

In some parts of the Northern Province, Ulster, a custom has long prevailed of an outgoing tenant selling the good-will (called Tenant Right) of his holding, generally subject to the veto of the landlord as to the purchaser, which power of veto was exercised but rarely, and when the proposed new tenant was for some cause (which was not necessarily stated) objectionable. Even where the land was pretty high rented, this Tenant Right fetched a fairly good purchase, in small holdings often more than the fee simple was worth.

One considerable and good effect of this custom was that a broken-down tenant of a little farm, say of £10 a year, when he was obliged to give up his land and go, did not become a pauper. He had no legal claim on the permission to sell the goodwill, but was for that dependent on the goodwill of his landlord to permit him. Now, before a poor Irishman will give up all hope of retaining his home he will use all the credit he can get to obtain means to crop his land and pay his rent and here, as everywhere, there are both tradesmen and money-lenders ready to give credit upon exorbitant terms to persons in distress, and many a poor cottager is utterly ruined by these. The lenders, however, could not seize upon the purchase of this Tenant Right. So if a poor man owed his landlord a couple of years' rent, and sold for twelve years' purchase, he had £100 over at his landlord's goodwill, who generally protected the poor man from unreasonable demands, and he had a sufficient residue to enable him to emigrate with comfort, or to begin again on a smaller scale in a new location.

This permissive Tenant Right has been made law [Tenant Right Act, 1870.] not only in Ulster where it originated, but over all Ireland giving the tenants, where the custom did not prevail, the advantage . . . The poorest Irishman, as well as the most sensible Englishman or the canniest Scot, ought to be manly enough to hold his own advantage in any lease to which he puts his hand. If he is not equal to this, then indeed he has no business with either lease or farm, and will trust in vain to Acts of Parliament to protect him where he ought to protect himself in his bargain. It is a great mistake to think the Irish tenant is incapable of making his own contract, the great thing is to make him feel that the contract must be observed.

DISESTABLISHMENT

The vast majority of the members of the Church of Ireland could hardly believe it to be true when they first heard that the British government planned to disestablish their church. Many of those opposed to it, the Antidisestablishmentarians, saw the move as nothing short of an act of treachery, reneging on a solemn promise given at the time of the Act of Union. Some were against it simply because no one could be sure of its after-effects, while others – like Hamilton – took the view that establishment had been a bad thing in the first place, not only for Catholics and Presbyterians, but for the Established Church itself. Anyway, after the general election of 1868, when he gathered 66 Irish followers on his side, Gladstone pressed ahead with the plan. John Hamilton wrote on the subject on a number of occasions between then and 1870, expressing himself clearly in favour of it – not because he had to pay £21 per annum in tithes to the Rectors of Drumholm and Donegal, but because of the wider issues and the evident wrongs:

I always looked upon an Establishment of the Protestant Church in a Roman Catholic country as, first, a great hindrance to the spread of true religion either by improving the Protestants or converting the Catholics, and secondly, as a monstrous injustice and political grievance. Indeed, I look upon the establishment, as it is called, of Churches as an evil, which for the time prevents a greater evil, and is therefore a blessing while men are so unchristian as to require such a medicine, and till they are in such a state as to take to wholesome food instead of drugs. The high Orange party will rage, and many good conscientious folk will prognosticate all manner of evil, and if the Church is in so low a state as to depend for its vitality upon State support and pay, we may have days of trial to mend us.

> I grieve that the Church question should have been made also a battle question between Conservatives and Liberals. It has caused both parties to stir up their followers with everything that animates them with hatred and provokes to violence, and decidedly the Orange party has now been the worst. For myself, I look to a much greater reformation from within the Roman Catholic Church than anything we have seen yet . . . however, those who dread rightly the bad effects of throwing off all religious ties, see no alternative but in holding to and increasing the dominion of Pope and priest, whereas in these countries there is the obvious alternative of free religion, which even among Protestants, is only beginning to be understood.

In the event, the terms of the 1869 Act disestablishing the Church of Ireland were quite favourable and while its passing caused deep resentment at the time, it caused no great permanent stir. John Hamilton wrote a pamphlet entitled *Should the Established Church be re-established*? but, 'for fear of unpleasant differences', he decided not to publish it. In it, he outlined not only his thinking on the subject matter, but also on what he thought of formal religious structures in general. He began by agreeing that the endowment of religion might have been helpful in certain respects in the past but went on to question (not for the first time) whether or not people might have been better Christians if, as he expressed it, 'clergy, separated and salaried as they have been, had never been invented':

> This treatise was written above a year ago, but I refrained from printing it, chiefly because I shun unpleasant differences with my brother Christians to such a degree that I have held my tongue, when I believe a higher motive, a more fervent love, would have been as a fire burning, and urging me to speak out. I have already been accused of indifference to religion, and of niggardliness, because I have declined to contribute to the so-called Church Funds. I can hardly believe that those who thus accuse me really suspect me of these faults. But they perhaps thought, and rightly too, that I am tender on these points, so indeed I am, and that I should be moved to give, rather than be accused of being indifferent to the religious welfare of my neighbours, or of stingy conduct towards them. Perhaps if it were not a case of conscience, I might have been vexed into contributing, but I here give my reasons, and as for any accusations brought against me, I make no reply; you who are my neighbours know me.
>
> I do not only want to tell others why I wish to decline to support any kind of endowed clergy, I also desire to show a reason why others should do as I do in this respect, for the advance of religion, for the glory of God, and for the improvement of people in all holy life. The things I

> read and hear since I wrote these reasons do not give me a better notion of the effects of paying the clergy a salary secured by endowments. They seem to forget that the ministry are servants, and that we are the paymasters; this is a great mistake.
>
> But it is not the men I blame, it is the system, and I declare the clergy are wonderfully good considering the system of which they are the slaves – many of them excellent men, for whom if we are Christians we shall pray God to prosper their work, and to free them from their fetters.
>
> However, it is not denied here that the endowment of Churches, so as to secure a salary to the clergy, and thus to make a class whose profession is to teach the people, and especially to instruct them in divine things, may have been on the whole, and probably was, a benefit, but when this is admitted, it by no means follows that a perpetual continuance of secure endowment may not be most injurious.
>
> One evil resulting from the endowment of a Church is that a caste or class of men looked upon as different, and separated from all the rest, is created. Presently, this caste calls itself, and gets itself called 'The Church', and in the end it claims the endowment as its own property in which it has invested rights.

Hamilton remained steadfast to his view that the whole spirit of Christianity was at variance with a system of paid clergy, feeling that this applied to almost every other denomination in addition to 'the Church disestablished and partially disendowed in Ireland'. Soon after disestablishment, he also expressed the view that:

> The dis-endowing and disestablishment of the Episcopal Protestant Church has not, as yet, had the extent of either good or bad fruits that different parties looked for from it. The Protestant clergyman was, in general, looked up to by all sides as a friend who had a will and some means to befriend his neighbours. It does not seem to have had any results as to the standing or influence of the Roman Catholic priests, most of whom are either good or wise enough to counsel their flocks to obey the laws.

VIEWS ON CATHOLICISM

Given his background, class and education, and the thinking of the time, he had a remarkably balanced view of other religions, feeling it grossly unfair, for example, that Roman Catholics and Presbyterians had to pay tithe money to support the Established Church. He claimed that he bore no ill-will against Catholics, though he felt very strongly that what he called the Roman Catholic *system* 'independent of the question as to truth or error in a strictly religious

Family group photographed at St Ernan's in 1872. John Pakenham and his sister Katherine are to the left in the front row along with Frank, Marjorie, Mary and 'Tiny', orphaned nephew and nieces of Mary Simson, who were reared along with John Hamilton's second family.

point of view, keeps the laity so enslaved to the priesthood. . . . ' He contrasted his own questioning spirit with what he saw as the almost complacent, unquestioning acceptance by Catholics of the doctrines of their church, describing them as 'those who feel a want of something to *repose* upon (which is something different from something to hold fast to)', adding that 'to repose is for the moment pleasanter than to grip, or to feel that one is gripped, and the Roman Catholic scheme is a feather-bed'. He could be, and was, just as critical of aspects of Protestantism:

> There is a good deal of bad feeling kept up by well-intentioned but ill-judging Protestants, who think it their duty to attack the Roman Catholic religion on every occasion, and often in very offensive terms.

In the space of less than a dozen lines, he summed-up the root causes of the strained relationships between Catholics and Protestants, and also looked forward to a better future:

> But in all times of political excitement, the wrongs the Roman Catholics suffered from the Protestants and the atrocities committed by them in bloody revenge, are made capital of by the leaders of the different parties. They are made afraid of each other, and filled with hatred, which, however, abates after the special occasion is past, but unhappily, only to be revived on the next opportunity. There is, nevertheless, a considerable portion of both sides which have a more Christian feeling towards those who differ from them, – indeed the great mass of the people do not know what the difference is, but having been on one or the other side, they stand up for their religion. . . .

This reminded Hamilton of a conversation he once had with 'the Hibernian son of a Scotch soldier':

> The soldier mentioned that he had been the evening before at a wake 'where', said he, 'there was a good gathering – and one fellow out of America stood up and blasphemously declared there was no God, and that everything came by chance'. Being asked if no one answered him, he replied: 'Troth it was myself answered him'. 'And what did you say?' 'Well, you see I was bound to put him down. I am an Orangeman, and most of the people there were that sort, so I up and says to him: 'That's all rank Popery. I knew they would all be with me there. So they hooted him and hissed him, and he had to fly, for the bare life'.

To this Hamilton added a point which he had stated before: 'For myself, I look to a much greater reformation from within the Roman Catholic Church than anything we have seen yet . . . '

A Story from Brownhall

Various stories used to be told about unusual or unexplained happenings around Brownhall. One of these concerned a very tall man from nearby Ballydermott who, just before the turn of the century, one night he left his house, his wife and his daughter and simply disappeared. Some time later there were rumours that he had been seen in America and this prompted his wife to sell their property after which she and her daughter left for the United States in the hope of finding her husband. Some forty years later, in the late 1930's, following an unusually severe storm, many trees were uprooted in Brownhall Estate, under one of which was found the skeleton of a six foot man. Some of the older local people speculated that the bones were the remains of the husband who, the story went, had been snaring rabbits or pheasants and, when caught in the act, had been shot and – possibly unintentionally – killed. Trees were being planted in that part of the estate at the time and the game-keeper involved – or so it was surmised – secretly buried the man where he was least likely to be found – under the roots of a newly planted tree.

TWELVE

Old Age

With advancing age, Hamilton's writings concentrated more and more on religious topics. Responding to a friend's question in February 1871, 'what would you plead before God when you present yourself for admission [to Heaven]?' he wrote an essay with the title *The Spirit of Religious Enquiry*. He regularly corresponded with Helen, his youngest daughter, now married and living in Paris, often on religious themes and, in a letter written after a visit to his wife's family in Scotland, he made a strange allusion to some kind of messianic aspiration:

> In addressing a meeting at St. Andrews some time ago, and urging upon my hearers the blessedness of being like Jesus, it occurred to me to say: 'If I *really like Him,* heaven would not satisfy *me* while one of you remained, by your character, necessarily excluded. I should not ask your Father then to *let you in,* such as you might be, but I would certainly ask Him to *let me out.* Aye, out of heaven and its joy to go to earth and its woes, if only He could send me so that I might save you from your sins and lead you to that love of God and good to which I should have attained'.

Among the Hamilton papers there is a letter, sent to him in 1876, with from the address Glas, Stranorlar, and signed 'Lifford'. This was the third Viscount Lifford who lived at Meenglas, near Stranorlar, and who, though this is not mentioned in the journals, had strong evangelical leanings and became secretary of the Hibernian Church Ministry Society when it was founded. He sent his letter to John Hamilton while the latter was staying with the Simson's near St. Andrews, an indication that Hamilton was now spending more time there and rather less at St. Ernan's. Lifford wrote: 'I hear no rumours of your coming home or I should not venture to ask you the question I am about to put – are you disposed to let St. Ernan's for a year, with the probability of its being taken for a longer time if you liked?' Lord Lifford added that he thought it would benefit the house to be occupied, and he knew a possible tenant for it 'without encumbrances, as the servants say, that is, with no children to break the furniture'.

On his 78th birthday, 28 August 1878, Hamilton wrote a general letter to his family:

> I know you are all with me today and I am truly thankful to think so, however we may be separated, even separated by bodily death. The seventy eight years tell me that, as men's ages go, I am old, but how young three quarters are to a spirit existence! My voice is weak from a continued gouty affliction of the bronchial region, which quite prevents me from speechifying with any degree of loudness, but I do hope to have *utterance* given for Raroy meeting [a reference to the annual Harvest Festival service in Raroy church which he hoped to address] at the end of harvest which is now beginning very favourably.

A couple of years after this, on his 80th birthday, he wrote to Helen:

> I expect you will get this greeting tomorrow, my dear child [Helen was then almost 50 years old], yet how young we are in comparison with our future! Eighty years! (my age), what are they? And yet we have perforce learnt much in our little span of life. How much do we know even now, that we could not have had the vaguest idea of in our young days, and if that is the case in a few easily counted days, what may we expect to know of God and of good in a few million years! If I ever have done any good, it has been in unsought and even apparently unfavourable circumstances. So I am perplexed, but all this is not like a birthday greeting. So I stop it, and send for your affectionate acceptance, as a small token of my affection, the value of which is not pecuniarily great, to my child. God bless her and make her a blessing.

In that same year, Hamilton briefly recalled the Famine of 1845-1850 once more, a period which, rather strangely, he described as

> The happiest years of my life, not excepting 'Love's young dream', were those closely pinched years at St. Ernan's in the great famine, when you all, and your mother, held up your hands, and by your affection and self-denial enabled me, by God's blessing, to go through the work I did in those terrible times.

A year earlier, John Hamilton alluded to six books which he had been reading, evidence of the breadth of his reading – even in old age. He had been quoting from *Memoirs of Matthew Davenport Hill* the Recorder (or judge of quarter sessions) of Birmingham who had written on jurisprudence; and went on to mention that he had read Roscoe's (Pope) *Leo X,* Stahr's *Preussische Revolution* (in German), Compte's *Politique Positive* (in French), deTocqueville's *The State of France before the Revolution*, and also a *Life of Napoleon*. Two years later, in his eighty-first year, Hamilton almost casually mentioned that he had just translated *William Tell* into English, adding that he had 'in a few days, translating it back [into

German] till it is almost perfectly got by heart'. 'There is nothing like it', he added, 'for *getting* a language – you quote your author and get *au fait*. I am also for using all 'cribs' [methods of cheating] and everything that gives facility to translation. Also, not learning much grammar, which should first be intelligently read more than once by the pupil so as to have a clear idea of what is in it'.

THE STATE OF IRELAND IN 1880

During his 79th year he wrote a long and wide-ranging discourse on the state of Ireland during the latter quarter of the nineteenth century, all the more interesting because it represents the view seen from the perspective of someone near the top of the social ladder who was well aware of conditions for those at and near the bottom. Naturally, as might be expected, he saw Ireland's place being in the United Kingdom – but he stressed that it should be as an equal partner, and belonging also to the Empire. It may seem strange to see that he used the word 'partition' – not in the sense of a divided Ireland as was to be the case some four decades later – but rather to describe the possibility if it being partitioned from Britain as a result of the agitation for Home Rule. Hamilton, who was in favour of a form of devolution with a parliament or assembly in Dublin, also demonstrated that much else of his thinking was well ahead of his time; for example his concern that too much emphasis was being laid by the schools on getting good examination results and not enough on preparing children for life. As a summary of his views about Ireland, his reading of its past history and how he saw its position at that time, only a few years before he died, it seems worth reproducing here at some length:

> There are several things that influence Ireland as to her condition and treatment, which each and all have their effect both on her past history and on the questions that now arise as to her true position, the nature of her connection with England, and as to the most practical way of furthering her welfare.
>
> The chief of these influencing causes are her geographical position, soil, climate, races, religions.
>
> Though lying so close to Great Britain, Ireland interfered little with her neighbour, and called for little interference as long as the island, split into numerous petty kingdoms, was busy about its internal affairs, and the leaders and people found a sufficient outlet for their combative propensities in wars among themselves. For all that affected England, Ireland might then not have existed.
>
> It is not very clear what benefit the English promised to themselves in the acquisition of Ireland. There might be a growing fear that so near

a neighbour would, when stronger, prove troublesome. There could hardly have been an idea of adding to the national wealth by the conquest of such a people as the Irish then were, but there was something which went along with the lust of conquest and rendered Ireland covetable, for coveted she was, and gradually taken possession of with all the painful details which conquests bring in their train.

Once coveted and attacked, Ireland could not be left alone. She was made an enemy, and the obligation was evident to make her a friend or a slave. Her position and condition rendered this imperative. From that time it became impossible for England to do without Ireland, either as a bond-servant or as a free member of a united kingdom.

It is a very curious fact in the course of events, that a gift of Ireland from the Pope should be a strength in the claim of the English king (Henry II. A.D. 1172) to be lord of Ireland. The story of the wars in Ireland, beginning with Strongbow's expedition, of the atrocities committed, the districts confiscated and given to English nobles or adventurers, covers a long period. The conquerors became settlers, became Irish, and after that were among the fiercest and most implacable enemies to the new influx of hungry or valiant Englishmen; a state of things that tended too surely to make hostile feelings between Ireland and England bitter and strong. That Ireland is there and will be there, is certain. There, to be a thorn in the side of England on account of past centuries, and a disgrace to the tyrannical and short-sighted treatment of the weaker by the stronger, as all sides now admit. Long was the sowing time while the wind was sown; high and blasting has been the whirlwind reaped.

A new era is now (1880) opening, and in seeking to bring about a happier state, it must be kept in mind that those days of injustice did once exist. The physician should consider what the patient has gone through which would affect his general constitution, and must prescribe not only for one who is then showing certain symptoms, but also must bear it. Her position geographically cannot be altered. . . .

AGRICULTURE AND GEOLOGY

A considerable portion of the Irish soil is very good for agriculture, and now some districts are really well cultivated. But the dampness and the mildness of the climate render the growth of grasses and green crops more certain than that of corn . . . .

Hence the almost exclusive industry of the people is necessarily agricultural and pastoral. The linen manufacture has long attained a prominent place in the north-east; it depends less on the mineral productions of the soil than most other industries do, and somehow it escaped the obstructive interference of English law, which slew in their early days many Irish attempts to set up manufactures. This manufacture has rendered the districts where the linen trade has long prevailed perhaps the most prosperous section of Ireland.

In some parts the soil and climate united give an abundance of grass, and a continuance of it which is hardly credible. Grass fields have been mown for hay for twenty years without requiring any manure, yielding as good a return at the end as at the first. Sometimes these grassy fields are low-lying and rich-looking, but a large hill has been observed where crops of hay were cut for several years. A tenant of a part of this hill was asked how long it had been the custom to keep this hill all for hay. He replied that 'his grandfather told him that his father had told him that it was always cut for hay'. 'What sort of usage do you give your fields that they can yield such a fine crop as I see you cutting?' asked the inquirer. 'Well, your honour, not a bit of usage we give it, barring the *hoigth* of bad usage, for we feed the [livestock on] grass into the very roots till May, or often later, and then we let it grow and it does'. Many high and many noble families owe their rise and fortunes to Irish grazing.

CLIMATE: The soil and climate, which have so much influence upon vegetable life, have also some upon animal life. Cattle lie out in the mild Irish winters, and except in heavy and long snow, they require neither shelter nor feeding other than what they pick up, and they keep in fair condition . . .

'WHY IS IRELAND SO BACKWARD'?

As to religion, all call themselves Christians. By far the greater part of the population are Roman Catholics who, considering the treatment they formerly received, and the way they are kept in mind of that treatment, are perhaps as well inclined towards their Protestant neighbours as could be expected . . . . There is a good deal of bad feeling kept up by well-intentioned but ill-judging Protestants, who think it their duty to attack the Roman Catholic religion on every occasion, and often in very offensive terms. The proselytism on the other side is more quietly and less obtrusively carried on, but it is believed that on neither side is there much loss or gain.

It was Hamilton's view that most of the Catholic priests came 'into the closest contact with the poverty and misery of the poorest people, and no doubt are led by their very humanity to use exaggerated expressions both in calling for aid for the distressed, and in raising expectations in the sufferers which can only end in disappointment. The better class of priests, and this includes the large majority, are of great political use, but a fanatical, disloyal priest is a curse to the country, to the cause, and to his own flock in particular'.

> In thus considering Ireland, where it is, its soil, its climate, its religion, and its people, the questions press themselves upon us: Why has Ireland been what it has been? Why is it what it is? And as to the future, what is it to be looked forward to? The more these questions are considered with earnestness, and from different points of view, the more will it appear that on Ireland's condition in the future will depend much of the hope of prosperity for the whole United Kingdom, and the more this is felt, especially with the prevailing British desire to see Ireland in a good condition, the greater will be the effort and the probability of bringing about a better result.
>
> The question is often asked: Why is Ireland so backward in all that concerns national improvement when it possesses so many local advantages? Especially it is asked: Why does not Ireland present a model system of improved cattle-feeding and dairy-farming, seeing that the climate and much of the soil are so admirably suited for these pastoral branches of industry, which if carried on prosperously ought to make a prosperous people? In the first place it may be replied: There is very great improvement in almost every respect. Though the condition of the industries and of the people is far behind that of England and of Scotland, yet one who has known Ireland well for more than half a century can see very great advance in almost every direction; the houses are better, the roads much better, the people are better clad and fed, and are better educated than of old. What is true of one district will give a fair idea of what is going on in many districts, and doubtless will go on even more, for many hindrances are now removed which formerly obstructed every effort at improvement. However, there may seem to be one direction in which improvement appears questionable. It may be asked: Are the people more contented now than formerly?
>
> There is contentment and contentment – there is a desirable contentment and a very undesirable one. When people have been long oppressed and in hopeless bondage, they lose all energy of will and of effort, and try to make the best of the present moment, as negro slaves do who, though suffering in some respects and so degraded by their sufferings, yet can be merry and contented with a low kind of content. When the poor law system was first extended to Ireland a commissioner was sent, one of many, to see how matters were going on with the people. He went among the little tenants in a district inhabited principally by Celtic Irish of a very poor caste, as well as poor in means of livelihood. When he described their poverty, it was remarked: 'Is it any wonder the people are discontented?' 'Discontented!' he replied. 'No. They are as merry as crickets, – most damnably contented in their misery. I can find no fitter

expression for their state'.

When men are stirred up to see and seek the advancement in well-being that is within their reach, and which has to their knowledge been reached by others, they often do become discontented. But too frequently a rather rough manner of speech and action in seeking to better their condition, is mistaken for more than it really means. It may be affirmed that with a manly kind of contentment the Irish peasant is more contented than he was sixty years ago . . . . Few among the Irish tenantry, it must be confessed, have attained to such a position that they should be content with their present advantages and wealth. It is observable, too, that a people or race contented in the lower sense, are apt to alternate their quiescent state with unreasonable outbursts attended with atrocious cruelties which leave sores on both sides difficult to heal and long in healing.

THE FORTY SHILLING FREEHOLDERS

A root of much suffering and hindrance to advance in Ireland was the law which at one time gave a vote for members of Parliament to holders of land under certain leases of the value of forty shillings a year. [In 1793 this voting power was extended to Roman Catholic forty shilling 'freeholders'. The forty shilling vote, Protestant and Catholic, was abolished in 1829].

These holdings were called 'freeholds', and were required to be on lease for no specified time – for example, a lease for the life of a man already eighty years of age gave a vote, but a lease for ninety years or more, gave no vote. The result was that many estates were cut up into freeholds by proprietors who sought political influence, thus creating a pauper tenantry – and where this had been done, the occupiers are so contented, in the worst sense, that they not only cleave to these little spots but work and save chiefly to purchase the Tenant Right of one of them.

The writer knows of an estate [his own] where a hundred years ago there were about half a dozen tenants, – but when the proprietor also wished to represent the county, he increased the number to above 200, and though the present proprietor greatly wishes to diminish the number, and make the remaining tenants more comfortable, nothing can induce them to move, and a little holding of two pounds ten shillings a year has brought on that estate fifty pounds purchase for the good-will or Tenant Right! The landlord of such a property must desire for his own benefit as well as for the welfare of the occupiers, to improve their condition and consolidate the holdings, for under the poor law the landlord pays the whole poor rate for all tenants valued under four pounds a year. This estate is by no means a solitary exception. There are others worse off, but even here there are certain circumstances that are forcing an improvement.

All the children of these tenants cannot get holdings on the land, and are obliged to push out into the world, yet they love their miserable old home, often visit it, and not infrequently spend the savings of years in the purchase of a Tenant Right . . . . The estates in this condition are chiefly moory and mountainous districts where generally the Irish language is spoken, a few men and the majority of the women cannot speak English fluently. If patience is required in seeking the improvement of Ireland, it is doubly needed in these unfortunate localities. In Froude's *English in Ireland* the right way of dealing with the Irish difficulty is summed up in very few words:

'There are two classes of characters to be considered. One which is to be *won to the right view* by reason and conviction, and the other to be *reduced to obedience*, because resistance is hopeless'. Froude's words, though alluding to the condition of Ireland in former days, are as applicable to the present as to the past. He says: 'It was essential to convince the Irish that they were a part of the British empire, and that if they attempted to free themselves (from the British connection) England had both the power and the resolution to crush them'. True, but in former days it would have been a vain attempt to convince the Irish that they were a part of the British empire, for they were merely a conquered country, treated as conquered people generally were in those days. The story of their wrongs and sufferings, and of their rebellions and revenge, is now very generally known . . . .

The case in Ireland is the same. The possession of land had changed as frequently as one petty king conquered his neighbour and seized his territory, and the former proprietors could make no better title than the law of the strongest.

And now that by the advance of civilisation the law is happily among us the strongest, the property acquired and held by each possessor is secured by a better title than by brute strength. As long as mere force held Ireland for the English, and England had possession of Ireland as a conquered country, it was to be expected that a spirit of disaffection would prevail, occasionally bursting out into rebellion, while the intermediate periods would be disturbed by individual attempts at revenge and reprisals. One of the hindrances to the complete unification of Ireland and England is the difficulty of bringing about that the people who were long treated as a conquered people, should at once amalgamate with the conquerors as soon as these seeing their double mistake, political and social, not to mention Christian – changed their policy and way of treating Ireland, and admitted the Irish to a participation of the citizenship of the United Kingdom . . . .

This hostile feeling between people of different race and religion is kept up by several causes. Both in England and in Ireland, in speeches of public men and the articles in the public prints, the rule of united legislation and government is spoken of as 'British rule', – keeping up the false idea that because the Parliament and Government have their seat in London the government of Ireland is therefore a 'foreign rule', whereas every effort should be made to cultivate the true notion that Ireland is as integral a portion of the empire as London itself.

Another cause of estrangement between the people of Ireland and England is the insulting tone indulged in on both sides, especially, it must be confessed, on the side of England, which is accounted for by the plain fact that the estimate of Irishmen is gathered in England from newspapers, and it happens that all the worst characters and actions figure in these, while the well-conducted and loyal are not heard of. The well-known adage of 'Give a dog a bad name', etc., tells here against Ireland, and tends to keep up a spirit of hostility between Irish and English. It may be observed here that the descendants of English and Scotch settlers in Ireland are included in the term 'Irish'. Though in some parts of Ireland the Celtic and the Saxon races are opposed to each other, and this is specially brought out when religious controversies inflame them, the Saxon and Protestant portion of the population is as much disaffected by any unjust treatment or vexatious legislation as is the Celtic and Roman Catholic portion. This may be noticed in the names both of prominent agitators and of persons taking a lead in tumultuous opposition to the laws, which are by no means confined to Celtic denominations.

Difference of religion is an element terribly used in stirring up the people to take one side or the other at elections or political demonstrations. It is hard to bring any direct means to bear against this difficulty, but it may be hoped that benevolence, the chief element of Christianity, will become more powerful, as it is in theory admitted by all denominations to be *the chief.* A symptom of such a spirit appeared some time ago, when, in the West of Ireland, on the occasion of a public dinner there were in the company two bishops, one of each religion. On the health of the bishops being proposed, the Roman Catholic bishop rose and spoke to this purpose: 'Let us on each side keep up a never-dying contest, each denomination struggling to prove itself the most faithful follower of Him who said: 'Love one another'. To this contest I challenge my brother-bishop here, with his hosts, and to my side I invoke my brother-bishops and their hosts, and God will bless that battle in which, contrary to the proverbial fate of those who war, both sides will gain'.

The other bishop replied in the same spirit, a spirit which is not dead but less active than might be desired, and is overcrowded by a more noisy spirit of controversy and proselytism, showing too often more zeal and energy against opponents than real furtherance of real Christianity.

If legislation can do little to directly remove the religious difficulty, nevertheless it requires great care and judgement to avoid all that would tend to increase this evil. But there are other vexed questions where legislation and government may act more directly and beneficially.

With regard to the inefficiency of Acts of Parliament when these interfere arbitrarily between two parties making a bargain, the following conversation between the writer and a small farmer, on the proposition that rents should be legally fixed by a land court, is suggestive.

Landlord. 'Suppose you wanted to take this farm on which I have spent a large sum, and the rent was by law to be settled by arbitration, and that the arbitrators fixed on a less sum than I would take, but also a sum less than you would give sooner than to lose the farm'.

Farmer. 'What would happen then?'

Landlord. 'Why this would happen – I should be obliged to keep the farm that I would rather let, and you would not get the farm you would rather have'.

Farmer. 'But couldn't we make our own bargain different from the arbitration?'

Landlord. 'Certainly, not. The law, if made at all, must be binding, and allow of no more rent than the arbitrators arranged'.

Farmer. 'Well, sir, that looks curious, it does. But I do think that if you were for letting the farm for 40£ a year, and I was inclined to give it, all the laws couldn't hinder us from dealing, though the arbitrators said thirty'.

Landlord. 'How would you come at that?'

Farmer (after a little thought)'.Well, your honour, could they hinder me giving 10£ a year for leave to fish?'

However, in the matters of land laws, poor law, and the laws concerning education, legislation can do much for the Irish people . . . nevertheless all classes of people, both in Great Britain and Ireland, have a decided love for the possession of a home, a certain dwelling-place in which perhaps their forefathers dwelt, and where probably their children will dwell. This love of home is a passion of extreme power in the Irish . . . especially from the prevalence of small holdings, where each family dwells separately in its cottage or cabin, and has its homely surroundings – cow, pig, poultry. However poor or squalid the whole may be, yet it is a home, and to them a sweet home

EDUCATION

As to the education of the people. If State assistance be given to schools, it should be given to all schools of above a fixed number of pupils under proper regulations, and irrespective of religious teaching. The religious teaching, if there be any, should be under the direction of the head or heads of each school.

At present (1880) education, such as it is, has made the people more capable of knowing what is going on in the world, and in some degree of judging also. The mere power of being able to read renders them easier to get at, for good or for evil, and those who desire the good should energetically use the press for popularising sound literature. This would make even imperfect education the means of advancing itself. As it is, there seems to be a system of utilising the scholars in the schools to gain pay for the teachers, the object being to please the paymasters who are not chiefly the parents, and to fit the scholars to acquit themselves creditably at examinations rather than to fit them to get on in life. There are bright exceptions to this, but such is the apparent character of the schools for the people.

There might be much impulse given to education, if political disability were made a consequence of gross ignorance. Real education is so essential an ingredient in real national liberty and personal freedom, that the subject could not be here passed over for, after all, the great question for Ireland as it is for any country, is rational and personal freedom.

HOME RULE

This subject brings us to the, at present, culminating object of Irish aspiration, Home Rule. As if Home Rule would assuredly, probably, or even possibly, bring freedom to Ireland. The difference between a free nation and a free people is great. Ashantee and Zululand were free nations under the sway of no other nation, but their people were subject to the most arbitrary and fearful tyranny. But the cries 'Home Rule' and 'Ireland for the Irish', have become popular, and when this is the case, mere opposition will not quench the flame. Patience, and it will burn itself out. In the meantime justice in legislation and justice in the executive will do their work. The people to be worked upon are very different from the Irish population of 1798, and require different handling. Imperfect as their education has been, they are far in advance of those of former days. They can be got at to be raised in the scale of the peoples, as the insurgents of 1798 could not be got at, and they cannot be put down and quenched as the men of 1798 were by brute force. It is true that stirred up by agitating orators, they seek and some expect things which in no possible case they can get. Their leaders or mis-leaders generally know this well, but find it suits their purpose to excite the masses by false hopes of rising suddenly into prosperous possessors of the land by throwing off the Saxon yoke. It is not to be denied that some who formerly led the insurgents in Ireland had some of the qualities of patriotism, but they lacked the judgement which goes essentially to the completion of a true patriot and so became miserable failures, miserable themselves and involving multitudes in their misery, leaving also a legacy of vain aspirations of national glory as a little independent nation, instead of the truly glorious position of being an essential part of the United Kingdom, and having an equal share in the Government and in the prosperity thereof. Every time such agitators have stirred up the population of Ireland, their followers have shown less and less inclination to follow them to the bitter end, and this for two reasons. The Irish of to-day are wiser both from better education and from bitter experience, and the English have become wiser and juster, more ready to admit their brothers of next door into their family. Still it has proved nearly if not quite as hard to root out English prejudice as Irish hostility, and unhappily these keep each other alive and the evil dies but slowly. There is, however, a kind of Home Rule which is looked upon as not only possible but desirable by many English statesmen, such as that a committee of Irish members should sit in Dublin and transact a quantity of Irish Parliamentary business, which cannot be as well transacted, if at all, in England; or that local councils should be appointed for the four provinces of Ireland. Some such modification of Parliamentary powers might probably be of advantage to both countries.

TO CONCLUDE: We must have patience. Every time the case of England and Ireland is considered, a brick is taken out of the wall of partition which separates the two countries, and even a few pages such as these, may have some effect in promoting harmony and banishing discord.

In July 1882, John Hamilton wrote what was to prove to be his last address to his tenants in which he averred that his rents were reasonable, but if the law showed them to be otherwise, he would not oppose it. He also looked forward to the time when some of his tenants became owners by being enabled to purchase their holdings:

TO MY TENANTS, July 1882

MY FRIENDS,– If we understand one another, we shall, I hope, always be good friends, even when troublesome times may test us, and troublesome people try to vex us with each other. There were days, which some of you can remember, when your landlord was the friend who was looked to in time of famine and of pestilence. A landlord was worth something in the eyes of a tenant then, and such days of trial may come

79 North Street, St. Andrews (next door to the tower building), where John Hamilton lived for the last few years of his life with his second family. (Photograph from the Cowie Collection, courtesy of St Andrews University Library).

again. I wish to have such an understanding with you as may help to keep us friends, and therefore I will mention two or three matters which require a little explanation.

First, then, as to rent.

If I am asked to reduce my rents, I answer: 'I would have reduced them if I considered them high', but I make yourselves the judges whether they are so.

You know very well that any tenant on my land could have got about ten years' rent, or often more, in his hand for the Tenant Right of his holding, without counting anything for his improvements. Plenty of purchasers who had money to lay out were always ready to step into his place, paying the input, as it is called, and willing to give it to get the place at the rent. And while a tenant could get such a price for his bargain, I cannot see that it should be reckoned a bad bargain or a high rent.

But if there is a law made by the Parliament of the United Kingdom of Ireland and England that gives tenants a better bargain, I cannot resist it, nor complain of you if you take advantage of it, though I may think it is not a fair law, and if I lose by it and you gain, I reckon that it would not mend matters if we let it spoil our old friendship and make a quarrel between us.

So, as far as lies with me, I intend to be no less friendly with you although the Land Court may give me less rent and give you a better bargain.

Whatever the commissioners allow as a fair rent must no doubt be most regularly paid, and a tenant who has a clear receipt will meet his landlord with cheerfulness, as I have long been in the habit of meeting with my tenants, for they generally paid me well.

I hope some of you, however, will soon cease to be tenants, not by leaving your place, but by becoming owners of it. I have long been favourable to the plan of enabling tenants to purchase their holdings, and I hope to see it in practice; and with any of my tenants who become owners, I expect the friendship as neighbours with me and my family will be no less than it has long been, and with the blessing of God will long be. And so I sign myself, your old and lasting friend,

JOHN HAMILTON, *St Ernan's.*

During September 1882, he wrote that he had made arrangements for his wife:

> to get her money, which is in my name, in the bank (the Royal Bank of Scotland) in case of my being taken with a fatal illness. But in case of my sudden death, I write to make it known that all the money to my credit in the Bank or on deposit is really my wife's, independent of my right. . . .

What has survived of his writings during his final two years are mainly the reflections of an elderly man on his past times and present frailties:

> I feel more drawn out of the common days of the year than ever, as my body waxes old, Til my eightieth birthday, I never felt a bit old, and often felt the want of that warning sensation which has its use, though a youthful feeling is a blessing too. But now the sense of old age comes, not as some seem to find it, as a cloud, but much more as a gleam from a better life, by the light of which I read the Gospel, the good message, as a certain reality, saying: God is good and you shall be good therefore'.

He followed this with the remark that 'Moody and Sankey [Evangelicals, noted especially for their hymn writing] have been campaigning at Cambridge with considerable stir among the young men' No doubt he was recalling his own student days there where he found a general indifference to religion shown by many of his fellow students. A month after this, he again mentioned his health: 'I find that, bodily and mentally, every time I suffer (from gout in particular) I lose permanently in elasticity'. He went on to add that this did not result in any loss of spirituality – in fact he felt the reverse was the case.

One of the last letters, written by John Hamilton just before his eighty-third birthday, was a response to his daughter, Helen, who had sent him a copy of an article on clericalism, written in France by a Hyacinthe Loyson. Hamilton warmed to Loyson's view – because it conformed to his own, which he had enunciated several times before – that clericalism was 'a great enemy of advance in *goodness*, that is, in the root of true faith and real progress in civilisation . . . '

What appears to have been an even later letter, probably written about six months before he died, received a response dated 14th January 1884. Hamilton had written to MacMillan and Company, the London publishers, enquiring about his tract, *Truth and Error*, and also about his novel, *Arthur's Seat.* He had wished to know how many copies of each remained in stock with the company. The reply, written by George MacMillan himself, informed Hamilton that of the former work, 1,500 were printed and 1,000 remained, and of the latter, 500 had been printed and 340 were 'still in hand'. In an age when publishers off-load most of their unsold books at reduced prices after only a year or two, MacMillan's reply was remarkably restrained and courteous, especially considering that the publications had been printed twenty seven and fourteen years earlier respectively! The letter ended saying that the company 'would gladly have four copies of the one, and two of the other work bound in half calf and the same number in cloth'.

⋆ ⋆ ⋆

Almost nothing is known about the last years of John Hamilton's domestic life except that he was staying for longer periods at or near his second wife's family home in Fifeshire. If one is to believe his grandson (who, however, was factually incorrect in a number of matters), John spent his last six or seven years there, yet this must be at least partly incorrect as John had written various letters, including one to his tenants from St.Ernan's, during that period. He appears to have spent almost all of the last three years of his life in a rented apartment consisting of seven of the twelve rooms of a modest, three storey, terraced lodging house at 79 North Street, St. Andrews, next door, as it happens, to the student home of James Crichton, later immortalised by J.M. Barrie in his play, *The Admirable Crichton*. The 1881 census showed him living at this address with his second wife, Mary, then aged 56, and their daughter, Katherine, aged 14. John Packenham Hamilton, their son (then 20 years old), may have been away at university at the time of the census. Also in the household was Katherine's 28 year old governess, Charlotte Hay, and the census returns also show that the house was shared with the owner, her nephew and a servant girl, which may indicate something of John's financial circumstances during his latter years. It was in this house that he died at six o'clock in the morning on 13 June, 1884, just over two months short of his eighty-fourth birthday, predeceasing his second wife by twenty-two years.

John Hamilton's son James travelled to Scotland to be with his father at the end and signed the Death Certificate three days later before taking his father's coffin back to Donegal to be interred in the family vault in Drumholm graveyard, on 18 June, a melancholy journey which must have had, for James, echoes of the long journey to Carlsruhe with his eldest sister's remains 44 years earlier.

How much money John left for his second wife in his Royal Bank of Scotland account is not now known but when, just over two months after his father's death, James wrote to the Manager of the Ulster Bank in Donegal requesting a statement, he received a one-line reply: 'Your father's account is Cr. £54. 19s. 1d'. This was only the beginning of the bad news, for James was soon to learn – if he did not already know it – the full extent of the problems which he had just inherited. Besides the fact that there was no money left, he had just inherited a heavily mortgaged estate which was going to take two or more generations of patient work, and the sale of part of the estate, to restore the property to something like normality. Nearly four years after his father died, James was to write in despair: 'This Probate business seems never to end' and at the time of James's own death in 1915, more than half of the 1847 and 1850 mortgages, as well as further ones arranged in 1878, still remained unpaid.

While some of the problems which John Hamilton left behind him were due to his youthful inexperience, there can be no doubt that the remarkable generosity which he had shown to his tenants contributed greatly to the 'pinched' (a word he used several times) circumstances of his old age. At the end, there was a certain poignancy in the fact that he died far from St Ernan's and Brownhall, the area of which he had written as a young man, 'I have an intense love of this place', a place where, on hearing of John Hamilton's death, several thousand people had very good reason to sincerely regret the passing of this complex, but remarkably benevolent and recklessly generous landlord.

THIRTEEN

Tributes to John Hamilton

Different people, at various times paid tribute to John Hamilton for his humanity and generosity. The late Professor Beckett, as quoted in the Preface of this book, was one of the very few who, in recent years, seems to have remembered this almost forgotten man, whose experience, he wrote, 'is worth examining in detail'. Beckett continued: 'Hamilton was certainly not typical; indeed, men of his stamp are rare in any community. But it is the very fact that he was untypical that makes his experience instructive. Here was a landlord of determined character, impelled by a strong sense of duty arising from religious conviction; in the course of a long life he won the affection of his tenants and the approval even of those who were opposed to landlordism in general'.

The Rev. H. C. White, whose book based on some of John Hamilton's writings was published only ten years after his death, wrote that his memoirs 'show him as a man of very benevolent nature, having a kind heart and generous sympathies . . . [and they] convey . . . the records of a man whose life is worthy of being remembered'.

Not unexpectedly, many tributes were paid to Hamilton while he was still living, especially around the Famine period: One such came from James Hack Tuke, who visited Donegal on behalf of the Society of Friends during 1847, when he reported that John Hamilton was 'one who was devoting his whole energies to the service of the poor', adding that he 'had employed a hundred men on improving his estate, to whom he gives high wages; he had imported meal, rice and beef for making soup, which he was daily dispensing, and . . . seemed most deeply sensible to the calamity which surrounded him. . . . '

Two of the most generous tributes paid to Hamilton during his lifetime came from the pens of local parish priests. The first, by Father Eugene McCafferty, P.P of Donegal in 1841 came in a letter thanking him for help in repairing the chapel there, and he prayed 'that the Lord may grant you happy and lengthened days here among a people to whom you are and always have been so useful, and reward you with a crown of never-ending glory hereafter'.

Generous as those words were, there can be little doubt that the most handsome tribute paid to John Hamilton came, almost forty years after this, from a most unexpected source, from the pen of the Rev. John Doherty, Parish Priest of Donegal Town, who was a noted outspoken critic of landlordism.

Father Doherty, who knew better than most the state of the relationships between Hamilton and his tenants, wrote his testimony in a letter to the editor of the *Derry Journal* in October, 1880:

> SIR, – I see by the circular addressed to his tenants and published in Friday's *Journal*, that John Hamilton, Esq., J.P., D.L., of St. Ernan's, feels more or less uneasy lest 'the things spoken in the address presented to the Right Hon. Mr. Childers at Donegal' in reference to rack-renting should be imputed to himself, and lest it should be inferred that his relations with his tenants were not of a friendly and reliable nature.
>
> As one of the deputationists, might I ask you in my own and in their name for permission to assure him, that nothing was farther from our thoughts and intention than directly or indirectly to include him, or any of the Hamiltons, among the rack-renting or oppressive landlords of this country? There are not, nor were there ever, any grounds of complaint against them in the discharge of the duties of their properties. In all Ireland there never was, nor is there, a more considerate and humane landlord than the good and kind-hearted proprietor of St. Ernan's. I know the pulse of his tenants well, and I know of my own knowledge that they honour him, respect him, and love him for his personal kindliness and friendliness towards them, and for his sympathy in all their worldly fortunes and mishaps. They regard him more in the light of a friend and benefactor, like his Master 'going about doing good' – than as a landlord.
>
> His many social virtues, the kindliness of his disposition, and the natural warmth and goodness of his nature have endeared him to his tenantry as well as to all who know him, and his character among his many old friends in Donegal is too sacred and too well guarded to be touched, nor indeed was it aimed at, by 'the things spoken in the address'.
>
> In this respect I will only add that we think Mr. Hamilton much over-sensitive. When bad and oppressive landlords are spoken of, no one intends to include the late Thomas Conolly, the Hamiltons, the Marquis of Conyngham, Mr. Brooke of Lough Eske and some others, in the category. Would they were all like these and that we were spared the darkness and the black pall that is over the face of our country. If it were true, it would be, by far, more pleasant to speak of all the landlords as we speak of those I have mentioned. But Mr. Hamilton himself admits, in fact no one can deny, that 'some landlords are oppressors and some tenants cruelly treated'. And he asks: 'Are they that are oppressed to submit quietly to be wronged?' And he answers: 'No; but they must seek redress lawfully like men, and the Government will interfere for them'.
>
> Precisely what the deputation has done. They have 'sought redress lawfully' (how could it be more lawfully?) from one of her Majesty's

John Pakenham Hamilton, John's son by his second marriage, photographed in his Donegal tweed suit in India in 1888 when he was 27 years old.

Cabinet ministers, and requested 'the Government' through him 'to interfere' for those tenants that are 'cruelly treated'. In this procedure, then, we have the sanction of one of the oldest and best landlords in Donegal, or in all Ireland, – of one whose life is the ornament of, and his dealings with his tenantry a model and bright example to his class.

The address dwelt with some emphasis upon the evils of absenteeism, and the unfriendly relations between the absentee landlords and their tenants. For this opinion we were rated by some of the landlord organs. I find, however, that our views are not only confirmed, but that absenteeism itself is much more strongly condemned by the *Pall Mall Gazette* of last week. That highly respectable and influential organ of the upper ten thousand is more severe and outspoken against its social and political effects than our deputation. Would you allow me to quote a few sentences?

I will italicise those that are identical with those in our address.

The *Pall Mall Gazette* complains that £3,000,000 are regularly paid out of Ireland to proprietors who never reside there. Surely here in itself is no little cause for dissatisfaction. The capital that might be expended in feeding the people of Ireland, and improving Irish estates, is spent in feeding English people and improving English estates. Have we any right to permit such a system to continue? Have we any right to allow more than one – fourth of the valued rental of Ireland, where the tenants make the improvements, to be paid out of the country when we know the effect of this? Even so fierce a Tory as Lord Salisbury has declared that *the land of Ireland should be more in the hands of the people of that country*. Of course it should. But there is a terrible fuss if an attempt is made in that direction. But apart from the mere injury done to Ireland by what they

John Hamilton's son, Major James Hamilton, photographed with the Donegal Grand Jury c.1898 (front row, third from right). James's son, Captain John Hamilton, is seen standing behind, to the left with his hands clasped, in the second row

take out of her for nothing, there is the political and social side of the question – such landlords deal with their tenants solely through agents who act harshly in the interests of their principals, and of course, there is no community of sentiment whatever. What more natural than the feeling that such persons should be dispossessed, who in the majority of instances have done nothing whatever for the farmers over whom they claim the absolute right of eviction? It needs some little patience to hear these pauperisers of Ireland, these habitual neglectors of every political duty, clamour against confiscation, when they themselves are doing all the mischief in their power. If we use language one-fourth as strong, there would be a 'terrible fuss' among the 'pauperisers of Ireland' and a terrible 'clamour' in their organ against the Donegal deputation. This 'natural feeling against such persons' is strong and breast high, we should be sorry that the good landlords of Donegal should be borne down in this strong current of popular feeling, or that, as sometimes happens, the innocent should suffer for the misdeeds of their class.

But above all we should be sorry that the good and charitable proprietor of St. Ernan's – whose purse was ever open to relieve, and whose heart ever felt for every kind of distress – should suffer in the least in the adjustment of the land system of Ireland. We know well 'whether the new landlords are better than the old' and we know also that in sentiments of honour and in feelings of humanity Mr. John Hamilton is at the head of the roll, and is deservedly ranked among the finest and best of our 'real old Irish gentlemen'.

I remain, most sincerely yours,

JOHN DOHERTY, P.P.

THE EFFECT OF GOOD LANDLORDISM

In the same issue of the *Derry Journal*, 6th October, 1880, along with the Rev. John Doherty's letter, there appeared the following leading article entitled *The Effect of Good Landlordism*:

> A warm tribute to good landlordism is paid in our columns this morning. We allude to the letter of Rev. John Doherty, P.P., Donegal, in a comment upon the circular of Mr. John Hamilton, St. Ernan's, to his tenants, and which appeared in our impression of Friday. We need scarcely remind our readers, that during the recent flying visit of Mr. Childers to Ireland, he was everywhere received with a courtesy which he admitted impressed him very favourably. Nowhere was the reception accorded the right hon. gentleman more cordial or more earnest than that bestowed on him in Co. Donegal.

The recognised leaders of the people gathered round him, not only to accord him unstinted welcome, but also at the same time to instruct him on the spot as to existing grievances, and to show him the sincere desire that prevailed for their removal. It is right to have done so. To have omitted such a duty would merely have been placing a weapon in the hands of opponents to enable them hereafter to fling the taunt that, when a member of her Majesty's Government visited the country with the avowed intention of examining the state of affairs with his own eyes, there was no one dared repeat in his presence the complaints made so frequently in his absence. Mr. Childers was fearlessly told the truth. He met the people and their genuine sympathisers, and from them he heard the plain unvarnished tale that ever carries conviction with it. From Letterkenny to Ballyshannon his course was a species of triumphal progress, and everywhere he was greeted with the self-same story, the necessity for amending, fostering legislation.

He saw the evils of bad, and was pointed out the blessings of good, landlordism.

At Donegal he was told by a deputation of representatives of tenant farmers that 'we are tenants at will, that is, the landlords at will can and have enormously rack-rented our farms, on which they never expended a shilling in improvements, but have, on the contrary, confiscated our improvements and destroyed our Tenant Right and the Ulster Custom by an arbitrary and unjust increase of rent'. This may no doubt be considered strong language, but who that knows the circumstances of land management in Ireland dare undertake to disprove its correctness? Only the other day we quoted an instance of an increase of 125 per cent laid on the rent of a certain holding in Co. Donegal last year, a year painfully memorable for its great agricultural and commercial depression. Facts speak trumpet-tongued, and are stronger than a thousand theories promulgated by interested economists. The deputationists of Donegal spoke from experience or from facts within their knowledge, and they therefore felt justified in speaking forcibly to Mr. Childers. But in their statements they did not include all landlords, much less all local landlords, though what they said might to some 'make it seem as if all tenants were oppressed and all landlords oppressors' as Mr. Hamilton states in his circular already mentioned . . .

'His tenants', continues Rev. Mr. Doherty, 'honour him, respect him and love him for his personal kindness and friendliness towards them, and for his sympathy with them in all their worldly fortunes and mishaps. They regard him more in the light of a friend and benefactor – like his Master 'going about doing good' – than as a landlord'.

This is high, but we are sure, not unmerited eulogium on Mr. Hamilton.

'When bad and oppressive landlords are spoken of, no one intends', proceeds our reverend correspondent, 'to include the late Thomas Conolly, the Hamiltons, the Marquis of Conyngham, Mr. Brooke of Lough Eske and some others, in the category'.

That there are good landlords in the county has long been unquestioned, but that there are many bad ones is also true. The good ones are so, however, solely by their own good-will. Their removal, by death or otherwise, may eventuate in a regime which tenants will feel only the more severely from the preceding good treatment.

Much of what is needed to settle the Irish land question would be found in an Act of Parliament legalising what has always been conceded by good landlords, and prohibiting the oppressive practices of bad, ones. If there were no rack-renting proprietors, none ever ready to employ the terrorism of notices to quit, or enforce the operations of 'office' rules, it made comparatively little matter what land laws prevailed, for all tenantries would be secure in their holdings and assured the profits of their improvements. If, in fine, Irish landlordism could be truly described in the complimentary terms applied to Mr. Hamilton's management of his estate by Rev. Mr. Doherty, and if such management were inalienably secured to tenants, Irish agriculture would rapidly flourish, and Irish contentment burgeon and bloom in undisturbed luxuriance. 'I do not want to rack-rent you'" writes Mr. Hamilton, 'much less to turn out any tenant who has a mind to stay, and still less do I wish to hinder any one who may have to leave, from getting the fullest value for his Tenant Right'. This is surely practical recognition of the principle of fair rent, fixity of tenure, and free sale, and it is therefore no wonder that the effect of such good landlordism is to have tenants honouring and loving their landlord. The whole story points a moral and adorns a tale which many landowners in Co. Donegal and elsewhere could study with advantage to themselves, their tenants, and the State.

John Hamilton's drawing of the spectacular sandstone formations towering above the River Elbe as it emerges from Bohemia into Saxony, near Bad Schandau, south of Dresden.

Epilogue

While John Hamilton's tenants had good reason to be grateful that they had such an unusually generous landlord, it is understandable that his immediate family successors recalled this side of his character with dismay – or worse. More recent generations, less affected by the debts left by John Hamilton, acknowledge his enormous contribution during extremely difficult times.

There can be little doubt that the picture which comes across more than a century afterwards is that of a person who was deeply religious, impatient to get things done, and often very determined to have his own way. For all that, it must be said that he appears to have been an exceptionally kindly landlord, one who – perhaps uniquely – addressed his tenants as 'Friends' and 'Neighbours'. The eloquent praise publicly extolled on his behalf by two of the Parish Priests of Donegal was all the more notable given that one of them, Father John Doherty, was an outspoken critic of the worst abuses of landlordism. Hamilton claimed that only the exceptional few of his tenants went to the Poor House, or on the public works or to the soup kitchens, and that those people did so because they preferred what he called 'the drone's fare and the lazy work upon the public roads'. However, if it is true, as he claimed, that only one of his tenants died from starvation during the Famine years, and that his efforts to improve drainage and sanitation resulted in the virtual disappearance of fevers on his estate, all this must surely rank him as one of *the* most benevolent of that now rarely remembered class of good landlords.

* * *

In more recent times, the widely held view that all landlords, without exception, were cruel evictors has been called into question. Hamilton was as critical as anyone – with very good reason – about those proprietors who made no effort to alleviate the plight of their tenants, but he was also careful to point out that there were at least five in the southern half of Donegal who were *not* in that category, including Lord Arran, Thomas Brooke, Thomas Conolly, Lord George Hill, and the Marquis of Conyngham who, along with himself, brought the number in the area to half a dozen. In this respect it is interesting to note that Elizabeth Smith, the wife of a West Wicklow landlord who, like John Hamilton, kept a detailed journal, was equally critical of those landlords in her locality who, as she expressed it, 'failed to do their duty'. She, too, named a number of caring proprietors in her West Wicklow neighbourhood who, along with her husband, coincidentally equalled Hamilton's half dozen.

It was proprietors like these that Professor Beckett had in mind when he wrote that 'a good many Irish landlords – more than is commonly recognised – did, in fact, try to improve the lot of their tenants and promote the general welfare of their neighbourhoods'. Evidence of the existence of numerous improving and humane landlords should induce historians to rethink and further research the record of landlordism in the nineteenth century.

Understandably, the generally negative picture of landlords has its origins in the immediate aftermath of the Famine. Such a picture has been described by Professor Terry Eagleton, in his book *Heathcliffe and the Great Famine* (1995), where he wrote that the Irish landlords 'were widely bruited as a brawling, gluttonous, chronically inebriated crew, given to murderous aggression and extravagant rituals of consumption' and were in addition 'venal, foul-mouthed and nepotistic'. This colourful description may well have been appropriate for many, if not the majority of the landlords, but as a generalisation it seems very unfair to those others, whatever their number, who tried to act humanely. Eagleton's comment that: 'Modern day historians have been zealously combing the estate papers in hot pursuit of exemplary landlords' could give an impression (almost certainly not intended) that he disapproves of those who take the view that the names of the benevolent landlords should be rescued from oblivion. While anyone familiar with the main events of the Famine will readily identify both Lord Leitrim and Sir Denis Mahon as the personification of evicting landlords, few could name a single exception. William Shakespeare's well-known lines are, in this respect, remarkably apt:

The evil that men do lives after them,
The good is oft interred with their bones.

In Donegal, the third Earl of Leitrim and George Adair were two who were notoriously cruel to their tenants, and neither they nor their ilk deserve much retrospective sympathy.

A much more difficult area concerns those proprietors who, when they were convinced that they had no alternative, evicted with some reluctance and tried to mitigate the plight of the dispossessed tenants with assisted passages to America. In Mahon's case, there is this other side to the story – beyond the scope of this book – which shows him to have been nothing like the brawling, gluttonous, chronically inebriated (etc., etc.) landlord.

In her book, *The Great Calamity* (1994), Christine Kinnealy challenged many of the conclusions reached as a result of recent studies of the Famine period. Nevertheless, she wrote:

1861–1965

Extract of an entry in a REGISTER of DEATHS

Registration of Births, Deaths and Marriages (Scotland) Act 1965

No.	1 Name and surname Rank or profession and whether single, married or widowed	2 When and where died	3 Sex	4 Age	5 Name, surname and rank or profession of father Name and maiden surname of mother
57	John Hamilton Landed Proprietor Married (1st) to Mary Rose & (2nd) to Mary Simson	1884. June Thirteenth 6h. om. a.m. 79 North Street St Andrews	M	83 years	James Hamilton Barrister at Law (Deceased) The Honourable Helen Hamilton m. s. Pakenham (Deceased)

6 Cause of death, duration of disease and medical attendant by whom certified	7 Signature and qualification of informant and residence, if out of the house in which the death occurred	8 When and where registered and signature of registrar
Senile Debility Prostatic enlargement & urinary retention 5-6 Months. As cert. by Wm. H. Moir M.D.	James Hamilton Son Brownhall Donegal Ireland	1884. June 16th At St Andrews John Kirby. Registrar.

B

John Hamilton's death certificate, issued a few days after his death, bears the signature of his elder son, James who brought his remains back to Donegal for interment in the family vault at Drumholm.

The role of the landlords, despite being an easy scapegoat for the ills of Ireland, was diverse, ranging from those who mortgaged their estates to help their tenants, to those who, insulated by their absenteeism, chose not to set foot in the country during this period.

Much later in the same volume, after commenting that Irish landlords were an obvious target for the wrath of the British government, Dr. Kinnealy was to use the word 'scapegoat' again:

Some of the criticisms levelled at the Irish landlords did have a basis in

> truth. However the invective with which such criticisms were delivered frequently was petty and politically motivated. More significantly, by its insistence on local responsibility, the government was able to minimise its own role in the provision of relief, and at the same time offer an easy scapegoat to blame when the level of suffering appeared to be unacceptable.

Cormac Ó Gráda is yet another historian whose writings, reflecting new research, demonstrate a recognition that there were many shades of grey in Irish history where, formerly, it was perceived to be in black and white. Writing about the pre-famine period in his *Ireland, a New Economic History* (1994), Ó Gráda stated that: 'Taken as a group, Irish proprietors were far removed from the cruel and destructive stereotype later presented by farmers and nationalist propaganda'.

The truth of the matter is that, besides the landlords, the Famine presented many other groups, including middlemen, shopkeepers and moneylenders, with an opportunity to enrich themselves at the expense of the weakest and poorest, and it may be worth adding that Hamilton, not always noted for writing favourably about his own class, once commented that 'the worst landlords were not so hard on the tenants as the tenants were on each other. For I know that if a tenant lets a field or two to his neighbour, he will extort a far higher rent than any proprietor of an estate would think of asking'.

It would seem that there is a book about Irish landlordism waiting to be published.

⋆ ⋆ ⋆

After John Hamilton's death, most of his journals passed to his son by the second marriage, and this John Pakenham Hamilton, in turn, died while staying with the youngest of his four sons, Henry, who lived near Chester. Henry Pakenham Hamilton found the journals, along with a collection of correspondence and documents packed in several boxes among his late father's belongings, and these have since passed to his daughter, Judith Fearnall, living in Gwent. Meanwhile at Brownhall, a comprehensive collection of legal and estate documents passed down through descendants of John Hamilton's first family, much of which has been deposited in the Manuscripts Department of Trinity College Library, Dublin.

While the main Brownhall Estate passed to James Hamilton, that part of the land attached to St. Ernan's was to have been left to John Hamilton's three surviving daughters and it was arranged that his son would hand the property over to the eldest, Arabella. She had, in 1863, married Arthur Hamilton Foster, nephew of the Speaker of the Irish House of Commons, and the couple lived at Belle's Isle on the south side of Donegal Bay, a wedding present from her father and named after her. Arabella's sisters, Mary and Helen, were then to be compensated by Foster through a mortgage arrangement which, however, he later repudiated on a legal technicality, obtaining vacant possession for himself. The legal point was that the gardener's cottage had been rented out for the sum of one shilling a year, infringing the terms of the mortgage which required that no part of the property was to be let. After commenting on this, John's grandson recalled that Foster raised the rents on his land by twenty per cent while the Hamilton rents remained unchanged since 1824 but, despite this, 'when the Land Commission valuers came along, they lowered *both* by about the same amount so that the worse a landlord acted, the better he got off'.

When Arabella died, St. Ernan's was sold to a solicitor and, later, to Cecil Deane-Morgan who was to become Baron Muskerry. The property subsequently passed to the latter's cousin who lived in England and, because she had no desire to move to Donegal, and prevented by the terms of the will from selling it during her lifetime, offered it as a gift to the Representative Body of the Church of Ireland. The church's administrative body ran it as a combined home for retired clergy and guest house for fourteen years, after which it was sold, and became a hotel. It was later acquired by Brian and Carmel O'Dowd who continue to run it as a delightfully situated, country house hotel.

When John Hamilton moved to St. Ernan's, the house at Brownhall became his clergyman-brother's home until the latter was appointed Rector of a County Meath parish, after which several uncles lived in the house until John's son, James, took over. Following his father's death, James (1824–1915) inherited the entire heavily mortgaged estate and, presumably in order to make ends meet, acted as agent for the Conolly estate near Ballyshannon. Because there is virtually no written record of what James Hamilton actually did, details about this period are vague, but the important thing is that he managed a holding operation that proved vital for the future of Brownhall.

James's son, John Stewart Hamilton, (1864–1952), was over fifty when his father died and he returned from Canada to take on the management of the estate which was still in a very precarious situation. In his autobiography, he wrote with evident bitterness about its condition and about the profligate manner with which the family fortune had been spent, and he also had some caustic comments to make on the old man's religious fervour. Obviously it would have been difficult, if not politically tactless, for him to have openly faulted John Hamilton for his generosity to his tenants; but what the grandson – and other members of the family at the time – found difficult to accept was that much of the money was wasted because of impulsive decisions and impatience, even though John Hamilton had readily acknowledged his own foolishness in this respect. However, in fairness to 'J.S.H'. it should be said that he did much to stabilise the situation at Brownhall, and his single most impressive achievement was probably the planting of almost 60,000 trees on the estate.

John Stewart Hamilton's son, James, born in 1913, as well as James's son, the present John Hamilton – less burdened with the debts left by their ancestor

– have freely and proudly acknowledged the contribution made by old John Hamilton in helping thousands of people in south Donegal during extremely difficult times. By the time that the above mentioned James inherited Brownhall, the property was emerging from the worst difficulties of the past, and he is now especially remembered for his work consolidating the estate, for his efforts on behalf of conservation and agricultural progress, and his many contributions in print about wild-life management and game conservancy. His sister, Sheila, was a quite remarkable woman, decades ahead of her time. Living at nearby Coxtown, she devoted much of her life to helping to bring Irish agriculture to a competitive level and played an important role in the establishment of the mart and A.I. systems which are now taken for granted, and she was not only the first woman to be elected to the National Council of the Irish Co-operative Operation Society, but also chaired the meetings of the North-west Cattle Breeders Association in her latter years.

Despite all the odds against it, the very much slimmed-down Brownhall estate continues to be in Hamilton ownership, run by the present John and his wife Radine and as part of the continuing the efforts to rehabilitate the property, John is currently restoring a large lake abandoned more than 160 years ago. He is also an active member of the local committee which aims to breathe new life into, and encourage progress in the local community. Following a tradition going back to 1679 whereby the head of the family is named, alternately, John and James, the elder of their two sons is James, and their younger son, Edward, emulates his great-great grand uncle of the same name, in giving both support and friendship to his brother.

Old John Hamilton's son by his second marriage, John Pakenham Hamilton (1861–1946), was the ancestor of the second, separate branch of the family, most of whose descendants now live in Britain. However, following a business move, one of his sons, Michael Pakenham Hamilton came to Dublin and thus re-established a branch of John Hamilton's second family in Ireland, now represented by his son David Pakenham Hamilton and his wife, Joyce, and family, along with David's sister, Jennifer Hunter. After St. Ernan's was sold in several lots in 1981, David Hamilton bought the gardener's cottage and some land at St. Ernan's, so that there is a Hamilton presence at both Brownhall and St.Ernan's once more.

* * *

John Hamilton's grandson appears to have been the only person who wrote critically about his grandfather, but the evident bitterness which he vented in his autobiography, *My Times and Other Times,* even if understandable, contrasts starkly with the written views expressed by others who knew this kindly and generous landlord. The reader will have to judge *his* or *her* opinion against the opinions of John Hamilton's tenants and all those, already quoted, who saw him in a very different light.

Index to Place Names

Index to Persons

Note: References in the text to John Hamilton (1800-1884) are so numerous that they have not been indexed.

Also published by The Woodfield Press

The Wicklow World of Elizabeth Smith (1840-1850)
edited by Dermot James and Séamas Ó Maitiú

The Sligo-Leitrim World of Kate Cullen (1832-1913)
revealed by Hilary Pyle

Ballyknockan: A Wicklow Stonecutters' Village
Séamas Ó Maitiú and Barry O'Reilly

The Tellicherry Five: The Transportation of Michael Dwyer and the Wicklow Rebels
Kieran Sheedy